P9-EDA-627

THE LAST CHANCE

By JOHN MYERS MYERS

OUT ON ANY LIMB

THE HARP AND THE BLADE

THE ALAMO

THE WILD YAZOO

SILVERLOCK

THE LAST CHANCE

Old style Cochise County miners. The men who hacked
Tombstone's wealth out of the rock were mostly professionals
from England and Wales or hard-bitten immigrants from
Ireland and Germany. *(Frontispiece)*

THE
LAST CHANCE

TOMBSTONE'S
EARLY YEARS

BY JOHN MYERS MYERS

E. P. Dutton & Co., Inc.

PUBLISHER

NEW YORK · 1950

CONTENTS

LIST OF ILLUSTRATIONS

(*Photographs by C. S. Fly. Courtesy of the Bank of Douglas*)

MAPS

THE LAST CHANCE

To

JACK *and* ANNE KEATING
themselves connoisseurs
of unusual communities

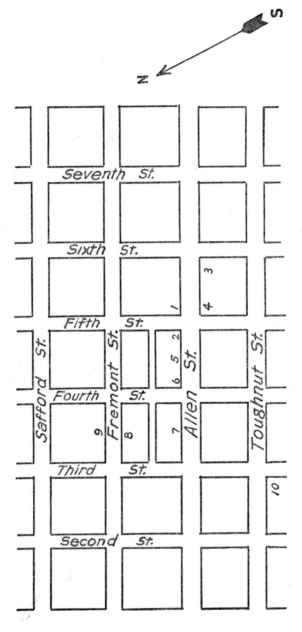

SCENE OF TOMBSTONE'S CELEBRATED GUN-FIGHT

1. Oriental Saloon. 2. Crystal Palace Saloon. 3. Bird Cage Theatre. 4. Cosmopolitan Hotel.
5. Campbell and Hatch's Pool Hall. 6. Hafford's Saloon. 7. O. K. Corral Stable. 8. O. K.
Corral Yard. 9. Old Courthouse. 10. New Courthouse.

CHAPTER ONE

EAST OF THE SAN PEDRO

SILVER was what drew men to the place. The time was the late eighteen-seventies. The region was southeastern Arizona. The name of the town was Tombstone. It sat, and in lessened glory still sits, high up on the eastern side of the San Pedro River Valley.

The remarkable thing about much history is that it is so pat as to seem contrived. Take that name. It was given in ironic triumph by a man who was probably as ignorant of social trends as the mules which bore his supplies and equipment. Yet he came out with the word which belonged.

It was not appropriate solely because so many people were soon to find violent deaths there. A tombstone is a marker for something unable to go any farther. That was what happened to the Old West of uninhibited enterprise when it reached this particular mining camp. It was the end of the road; the last spot on the map of the nation where destiny could be worked out on a large scale without governmental or other outside interference. When Tombstone's spacious days were over, "here lies the body of an era" could be read in the empty buildings and sleepy streets of what was left of the city.

There were western towns which boomed and bloomed later, but they were not in the same class. They could not be, for, like Wordsworth, the world was too much with them. Roads and railroads had let too many people in to enjoy the developed wealth of a country rapidly submitting to discipline. Wildness and outlawry did what they could under the circumstances; but they were simply crowded off the map by a hard working citizenry whose second demand, after prosperity, was peace in which to enjoy it.

Next to the presence of silver the most potent factor in the history of Tombstone was its isolation. For all purposes the town was the capital of an autonomous land, its integrity preserved by its distance from the nation's population centers, poor communications, and the inability of the Federal government to reach into inaccessible regions of a growing nation.

Two other factors contributed to make Tombstone the explosive end marker of the American migration phenomenon. One was that it was in the territory included in the Gadsden Purchase of 1853, which was the last addition to the United States proper. Another was that it was situated in the last region of Arizona to be surrendered by that most tenacious of Indian tribes, the Apache.

To return to the specific locality, the San Pedro rises in the State of Sonora, Mexico, and runs something west of north to the Gila, itself a tributary of the Colorado. Unlike most Arizona rivers it contains visible moisture the year round, often in quantities sufficient for water power. To make things better in this respect, the river has a declivity of six hundred feet for its first forty miles north of the international border. This has a bearing on the story.

The San Pedro Valley is here from fifteen to twenty miles wide, wedged between the Huachuca and the Whetstone Mountains to the west, the Mules and the Dragoons to the east. How steeply the land mounts from the river can be seen from the elevation of Tombstone itself. Fairbank, eight miles west on the San Pedro is 3853 feet above sea level. The height of the old mining city is 4539 feet.

The Dragoons were so called from the activities in those mountains of the Third U. S. Cavalry, designated as dragoons then because its members were armed with carbines rather than the traditional cavalry weapons of sabre and revolver. The Mules, south across Mule Pass, are said to have got their name from some army mules which went AWOL to mingle with wild horse bands which grazed the range in question. The town is in a jumble of hills likewise called Tombstone, although the early name was apparently the Burros, to distinguish them from the grander Mules.

Roughly speaking, these silver bearing Tombstone Hills are caused by a local upheaval of porphyry through a capping of limestone. Patrick Hamilton, who published a survey of Arizona in 1884, has this to say about the locality:

"The mineral belt of Tombstone extends about eight miles east and west, and may be said to extend south to the Bisbee copper deposits, nearly twenty-five miles. The geological features of the belt are an interesting study. Porphyry is the most widely distributed and is the formation in which most of the large ore bodies occur. The veins and deposits are nearly all covered by a capping of lime, and in some places large chambers of ore are found in this rock. As depth is reached the lime disappears, and considerable quartzite is encountered. This also gives way as the work of development proceeds, and at the water-level a feldspathic porphyry encases the ore bodies. . . . The country in which the mines of the district occur may be described as a series of rolling grass covered hills, being the northern end of the Mule mountains."

The climate of the region is that of a high mesa country, sharing some of the characteristics of both prairie and desert regions. The sun beats down with varying degrees of intensity most of the year, but rains, when they come, are apt to be torrential. The soil thus treated supports little but grass in the way of vegetation. However, the presence of that grass had a bearing on the story of Tombstone of the first importance.

"The upper San Pedro," to quote Hamilton again, "is a rich grazing region, as are also the rolling hills and table lands adjacent. . . Water is abundant in springs and streams, and the grass is sweet and luxuriant."

So much for significant flora; in fauna the district was much richer. Deer, antelope, and javalina or peccary ranged there, along with wild hogs. Mountain lions, wild cats and bear were occasionally encountered; so were skunks, jackrabbits, cottontails, and gophers. Rattlesnakes and gila monsters were the most dangerous of many reptiles. More apt to cause trouble were scorpions, centipedes, tarantulas, and black widow spiders.

The known history of the region makes quick reading; and even pre-history is not as helpful as it is in so many other parts of Arizona. The Cochise culture of archaeological findings was that of a semi-nomadic people whose national affinities have not been determined. Such was also the style of living of the Sobaipuris, a subdivision of the Pimas, whom the Spanish found there in the sixteenth century. These ranged elsewhere much of the year but returned annually to townsites along the San Pedro, which they called the Quiburi, to raise certain crops.

The brevity of the valley's history is all the more remarkable when it is considered that white men first reached there nearly seventy years before Jamestown was settled. Yet after three hundred years of so-called Spanish occupation the principal change was that the wholly nomadic Apaches had ousted the semi-nomadic Sobaipuris.

Arizona was first visited by white men in 1539, but by way of another break in the mountains. The San Pedro Valley wasn't used until 1540, when Francisco Vásquez de Coronado led his treasure hunting expedition north. Ironically he passed within a few miles of the wealth of Tombstone to find the drab adobe reality of the golden Cibola he counted on.

Spanish interest in the country lapsed with Coronado's failure and was not revived until it took the form of missionary zeal. The Jesuits began the work of converting the Indians in the seventeenth century. Eventually they established certain permanent missions — but not along the San Pedro. In this connection the old maps of Arizona are misleading. They show the valley dotted with names, and historians prior to Bancroft assumed these indicated Spanish colonial settlements. Actually they only marked "visitas" or periodic points of call for traveling padres. Visitas were often developed into permanent missions, around which Indians congregated to form settlements, but that didn't happen along the San Pedro. The reason is that at some time during the seventeenth century the powerful Comanche tribe squeezed the Apaches westward. The Apaches in turn forced the Sobaipuris to leave the valley — and the visitas could not safely be visited any more. The Apaches weren't mission redskins, and that was final.

If later Spaniards went to the San Pedro except in the course of retaliatory expeditions for Apache raids on the towns of Tucson and Tubac in the roughly parallel Santa Cruz Valley, there is little record of it. There is also little evidence that the region was prospected during colonial times or when it was a part of first the Empire, then the Republic, of Mexico.

American occupation of Arizona did not immediately change conditions. Reversing the standard trend of a westward push, settlers in quantity first entered from California as a sort of back-wash from the great gold rush of that territory. Mining towns were therefore thrown up along the Colorado while the Indians were still in relatively undisturbed possession of the eastern part of Arizona.

But though most that came to what was then western New Mexico after the Mexican War and the succeeding Gadsden Purchase were in search of mineral wealth, they left the vicinity of Tombstone alone. Prior to the War between the States, as well as for better than a decade after it, about the only whites active there were troopers of one unit or another of the U. S. Cavalry.

There may have been earlier prospectors, but they didn't get their names in the book. The first man definitely known to have staked a mining claim on the east side of the San Pedro was a Russian or Polish mineralogist. Probably he came from what was then called Russian Poland, but in any case his name was Frederic Brunckow and the date of his discovery was 1858. Rationalized into Bronco by topographers of a later day, his name still lives on Arizona maps. That's all the good Mr. Brunckow got out of his mine, however. Some Apaches caught him in his digging and shot him full of arrows.

The later history of his find isn't easy to follow. The only certain point is that it was absolutely worthless. Before that was clearly established during the Tombstone silver rush sixteen more men were supposed to have been killed at the Brunckow Mine either in quarrels for possession of it or because the ever lurking Apaches caught them with their heads in the hole.

Early records also contain references to a San Pedro Mining Co., the scene of whose activities was in all likelihood the Brunckow. Then there is one other reference to non-Indian occupation of the upper San Pedro. Following the separation of Arizona from New Mexico in 1863 a census of the new territory was ordered. This reported a handful of Mexicans at a settlement called San Pedro, which was somewhere in the Tombstone region. All the peons were listed as living without their families, although most were described as being married, and all were designated as laborers. What they were laboring at so far from any of the projects of civilization wasn't mentioned, but they may well have been working for the San Pedro Mining Co. on the Brunckow Mine.

How these laborers escaped the attentions of the Indians — or if they did — is an unanswered question. Traditionally the Apaches hated the Mexicans more than they did the Americans, which is saying a great deal.

At the outset, though, there is evidence that the Apaches viewed the newcomers without too much disfavor, purely because they differed from the Mexicans, their enemies of long standing. Yet inevitably they began to feel the pinch as settlers pressed westward from Texas as well as eastward from California. Then the Apaches started to fight, and when they did they meant business. They fought more stubbornly, more skilfully — and on the whole more successfully, in spite of their weakness in numbers — than any Indians with which the United States pioneers came in contact.

The eventual focal point of the Apaches' struggle to survive on their own terms was southeastern Arizona. Initially, however, there was only desultory warfare in that region for two reasons.

East of the San Pedro

On the negative side was the paucity of settlers for the Indians to harry. On the positive side, Cochise, war chief of the Chirichua Apaches, had decided to try to get along with the Americans on the excellent military ground that they had too many troops in the field to make fighting them profitable.

But that doesn't mean that Apache depredations did not take place in the region. Due to logistical problems raised by a dry, barren country the Apaches normally traveled in small bands. They seldom, if ever, gathered in such great encampments as marked the rendezvous of the Sioux or Blackfeet, say. As a result separate bands were necessarily autonomous, unless they chose to operate under a particular chief in time of war. Cochise, therefore was a lawmaker only to his immediate followers.

As far as he and his were concerned, his peaceful policy was maintained until the fall of 1860. In October of that year some Apaches looted the house of an Irish settler and kidnapped the son of his Mexican mistress. Following an appeal by the settler to the commandant of Fort Buchanan a Lt. George N. Bascom was sent out with orders to retrieve the boy. His first move was to interview Cochise, then camped near what is now Bowie, Arizona.

Bascom's method of procedure was at once underhanded and high handed. He invited Cochise and some of his associates to a parley. At the meeting Cochise said he knew nothing about the abducted youngster, which turned out to be true, but young Bascom refused to believe him and placed the Apaches under arrest.

Cochise himself promptly escaped, but his comrades, some of whom were his kinsmen, remained as hostages. Thinking he knew the answer to that, the chief captured three Americans and offered to make a trade. Whereupon Bascom added pigheadedness to his other sins. He refused to make a deal, although the three captured citizens were brought near enough to make a personal appeal. His refusal to listen was their death warrant. In full sight of the Lieutenant and his troopers Cochise dragged one to death behind his horse. The other two were tortured before being hanged. The soldiers retaliated by hanging six Apaches, including relatives of Cochise. Tribal law left him only one course. He vowed a war of vengeance and rallied other bands to him.

During the next few years the Apaches were aided by a much greater conflict, the War between the States. Before it was over practically all troops were withdrawn from Arizona, and the settlers who moved fast enough had either left the territory or withdrawn to the comparative safety of Tucson or Tubac. Yet even when the soldiers returned after Appomattox Cochise couldn't be stopped. In fact things grew steadily worse, for there were again settlers to be preyed upon.

The general situation has been vividly summed up by the Arizona historian, Frank C. Lockwood. "During the years '69, '70, and '71 Apache atrocities had mounted steadily to a climax of terror and bloodshed. Scouting expeditions were carried on all the time by army officers unsurpassed for bravery, and knowledge of Indian ways. But the territory to be covered was vast, arid, and mountainous. There was neither telegraph nor railroad; supplies had to be brought from great distances; the foe was as wily and resourceful, as any that ever arrayed itself against the white man. The Apaches struck simultaneously at points far apart; and so added distraction to terror. A herd of sheep was driven off while grazing only two miles from Tucson under the care of a Mexican herder; the stage stations both east and west of Tucson . . . were attacked. . . Tucson itself was taken by surprise, and a large number of beeves and work oxen were driven into the mountains. . . *The Prescott Miner,* in the autumn of 1871, published a list of Apache murders and atrocities occurring between March, 1864, and the fall of 1871. Three hundred and one pioneers had been murdered, two of whom were known to have been burned alive; fifty-three were wounded and crippled for life and five carried into captivity."

Considering the small size of the population this was an

enormous casualty list. It includes, be it noted, only civilian personnel. "All this time," Lockwood goes on, "the troops were on the move, trying to forestall these tragedies, and after the attacks pursuing and punishing the Apaches with relentless vigor. Most daring and resourceful among a score of officers of indefatigable energy and high courage was Lieutenant Howard B. Cushing. His death . . . in the Whetstone Mountains southeast of Tucson in a desperate encounter with Cochise. . ." And so on.

For nearly twelve years Cochise successfully eluded this implacable pursuit; and when he did finally come to terms with the United States it was not as a defeated renegade but as one sovereign power dealing with another. The American ambassador who proposed the treaty was General O. O. Howard, who had the courage to seek the chief out, with only one guide as a companion, and make a personal appeal to him in his stronghold in the Dragoon Mountains.

The general, as he recorded, saw an old man but a very impressive one. He had a large head, good features, and at six foot-one was tall for an Apache. Moreover his bearing was that of a self-assured statesman. The general also reported that he had been allowed to observe the defenses of the natural fortress and that there wasn't an officer in the United States Army who could have made better use of his forces than did Cochise.

The chief must have taken to General Howard, too, for he consented to talk things over. Whether he was influenced decisively by his knowledge that the Apaches would be wiped out if the war of attrition continued, his advanced years and a well grounded fear that the Chirichuas boasted no one capable of taking his place, or the feeling that his hanged kindred had been sufficiently avenged, he declared a wish for peace. He also agreed to live on a reservation — if the United States made the Dragoons one. He carried his point, too.

It was in the fall of 1872 that the treaty was made as a verbal agreement between two men who had decided that they could trust each other. It was faithfully kept on both sides for the two years of life which remained to the chief. He died in 1874 in his favorite haunt, still known as Cochise's Stronghold, fourteen miles northeast of Tombstone.

Being an Apache, he was professionally cruel, but withal he was faithful, as not too many have been, to his guiding principles. In the fine Spanish phrase he was "much man," and it is fitting that his country, extending from the Chirichua Mountains along the New Mexico border west across the San Pedro Valley, still bears his name.

He was as successful at bringing his people peace as he had been at leading them in war, but good times did not long survive him. Apache law did not call for a hereditary chieftainship. When he died there were too many capable aspirants, and no top notch one. Internal troubles finally took the form of civil war; and next members of the disorganized tribe began renewed raids afield. As a result the reservation in the Dragoons was nullified in 1876, and the attempt was made to move the Chirichuas to a place which offered them less of an opportunity for secret movements. Refusing to go, many hit the war path in open earnest. Anything less than a well armed group entered the San Pedro Valley with the betting against survival.

CHAPTER TWO

SILVER IN THE VALLEY

Such was still the situation when a man, hundreds of miles away in California, began stocking up for a prospecting trip. The story of Tombstone was in the making.

That story, in something resembling its full development, has been given in two earlier works, Frederick J. Bechdolt's *When The West Was Young* and Walter Noble Burns' *Tombstone: An Illiad of the Southwest*. In both instances the main reliance was evidently placed on the oral testimony of actual or self-styled early residents.

The temptation to act in kind has been in part removed by the dying off of the generation which participated in or were witness to the events here described. Their immediate descendants, or those who knew, or claim to have known, those descendants, still present a problem for the investigator. A considerable number of people, their sincerity not in question, know the facts — or know nothing. How can you tell, or what means have they themselves of assessing the veracity of what was passed on to them? Tradition may be a chrysalis for truth, but it can just as faithfully preserve slander, a misconception, or the bad memory of some early settler who had no close connection with the happenings under discussion in the first place.

Worse yet, tradition may be no more than an invention for the sake of saving face. A man who arrived on the scene after the big excitement may, in days to come, pronounce like a soothsayer to maintain his status of a knowledgeable old timer. For decades historians of the Old West have been hornswoggled by statements notarized by only long beards and a wrinkled, weather-beaten hide. Moreover, some of these oldsters, like the man Kipling's

German scientist pathetically accused, have "lied in print," publishing reminiscences in which facts have little or no standing. Hardly less dubious are books and articles which embody childhood recollections of the gossip of the day. Such items are not missing from the bibliography of Tombstone.

With respect to this chronicle the decision was made to eschew oral tradition and writings which looked to it for authority. It is recognized that something of worth may have been lost in so doing; but at this remove there could be no other guide than guess work in making selections from the mass of that material. It is furthermore recognized that much of what has been accepted as legitimate source material is written from the bias of personal interest. Still that very bias is a reflection of actuality such as the reporter is bound to respect. By gauging the degree of passion involved he also has some means of judging the relation of expressed opinion to fact.

Among documents of primary significance there are coroner's records and those of the county courts. For reasons which will be given later these are often sketchy and as often blank. Then there are old newspaper files, of two Tombstone journals in particular, though the files are incomplete due to fires which burned out the business section of the town. Supplementary are despatches to a Tucson paper which maintained correspondents in Tombstone.

There is also personal testimony of the first importance. If there was, alas, no Mark Twain to give life to Tombstone as he did to Virginia City in *Roughing It,* there is a volume of equal historical, if far less literary, value. This is the journal of a man called George Whitwell Parsons, whose noted impressions of facts and events was almost as immediate as those recorded in a daily newspaper. The word "almost" is used, because it is clear that although the entries in his diary are dated sequentially, he frequently waited to write up a number of entries at once.

Then there are two books incorporating the recollections of men who were themselves prominent actors in the feud which wracked the town. Of these men one was Wyatt Earp, who lived to give his biographer his own version of the facts in the case. The other was William M. Breakenridge, a member of the opposing faction, who wrote of his experiences in Tombstone under the name of *Helldorado*. Contrasting with the foregoing in their jovial non-partisanship, are the reminiscences of Billy King, by turns bartender, gambler and peace officer of the city. Also of great value are the miscellaneous writings of John P. Clum, mayor of Tombstone in the hectic year of 1881.

In addition to the items listed above there are an astonishing number of books, mostly autobiographical, which contain references to early days in the town. Some of these are suspect, and some are indicted outright by their own nonsense. Others supply points of information not given elsewhere, or serve to corroborate the more pertinent volumes.

One narrative whose importance is of the first order is yet to be mentioned. Edward L. Schieffelin, the discoverer of Tombstone's silver wealth, gave one of the town's newspapers a comprehensive account of the great event of his life.

As he became famous, there are pictures of the man. These were taken after he was prosperous and curried; but he caught the eye of at least one journalist before that. This newspaperman remarked of him in 1876 that he was about the queerest looking human article he had ever encountered. He was a gaunt six-foot-two, short of thirty and looking forty. His black hair hung down below his shoulders, and his full beard, a tangle of knots, was almost as long. His clothes, including his hat, had been so patched with pieces of rabbit skin that he resembled a scrofulous fur bearing animal.

Schieffelin was born in Pennsylvania, but before he was in his teens he was helping his father pan gold in Oregon. At seventeen he was on his own as a prospector. During the ten years or so before he entered Arizona he had wandered up and down Oregon, Idaho, Nevada, and California. Finding pick-up riches was the only existence he had, knew, or wanted. He had neither scientific knowledge nor technical skill, but he did have the things essential to his calling. He possessed an enormous patience and the unshakeable conviction that he would some day make his strike.

It takes a queer bird to be a long term prospector. The way of life makes him queerer. By the time he was nearly thirty Schieffelin had severed his ties with the world almost as completely as an anchorite. His only contact with even such civilization as the unsettled West had to offer was when he took a temporary job to grubstake himself for another trip. When he set out again, he traveled by himself. The only thing which can save a man's sanity in such a lonely existence is developing a counter-irritant in the form of fanaticism. This was to show up and have its way when the time came, but the time didn't hurry. In close to a dozen years he hadn't made peanuts. When he entered Arizona, for instance, he had twenty-five dollars in his kick, and no bank account.

Writers have tried to improve on the report which Ed Schieffelin made of his exploit. It is true that they throw in such an element as skeletons lying amidst fragments of ore and a near capture by Apaches that he doesn't record. But none of them have succeeded in showing, as he did so clearly in his matter of fact narrative, how his passionate faith in a hunch made the discovery possible.

The trappings of melodrama aren't needed when true drama is present. What happened was a tremendous thing: the dreams of all the weary willies who have ever made a career of prospecting were for once vindicated by reality. Nor was it a matter of stumbling over precious metals, like Wickenburg, say, or Sutter himself. It was not the result of following up leads furnished by other men, as in the case of Comstock. Schieffelin picked his locality, persisted until he had made his find, and cashed in for a prosperity that lasted all his life.

To follow his own statements, then, in January, 1877, he outfitted in San Bernadino, California, loaded his gear on a pair of mules, and headed toward the vicinity of the Grand Canyon to prospect for either gold or silver. He followed that plan but had no luck in northwestern Arizona. Therefore when some Hualapai

Indians were recruited for scouting service against the Apaches in the opposite corner of the territory, he decided to go along. He was counting on military protection to make prospecting in hostile country feasible.

The scouts were stationed at Fort Huachuca, west above the San Pedro, but beyond escorting him there they weren't much good to him. A man can't keep up with a hard riding military expedition and attend to prospecting, too. Perforce Ed chose practicality above safety and, while still using the fort as a base, started scouring the valley on his own.

By that time, nearly thirty years after the California heyday of finding money in the ground, the prospector was already looked upon as a somewhat comic ne'er-do-well. Ed's futile expeditions amused the garrison; and it was at this time that a name was impressed on his brain. A group of soldiers, by way of having fun with him, quizzed him as to what he thought he was up to. The answer they drew from Schieffelin was to the effect that he expected to find something he could use down in the valley. His interlocutors had been in that valley many times themselves since the Chirichuas had gone on the war path again, and they knew the sort of thing that took place there. "Yes," they agreed, "you'll find your Tombstone."

Schieffelin arrived at Fort Huachuca in April, 1877, but some time later he made his headquarters in an old adobe building by the Brunckow Mine, spelled Broncho in his report. There Ed found two men who had been hired to examine the mine for its latest owner, and he contracted to stand guard for them while they worked. It was then that he got his first close-up view of the Tombstone country, some miles to the northeast. Studying the jumble of hills through his field glasses, he decided that he would try there next.

As mentioned earlier, these hills were hardly more than a dozen miles from Cochise's old stronghold. It was very dangerous territory; and Ed himself recalled in his undramatic fashion that he had to proceed with care, because the Indians were continuously active. He dared not remain in such an exposed locality — the country, be it remembered, was treeless — for more than one night at a time. Consequently he made slow progress with what is at best tedious work.

The local upheaval of ore-bearing rock responsible for the presence of silver so near the surface had naturally taken place far in the past. During the ages which followed the veins and pockets had been covered over with earth and then vegetation. Ledges could be inspected with any ease only where erosion had eaten away channels, dry most of the year, leading to the river.

These gullies, too, were the places to look for float, or chunks of ore that had broken loose, and had been washed perhaps miles away, from the mother lode. A thorough job of prospecting meant going over all the gullies in the district inch by inch. It is not surprising that Schieffelin hadn't half completed the task by the tail end of summer. He had not found any impressive looking ore, but he wouldn't let go.

He couldn't let go. The blind faith in his fortunes which had kept him trying for so many luckless years had found a focal point. In spite of the absence of confirming evidence he had decided that this must be the place for which he had always searched. He kept on, working into more dangerous territory as he drew nearer to the Dragoons hideout of the Apaches, and finally found some float which looked good.

Laboriously tracing this to the ledge from which it came, he found an outcropping of rock which indubitably contained veins of silver. Remembering the grim joshing of the soldiers at Fort Huachuca, he gave the name of Tombstone to this first discovery.

After locating at least one more claim, he temporarily left the region. Most accounts imply that Schieffelin had been a lone hand all this period; his own narrative contradicts such statements. After leaving the Brunckow Mine, he had made his headquarters at a couple of abandoned ranch buildings — put up by some nameless person under unrecorded circumstances — a few miles down river. Among several others billeted in the same shanties was a

man called William Griffith, one of the men who had employed Ed
to stand guard at the Brunckow. Griffith had promised to pay for
the recording of anything Schieffelin found in return for a claim
of his own. As an interested party, he sometimes accompanied Ed,
who showed him the Tombstone before they left for Tucson,
the seat of Pima County, of which the upper San Pedro Valley was
then a part, late in August.

It was Griffith and not Schieffelin himself who actually recorded
the Tombstone on September 3, 1877. That, however, was his last
connection with the venture. Men to whom he and Ed showed
their ore were of one opinion: it was worthless. Griffith decided
that ranching would be a better investment for his money, and
Schieffelin had to carry on without a backer.

His first move was to go right back to the Tombstone country.
He was impelled to. No matter what anybody else said to the
contrary, he knew that silver was there. It was the country which
must repay him for his forfeited youth and young manhood, the
country which must prove that his years of self-deprivation
wouldn't be extended indefinitely.

Back on the east side of the San Pedro, he convinced himself all
over again that he was right; but by the time he had done so his
supplies were all gone. In cash he had exactly thirty cents. Looking
for credit in Tucson was useless, so he turned north. When last
heard from, his brother had been working at the Silver King Mine
at Globe, Arizona.

Al E. Schieffelin had changed jobs when Ed arrived, minus the
thirty cents, which he had spent for tobacco. Half starved, the
prospector had to go to work in a mine himself before he was able
to travel west across the territory to Signal. There Ed found his
brother and employment at the McCracken Mine.

He hadn't forgotten about Tombstone, but he took his time
about breaking the story. Al, as Ed noted, was a different limb of
the tree; a man, for instance, who was thoroughly disillusioned
about prospecting. Ed wanted him for a partner, but, knowing his
brother wouldn't be easily won over, he started in by merely show-

ing the latter his ore specimens. The plan backfired, for Al was as disparaging as the men at Tucson had been. Moreover, everybody else at the McCracken agreed with Al.

It takes a strong hunch to survive under the scorn of supposedly expert opinion, and Ed's almost did not. He threw most of his specimens away, yet he still had three when Richard Gird came to Signal. An assayer and mining engineer, who had made a tentative geological map of the territory, Gird was held to be one of the most knowledgeable men in Arizona.

This was Ed's first break. Al, who knew Gird, submitted the Tombstone specimens for assay, and the engineer promptly wanted to know where they came from. There was reason for asking. The ore from the original Tombstone claim was, as it happened, of such low grade as to be almost worthless, but a specimen from another ledge assayed at $2,000 per ton. This was better than the McCracken or any of the neighboring mines could show.

Gird promptly said he was willing to quit his job, grubstake the prospecting expedition, and investigate the new field in a professional manner. In return for the grubstake and his professional services he asked for a full partnership with the two brothers. When Ed, after some hesitation, agreed, there was nothing else to it. A verbal contract was all that ever bound Gird and the Schieffelins. It was unswervingly honored.

The expedition left Signal in February, 1878, on St. Valentine's Day, to be exact. Ed was so close-mouthed about his precious secret that neither Al nor Gird knew just where they were heading until they were well on their way to the San Pedro. And when they arrived, they weren't glad. The ledge on which they had been counting so heavily contained only a shallow pocket of ore. They christened that claim the Graveyard, because there their hopes lay buried.

At this point passion fought with disillusionment in the form of Al and science in the person of Dick Gird. They wanted to leave, but Ed wouldn't have it. Percentage, wisdom, and the facts as they had found them to be were all against him. Yet this was his place, the spot he depended on to give all his life some meaning. He *knew* silver was there, and he beat the others down with his faith.

Further searching forced Gird to admit that the geological signs were favorable. The engineer turned one of the fire places of the old adobe house at the Brunckow Mine into an assay furnace, and they settled down to it systematically. A factor in their favor was that the region was temporarily free of Indians. Schieffelin wrote that Cochise, dead three years past, was on the war path when he first entered the district. He went on to note that the old chief had died by 1878 and that his band had moved away. Actually the chief leader of the warring Apaches at that time and place was neither Cochise, of course, nor Geronimo, as is sometimes stated, but Victorio, who had led his braves into Mexico to avoid the pursuit of the United States troops. In any case a much more thorough job of prospecting was possible when every second glance was not one in search of possible danger.

Whether or not this was the deciding element, they eventually did make a big strike. It probably would have broken Ed's heart if any of the others had been the first to score, but poetic justice was on the job. He found a lode which assayed $15,000 to the ton, and Gird's investigations showed that the veins ran deep. This was the true beginning of the Tombstone boom. It was also the first genuine vindication of Ed's hunch. That probably meant more to him than the potential wealth of which he found himself possessed. One day had changed him from a stubborn damned fool who had wasted his life into a man of achievement. You can sense his new and relaxed attitude in the Lucky Cuss, the name he gave to the mine but meant for himself.

After the discovery of the Lucky Cuss, they worked faster. They knew that every mining man in Arizona was aware by then that Dick Gird had quit a fine position to disappear into the hills with a prospector. As soon as his whereabouts were discovered, the rush would be on.

But they knew which signs to look for now, and other finds

followed with comparative rapidity. Painstakingly tracing a low outcropping which left the Lucky Cuss, Ed found the Tough Nut. The reason for the name lay in the fact that a mining claim could be only 600 by 1500 feet. It was necessary, then, to make boundaries which would include as much as possible of the valuable veins at hand, but faulting made this a difficult business here. It was several days before Gird could satisfy himself that when he surveyed the Tough Nut he wouldn't leave anything he really wanted outside.

These were two of the three big discoveries that made Tombstone the richest mining camp in the country. The third, to Ed's great mortification, was found by another party. A pair named Hank Williams and John Oliver had moved into the district. Finding Gird on the scene, they made arrangements with him to assay their findings in return for a split in whatever claims they located. When Williams and Oliver did find something big, however, they forgot about the agreement until it was indignantly called to their notice. Because of the argument which took place before they got their rights, Gird and the Schieffelins called their share of the claim the Contention. The part Williams and Oliver kept they denominated the Grand Central.

By the time these claims were recorded, word of the bonanza had got around, and, indeed, the partners themselves were ready to publish it. They had, in Ed's phrase, "all they needed," and as it turned out, the major riches of the district had already been located. Plenty of smaller mines were to yield considerable sums, but there were no more really big finds.

Yet it is one thing to locate a good mine, and another thing to be able to exploit it. Capital on a large scale is needed, and in this field even Dick Gird's competence was of little use to the partnership. Traditionally the prospector who makes a valuable discovery ends up with little or nothing, while johnny-come-latelies whack up the treasure he found. That didn't happen here, although the Schieffelins and Gird did not get off to a very good beginning.

First off they sold the Contention for $10,000 cash. As this turned out to be the richest mine of the whole area, yielding $5,000,000 in the first five years, that was a bad mistake. Still ten grand, considering the buying power of currency at the time, looked like a sizeable chunk of money; and they were in need of operating funds.

Next they almost froze themselves out of the whole venture by offering the Lucky Cuss and the Tough Nut together for $90,000, to be paid in three months. They bonded the mines for that period, and so had, when the payment wasn't forthcoming at the end of ninety days, some thousands more to work with. By then they had a clearer idea of the worth of their holdings and turned down $150,000.

That was in the late summer of '78, and big scale operators began to take an interest. Some claim that John S. Vosburg, a Tucson promoter, helped to grubstake the Schieffelins and Gird when they first went to the San Pedro. These sources add that he was the one responsible for interesting Anson P. K. Safford, third governor of the Territory of Arizona, in the enterprise. On the other hand Ed, who recorded with particularity his dealings with everybody he encountered at the great period of his life, does not mention him. He states that the former governor arrived in the company of one Dan Gilette, leaving the inference that Vosburg's undoubted connection with Tombstone was of a somewhat later date.

Safford was a financier as well as a politician. He liked the looks of the claims and made the partners a proposition. In return for a quarter interest he would finance an ore reducing mill and would raise the capital to develop the mines. The mill would be built under Gird's direction, and he and the Schieffelin brothers would retain possession of it. As this was satisfactory, the Tombstone Mining and Milling Company was formed.

Water to run the mill and timber to build it with in the first place were alike absent from the Tombstone area. For the power they went to the San Pedro, picking a site a few miles from the Brunckow. In the Huachucas there was plenty of timber but no sawmill. To purchase this and other things he needed Gird took off for San Francisco. Safford headed east to talk turkey with high finance. His guarantee was that he would deposit adequate funds to Gird's account in a San Francisco bank by the time Dick needed them.

So agreed and so done; but it wasn't until June of 1879 that the mill was ready. Meanwhile the Western Mining Co., later to be the Contention Consolidated Mining Co., and the Grand Central Mining Co had been formed. Not much money had been taken out of the region, but a great deal was being put into it. There was need for a town; and one, in fact, had already been laid out.

CHAPTER THREE

THE TOWN AT GOOSE FLATS

THE ORIGINAL TOWN had neither its present name nor location. After the first big strike the partners had moved their headquarters up the valley from the old Brunckow Mine to the vicinity of the Lucky Cuss. Here, a couple of miles west of Tombstone, a settlement grew up around them. Called Watervale, it remained the center of population until the spring of 1879.

The presence of a water hole was, however, the only thing to recommend the site. Throughout the Tombstone region the terrain hardly offers ten yards of ground that is at once level and well drained except at one spot. Certainly there was elsewhere no place for the streets of a city; and everyone was convinced that nothing less than a city was in order. By then enough experts had examined the mines to make the permanence of the town a certainty. Growth seemed equally inevitable. The veins would not run out in the foreseeable future. It would not be a settlement for just pick-up-and-run treasure hunters but one where business men with a calculating eye for the future could afford to establish themselves.

The site chosen was Goose Flats, a mesa overlooking the Tough Nut claim. It was and still is a superb location. At 4500 feet above sea level the air is always invigorating and the temperatures seldom extreme. The land falls away on all sides, so although it is true that hills make a near horizon to the south and west, the impression of being at the top of something persists. No doubt the absence of trees to block the view aids this illusion, which is further amplified by the vista over the flat lands leading to the

Dragoons and through Mule Pass towards Sulphur Springs Valley. Whatever the causes, when you step outdoors in Tombstone your immediate reaction is of being in contact with the elements rather than in a town. It's an expansive feeling, and may account for some of the high jinks which took place there.

These did not take place on any scale worth comment until Tombstone began to feel its oats as a metropolis. It was a while before that happened. After reading of the excitement caused everywhere by the news of Schieffelin's bonanza, it is somewhat deflating to read further and learn how slim the physical response to that excitement initially was. At the demise of Watervale, nearly a year later than the discovery of the Lucky Cuss, the district had a population of only a few hundred.

Among the several causes can be listed first of all the tiny population of the entire West, which supplied the first wave of settlers. Next was the nonexistence of any regular communications, impeding both the flow of news out of the region and the entrance of men into it. Difficult and often dangerous country surrounded it for great distances on all sides. In the main a road was simply where anyone had the nerve to drive a wagon. There was not a foot of railroad within the boundaries of Arizona Territory. It goes without saying that mail service was sketchy.

If the original inhabitants were drawn from the citizenry of the Old West, there was a screening to throttle down even that scant source of supply. Tombstone was yet no place for a person who wanted to invest in any sort of real estate but a mining claim. At the time of its founding the town was in Pima County. Its county seat was Tucson, seventy-five miles west across the Whetstones. The territorial capital was Prescott, several days' journey to the north. There was no liaison in any regular sense between either of these places and the Valley of the San Pedro. Tombstone began then without official sanction and continued for months without official interference of any kind.

Trusting to get legal backing for its actions later, a townsite company was formed, and in March of 1879 one Solon M. Allis

Apache warrior group such as the ones which terrorized southeastern Arizona in the 1870s and '80s. (*Chapter 1*)

(*Courtesy of the Bank of Douglas*)

Ed Schieffelin (seated on ground at right) in the days after
Tombstone's silver had brought him prosperity. A younger
brother, Eff, is seated facing him. *(Chapter 2)*

laid out the town. It has been changed little if any since. The named streets run the length of the mesa, which is roughly three quarters of a mile long by a quarter in width. The numbered streets run at right angles to the others, pointing north and west toward the Dragoons. Of these streets there was room for twelve without spilling off the mesa, a thing which eventually became necessary. Crossing them were, reading from north to south, Safford, Fremont, Allen, and Tough Nut Streets.

Fremont, named after the renowned explorer of the West who was then governor of the territory, was made eighty feet wide and designed to be the main drag of the town. Incidentally, and although it was always spelled with one 'e' in older documents, just as the governor did himself, all the signs now on the street designate it as "Freemont." Yet the extra five feet of width became Fremont Street's sole claim to superiority. With the usual indifference to the schemes of city planners shown by communities, Allen Street, a block south, became the main business thoroughfare. Soon it grew clear that the hub of the city was the junction of Allen and Fifth Streets. So much, it can be added, is true of the town today.

By the fall of '79 Tombstone had a population of just under a thousand, living in wooden shacks, adobe huts, tents, and Apache-style wickiups of poles covered with odds and ends. When Parsons arrived in February, 1880, he found two thousand predecessors in a town which hadn't yet passed the camp stage. He himself was invited to share a cabin where he had the privilege of bunking on the ground which floored it. It was a privilege with drawbacks. "Rats and mice made a deuce of a racket last night around a fellow's head," he wrote soon after his advent. "Rolled over on one in the night and killed him — Mashed him deader than a door nail." There were no window panes in the shanty, and the winds entered elsewhere at will. There was a stove, but when the wind was from the wrong direction it blew down into the pipe instead of making it draw. In the end Parsons found it pleasanter to build an outside fireplace to do his cooking.

The Last Chance

Places of business were equally primitive. Parsons mentioned attending a theatre, a rickety frame shack with a badly torn canvas roof. Stores set up shop in tents, and restaurants were similarly housed. So were church services and dance hall girls — sometimes too close together for comfort. "Talked with . . . the minister," to quote an entry from the journal, "a while before service which now begins at 8 o'clock. Hard work for him to preach on account of dance house racket in rear. Calls to rally in that direction do not mingle well — hug gals in corner etc."

The single fault to be found with Goose Flats as a site for a town was that water had to be hauled in by carts from various holes and springs. It was priced, for all purposes, at three cents a gallon. Another scarce commodity of primary importance was wood. The nearest trees were in the Dragoons, but lumbering wasn't feasible while Victorio was alive. Timber was rather brought in from mills in the Huachucas, south and west across the valley. The price of $8.00 per hundred foot was exorbitant at that time, but even so the demand far exceeded the supply. An order of boards was a prize second only to a mining claim and was as readily stolen from the unwary. A man expecting lumber had to be waiting for it on the outskirts of town, prepared to outbribe competitors and ride his timber to the spot where he wanted it unloaded.

Another factor that slowed the growth of Tombstone proper to begin with was that it was originally more of a business center than anything else. Many men for reasons of economy, or to guard their presumptive wealth, camped on their claims. A batch of outlying communities mushroomed, such as Austin City in Emerald Gulch, on the eastern approach to the town, Richmond, where Parsons first lived, and Stinkem, a suburb he more than once noticed in his journal. In time these were completely or nearly abandoned as the advantages of living in Tombstone itself seduced the inhabitants.

There remained, however, more permanent towns which were considered a part of the community although they were at a considerable remove. Charleston, where Gird put his ore reducing mill, was one; Fairbank and Contention City, mill towns farther down the San Pedro, were two others. The nearest of them was six crowflight miles away, but because they were dependent upon the Tombstone mines for their existence they belonged. So, too, for reasons which will be dealt with later, did Galeyville, forty-five miles east in the foothills of the Chirichuas. The people in all these places floated back and forth, drank with each other, and betimes shot each other, also. If they died elsewhere and happened to have friends who thought they were worth the attentions of undertakers, they were brought to Tombstone for interment.

Such things as undertakers and coroners' inquests came later, though. For a year and a half the town had no legal standing, let alone any officially recognized government. Parsons stated flatly that there was no law but miners' law when he arrived. Wyatt Earp, who reached the place a few months before him, declared that he was appointed deputy sheriff for Tombstone, where previously no such officer had existed. Yet he was primarily appointed, he recalled, to collect fees missing from the coffers of Pima County rather than to enforce the law. As a matter of fact, to enforce the law was itself a legal impossibility in the absence of any courts.

Tombstone became an interesting demonstration of two phases of man's reaction to the lack of laws. On the one hand the situation fostered lawlessness in those not fundamentally given to it. On the other it caused a reaction which led men to fill the vacuum by organizing in favor of civic improvement. Lawlessness was to have its inning, almost without challenge, at first, and quarrels over the title to lots in town ranked only a little behind disputes over mining claims as causes of ill feeling in a dog-eat-dog society.

Granted that all sales were illegal, in as much as the town site company had no license, nobody seemed to be quite sure exactly what he had bought. As nothing could be officially recorded, there was no generally agreed upon starting point for a survey of property. To complicate things further, the town had been laid out after certain mining claims — which *had* been officially recorded — had been staked out to include a good part of town territory. The effect was to divide business men and miners. The feud of these two elements, which might otherwise have worked together in the interests of fostering stable living conditions, simplified the efforts of sharpers to maintain what was for them, a profitable state of chaos.

Such a state of affairs would naturally tend to make men leery of investing too much money in building. Undoubtedly this was the case, but a more forceful deterrent to the development of the town, during its first year, at least, was that few of its citizens thought it worth their attention. Most of the first echelon of settlers came there to be prospectors. It was only belatedly that some of them realized that they had a city — and as such a potential source of wealth — on their hands, too.

For these early hopefuls Parsons was a signally capable spokesman. To examine his dreams, successes, quarrels and disappointments is to understand the confusion which envelops boom town activities for all but the lucky and the indifferent.

Parsons was by parts from Maine and Virginia and had a mixture of the qualities traditional with the citizens of those two highly individualistic states. He wasn't a complete tenderfoot, as he had done a little knocking around Eastern oil towns and, as he was fond of remembering, Florida. But as far as the West was concerned, he had seen nothing much but San Francisco, where he was working for a bank when the Tombstone boom started.

His reasons for joining it were typical. Adventurers by choice are few, and the successful don't have to leave home. Parsons confided to his journal that, at almost thirty, he considered himself a failure. Moreover, there was a girl back East he wanted to marry. Tombstone looked like an opportunity, and he persuaded Milton Clapp, a fellow employee who was also dissatisfied with his prospects, to go with him.

Schieffelin's big strike had raised hopes of fortune for the finding in the hearts of hundreds, most of them as ignorant of mining as Parsons and Clapp. The latter, after taking a look at the situation, shopped around until he got an indoor job. Parsons plunged into prospecting, confident of becoming a tycoon. The town, it was clear, initially had no interest for him.

What is now evident but could not be to him and his ilk was that he didn't have a chance. By 1880 the men who could afford to hire A-1 engineers, of the stripe of Gird himself, were developing what was worth developing and only chicken feed was procurable elsewhere. Then, to begin with, silver is not valuable enough in itself to be profitable except where ore is produced in great quantities. The reading of an assay sounds so much more valuable than the actuality. If the report is that it should produce, say, $3,000 a ton, it does not mean $3,000 for every ton of rock removed from the mine, but only of ore — which had to blasted from its matrix of lesser stone.

To operate at a profit consistently it was necessary to be able to afford power hoists and other mechanical aids to mass production. Even the richest veins demand big money for exploitation, and, as has already been pointed out, the one-horse miners didn't have the richest veins. The lower the grade of the ore the bigger the investment needed to make it pay; but such a truth either was not realized or wasn't faced.

They worked their hearts out with inadequate tools, as Parsons, who shirked none of the labor, related. "Then came the ticklish trick of holding drills while the 8 pound sledge came down with force every second or so. More difficult than I imagined to hold drills properly — to keep them in proper direction and prevent their running away from true course . . . Some nerve required to hold hands just under the pound of the hammer. I tried the sledge too and that's equally as ticklish business . . . One must bury all fears and strike boldly. G clipped me just a little — nothing serious — might have been though. Terrible hard rock. Mixture of lime porphyry and iron. Used drills badly. We fired a number of shots. Several of the blasts doing good execution. This again is dangerous work. We used giant powder. Has to be handled carefully. Tamping is done very nicely — not too much — or cap explodes and one is likely to go flying out of the shaft. Black powder not so dangerous but bad enough."

There are other entries equally graphic and pertinent. "The terribly cramped and strained positions at times and strength required to manage a hole in soft ground enforces a great physical strain and much nerve when the swinger of the heavy sledge hammer has to aim over and draw in to prevent hitting you and sometimes will graze the edge of your moustache in striking a hundred pound blow upon a piece of steel ¾ of an inch in diameter . . . Drilled a hole myself today with single drill and 4½ lbs. hammer. Tasked my arm dreadfully and once I just clipped myself . . . Windlassing much easier than throwing dirt ten feet to surface after being shoveled up another ten feet from bottom of shaft."

In that last remark Parsons might be considered as showing himself grateful for small favors. The windlass in question was made out of a log and was operated painfully by hand, often under the full power of the Arizona sun. He and the others gave everything they had all right. They spent all the capital they could raise. Occasionally they killed each other over their largely worthless claims. Yet they remained the also rans of bonanza days. In rare instances they made a competence out of their mining activities; but wealth was beyond their reach, and they could no more understand why than does a fly on the outside of a candy store window.

There were three thousand claims in the area and, except for about fifty, their average worth was approximately that of the original Tombstone claim, which Schieffelin eventually sold for $400. A man would spend all the capital he had been able to earn and borrow for a claim — and wonder later how he was going to manage to develop it. And even after he had been stung a dozen times he came back for more. The notion that if you only dug a hole in the right place you could be rich held him there in spite of poverty, wretched living conditions, and homesickness.

There were plenty to lead him on. A claim broker was not above salting the mine he was selling, or showing the wide-eyed buyer pieces of float he had picked up on a sneak visit to one of the big finds. Many were not above selling claims to which they had a dubious or wholly imaginary title. "Just here I will say," Parsons bitterly commented, "that I was never in a place or business before where there was so much chenanniging (sic) carried on. It seems impossible almost to believe anyone. One must rely entirely upon himself and trust *no one* else."

Yet if a man did secure an unquestionably clear title, that didn't mean it would not be disputed. For every underhanded dealer in town there was an open crook who would start mining operations on any unwatched claim he thought promising. A man had to be willing to fight for what he had or forget it.

They were all, even the honest ones, on the make and suspicious of everybody else. Disappointed in themselves and their prospects, they were readily quarrelsome. All the same a credulous optimism lurked so near to the surface that they were willing to believe any rumor that suggested good fortune.

Parsons tells the whole story in its psychological as well as its physical aspects. At twenty-nine he was still young enough to feel romantic about coming to a genuine western mining camp. With prospects of wealth imminent the hardships could be taken in stride. Soon after his arrival he proudly laid out a claim which he named for himself. He came close to claim jumping when he did so, although he was justified, as he persuaded his journal, by the fact that his predecessor had marked the holding improperly. Perhaps his predecessor was one of the rare ones who had seen the light and turned to something else. There is no evidence that he protested. Nor is there any evidence that Parsons got around to working his so-called mine.

It was in order to be able to do so, or to buy into something better, that he hired out to swing a sledge, etc. He was thus equipping himself to be an operator in his own right in addition to earning a stake. Meanwhile he was putting out feelers for more capital. Enthusiastic reports of the local possibilities drew money in small amounts from relatives and friends in the East and in San

The Last Chance

Francisco. People with real money to invest ask more than a young man's optimism as security, and that's all that Parsons and his kind had to offer.

The small mines didn't earn more than bread and beans. The little holding companies which leased them soon used up their working capital and folded. Their only genuine chance for success was to discover a lode which would attract one of the big outfits. But those companies had their own prospectors, trained and professionally equipped. Only pure luck could help the amateurs.

In desperation the amateurs tried afield. They went into the Dragoons in spite of the fact that small parties were methodically killed and scalped by Victorio's braves. Always there were favorable reports. Things looked good. This was the strike that was to make it all worth while. Or a reworking of an old mine would raise similar hopes. An assay of a new vein would show they had struck it rich. Then the vein would run out, and new plans would be formed.

It was this state of affairs that eventually turned the attention of the more intelligent treasure hunters toward Tombstone itself. They never surrendered their hope of sudden riches. Had they done so, they would have left a spot where effort and enterprise had proved so unrewarding. But they commenced hedging their bets by trying to manage a respectable livelihood while they were waiting for luck to be kind.

Parsons, for instance, worked seasonally in the local branch of the Safford and Hudson Bank. Next he formed a business with one of his associates, the title searching and mining agency firm of Parsons and Redfern. Meanwhile he had begun speculating in Tombstone real estate; and so did many of his colleagues and rivals. For if mining claims were generally of dubious value there was no doubt as to the genuine worth of property in a rapidly growing town.

Once the financial interests of these men were vested in the place, they found themselves developing a zeal for its welfare.

They became, in fact, what they had by no means been while prospecting was their only concern, genuine citizens of Tombstone.

This was not only of moment to the town, it was indispensable to the most dramatic phase of the town's history. In combination with the merchants and professional men who were being drawn in increasing numbers by Tombstone's prosperity, the more or less reconstructed prospectors formed an element which asserted itself in the city's great struggle. The prize of that struggle was to be the control of Tombstone itself.

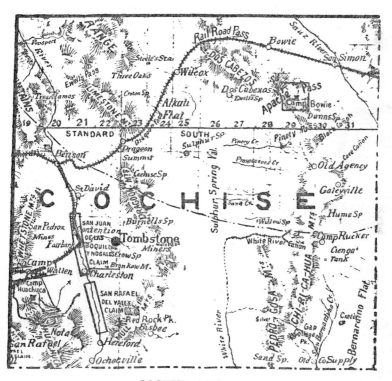

COCHISE COUNTY

CHAPTER FOUR

TOMBSTONE THE CITY

IT WAS NOT until the mining boom in the San Pedro Valley took on an air of permanence that the Southern Pacific saw fit to push its tracks east across the Colorado. When the rails got as far as Tucson during the first half of 1880 Tombstone celebrated. There would be a distributing point within comparatively easy reach both for incoming goods and outgoing bullion. Mail, which had been delivered only twice or three times a week, would now be a daily service. The town's liaison with the outside world was so strengthened that a new rush of prosperity resulted. The six-horse stages which brought the mail brought in new settlers; a half a dozen perhaps on top, and ten more jammed into the carriage.

Other things took place about then or in the ensuing months to boost Tombstone's stock as a place in which to invest capital as well as to make it. In September of 1880 a patent for land was let to the corporate authorities of the Village of Tombstone. That didn't signify the end of real estate troubles, for the corporate authorities proved crooked; but at least a legal basis for the ownership of town property had been established. Then official recognition of the town's existence furnished a taking off place for further political development. A movement was afoot to make the eastern half of Pima into a separate county. Tombstone would inevitably be its county seat. On the last day of January, 1881, the governor signed such a measure. Cochise County, named for the old Apache chief who had for so long dominated the region, was created.

Tombstone's most flamboyant era of lawlessness was yet to come, yet the tools of law enforcement, previously withheld from

Tombstone the City

the community, were at last accorded it. The more dubious benefits of political patronage went along with this new estate. Nevertheless, the town got an added lift, and one not reckoned strictly
in population figures. Professional men, a group not attracted in
strength during the town's formless stage, moved in to give the
place a more cosmopolitan flavor.

The fourth estate was already well entrenched. Earliest on the
scene was *The Nugget*, which began publishing in the fall of '79.
The press which printed this sheet was the first ever seen in Arizona, having been brought into the territory prior to the War
between the States by Lieutenant Sylvester Mowry. This enterprising young West Point graduate was one of the first to see the
possibilities of Arizona and to make a vigorous attempt to exploit
them. As part of this effort he had a press shipped from California
around to a port on the gulf of that name and brought overland
to the old Spanish settlement of Tubac. *The Arizonian* flourished
there and down the Santa Cruz Valley at Tucson. There the
veteran press was subsequently used to publish *The Arizona Star*
before being brought to Tombstone.

The Nugget's more famous rival was *The Epitaph*, still published and now Tombstone's only paper. It first came off the press
in the spring of 1880. Other journals, some of them the fly by
night rags of traveling printers, were *The Union, The Citizen, The
Prospector*, which *The Epitaph* eventually absorbed, and *The
Arizona Kicker*.

The advertisements in these papers reflect the commercial
development of the town. Saloons of one sort or another formed
the core of the business section. At one time there were 110 places
with licenses to sell liquor. Some purveyed food also, some had
dancing as a side-line, complete with girls for partners, most had
gambling tables, and a few of the bigger ones offered vaudeville
acts. The most famous came to be the Crystal Palace and the
Oriental, both occupying prize locations at the junction of Allen
and Fifth. Next in importance to the saloons were the hardware
stores, specializing in mining equipment and firearms. Corrals

47

also ranked as important business concerns. These were livery stables with the additional feature, suitable to the West, of open air pens where mounts could be checked and picked up with a minimum of formality.

For Tombstone was more than a mining town by then. It was the metropolis of a region of riding men. It was the focal point of every kind of business as well as the place where they counted on meeting both their friends and enemies. Nor was it necessary to pick your time in order to locate food or entertainment. The town was wide open twenty-four hours a day. A thirsty miner, say, getting off the graveyard shift could find what he wanted by entering almost any door for blocks on the north side of Allen Street.

That was the side along which women did not walk unless they were looking for a pick-up or were parading their wares with a view to encouraging future business. Other parts of town came to be partitioned off, too. The redlight district was in the southern part of town, east of Sixth Street. Not unnaturally the favored residential district was in the northwestern corner. Hop Town, the Chinese settlement, began at Tough Nut and Third.

By the time Tombstone had taken on such definite contours it began to call itself a city and had a right to the claim. The pushing through of the Southern Pacific to join the Santa Fe Railroad in New Mexico started boom days all over again. Benson, twenty-five miles down the valley, was the rail point, and there were hopes — to be realized not much more than a year later — of a line down along the San Pedro. Incremental prosperity seemed guaranteed, and the Johnny-come-latelies poured in by the gross.

There was reason for the enthusiasm of these newcomers. The big mines were living up to advance billing. They operated on a twenty-four hour basis seven days a week and paid hundreds of miners the then high wages of four dollars for an eight hour shift. As most of the miners were young men without families, they spent their money as fast as they got it.

To turn to the mines again, Hamilton stated that by 1884 they had produced $25,000,000 in bullion and were still going strong.

Tombstone the City

The Contention was 600 feet deep and ran 20 miles of underground passages on five different levels. The specifications given for the Grand Central were almost the same except that the main shaft was 750 feet deep; and the Lucky Cuss and the Tough Nut had been worked on a similar scale. Several dozen lesser mines, which yet were producing sound profits, were also listed by Hamilton.

Tombstone itself was burrowed under from all directions, and the mesa on which it sits is said to be a network of tunnels today. The form of most of these workings was stope mining, which is to say that when a vein was followed the rock above it was propped up by timbers to prevent it from collapsing. At Tough Nut and Fifth Streets there is a huge hole which testifies to the fact that this effort wasn't always successful. It also testifies to the wealth that was in the very foundations of Tombstone. After an enormously rich vein of the Tough Nut series of mines it was called "The Million Dollar Stope."

With an unfailing supply of silver to nourish its prosperity there seemed to be no ceiling to stop the growth of the city. Early in 1881 the population was estimated at 6,000. What it was at the town's peak is something that will never be known, for it rose and fell between the census takings of 1880 and 1890. Guesses range from 7,500 to 15,000. For its period a reliable one is probably that of Clum, who was at once mayor and postmaster of Tombstone as well as publisher of *The Epitaph*. The estimate he made from these three vantage points was that by the end of 1881 there were upwards of 10,000 residents of a still growing community.

It had grown and developed in other ways, too. Water was no longer brought in by wagons. It was piped to a reservoir which in turn served it to individual buildings. At first the supply came from Sycamore Springs, seven miles away in the Dragoons, but when this proved inadequate after the fire of 1882 a more ambitious project was undertaken. Among the citizens of Tombstone was a New York piano manufacturer called Haley who had made a comfortable fortune peddling his instruments to the music-starved West. His method was to travel around with his merchandise in a knocked-down form and have it set up for the purchaser on the spot by a crew of experts. Apparently believing that what could be done with pianos could also be done with a water works, he contracted to run a pipe line to Tombstone from twenty-three miles away in the Huachucas. Ordering the necessary sections of pipe from Pittsburg, he had it dumped in lots at strategic points between the source and the city, and arranged for soldiers from Fort Huachuca to stand guard against hostile Apaches. By September of '82 he had done the job. With a drop of 1500 feet there was pressure enough for the water to reach every house in town.

Telegraph service had been instituted in 1880. Gas had taken the place of oil for lighting by the next year; and in general the air was one of modernity for the times. Wooden awnings extended over the walks along Allen Street to shelter passers-by from the sun and occasional rains. The buildings supporting these awnings were no longer of makeshift construction. They were well-built frame, adobe, or brick buildings. The bars had elaborate fixtures, the restaurants, such as the Can-Can Chop House, the best of table ware. Shops had the latest thing in the way of clothes or mechanical devices.

Tombstone had become, indeed, a nationally recognized cosmopolis. It boasted the best food between New Orleans and San Francisco. It was a regular point of call for the better road shows making the westward swing. Newspapers and magazines throughout the country publicized its wealth as well as its lawlessness. It was the biggest town in the territory. Looking forward to the days when Arizona would become a state, many were confident that Tombstone would be its capital.

If the saloons and six shooters made the headlines, there was much else to the city. Schools had been established, not without protest from youngsters accustomed to running as wild as their elders. Many youngsters, especially those who rode in from the range, were accustomed to consider themselves men by the time they approached their teens. They did a man's work and went armed like men; and they were outraged when teachers objected to this practice in class rooms. In his reminiscences one man recalled that his teacher finally settled the issue by commandeering all weapons and throwing them into the stove. As he had neglected to unload them, there was quite a bit of excitement. Another man, one who went to school in Charleston, recalled that the teacher secured the backing of his pupils' parents to have all revolvers checked at the class room door, in the manner of men establishing peaceable intentions when entering a saloon.

There were self-improvement courses for adults in the evening, where everything from penmanship to sundry foreign languages was taught. There were dancing schools for old and young. Joiners could satisfy their needs by enlisting with the Masons or the Knights of Pythias. More serious entertainment was offered by the Tombstone Club, which subscribed to sixty periodicals, and certain rental libraries which made a point of stocking the latest American and foreign books.

There were four churches — a Catholic, an Espiscopalian, a Presbyterian, and a Methodist — and, true to the American norm, these became the centers of social as well as of religious life. The women gave church suppers, teas, and musicals. There were dances, Christmas parties, and literary evenings. Several amateur dramatic societies were formed, one of which was ambitious enough to put on the then comparatively new hit, Gilbert and Sullivan's *Pinafore*.

Professional shows were housed chiefly by two theatres, each catering to a specific type of audience. Bona fide plays, operas, operettas, revues, minstrel shows, and variety acts with any pretensions to refinement were booked by Schieffelin Hall. This building, erected by Al Schieffelin, is reputedly the largest adobe building in the United States. Certainly it is a sizeable edifice. The upper story is still, as it was originally, used by the local chapter of Masons, but the theatre itself has been dismantled. In its day, however, it was claimed to have had a stage which rivaled in size and appurtenances anything west of Broadway.

The Last Chance

Although Schieffelin Hall had previously been used by Tombstone amateurs, it was first used professionally by the Nellie Boyd Dramatic Co., featuring the actress who gave her name to the outfit. On December 5, 1881 these troupers offered *The Banker's Daughter*, a drama by the American playwright, Bronson Howard.

Miss Boyd had been a minor figure on the New York stage before forming her company. The Fifth Ave. Comedy Co., which subsequently produced *Minnie's Luck* or *The Ups and Downs of New York Life* may or may not have come from Manhattan, as advertised, but there was no doubt as to the standing of others who entertained Tombstone theatre lovers. William H. Lingard and his wife had been well established New York producers before they brought their troupe to Schieffelin Hall for a performance of Sardou's *Divorçons*. Frederick B. Warde, who thrilled Tombstone with his performance in *Virginius* or *The Roman Father* in 1885, was reckoned an actor of the first rank by critics throughout the nation. Three years earlier Milton Nobles appeared in the hall. Successful in New York in the joint capacities of author, actor, and producer, he presented and played in two of his own hits, *The Phœnix* and *Interviews*.

If some undoubted celebrities graced the Tombstone stage, some far greater ones did so in legend only. Of these mythical appearances the one which has achieved the widest publicity is that of the famous Lotta Crabtree. The story still persists, although it should have been scotched for good by the report of Claire E. Willson, who took the trouble to get in touch with John B. Wright, a lawyer concerned in the disposal of Miss Crabtree's estate. In his *Mimes and Miners* Willson published Wright's answer.

". . . I put in four years studying the Crabtree family, and went through a very long-drawn-out litigation in Boston, so I am perfectly confident that what I tell you is true. Lotta Crabtree never did appear at the Bird Cage, nor any other theater in Tombstone. She never even visited that town.

"The story evidently started because of the fact that she staked her brother, Jack Crabtree, who went there, and he repeatedly told people that he intended to build a big theater in Tombstone and his sister Lotta was going to open it.

"Among 66 old-timers whose affidavits I took, and who were there in Tombstone from the time it started until the boom was over, I never found but one who stated that Lotta Crabtree was ever there. This man . . . had been drunk for forty years and unquestionably was drawing upon his imagination."

Yet even better imaginations have been at work on the annals of the Tombstone stage. It is stated, for instance that Lillian Russell used to sing for the delight of those dining at the Can-Can Chop House. As Miss Russell was already well on her way to being the toast of the nation when the Can-Can first opened its doors, this can be safely denied without documentation.

A far more remarkable statement remains to be dealt with. The old Bird Cage Theatre is now a museum visited by dozens of tourists any day the weather is fine, which is most of the time in Tombstone. These tourists are told with a gracious confidence that almost enforces credulity that Jenny Lind once sang on the house's stage. If so, it was her only appearance west of the Atlantic in almost thirty years. Miss Lind would then have been not less than sixty-one years old, and a doubtful attraction to a bachelor audience that liked its female entertainers bare and spry.

One famous trouper who did appear in the Bird Cage was the comedian Eddie Foy. His comment on the architecture of the house was that it should have been called the coffin. Nevertheless, from the night it opened, late in 1881 or early in 1882, it was singularly successful. If its shoe-box design makes Foy's comment seem an apt one to someone viewing it from without, its interior was cheerful and intimate. Unlike the management of Schieffelin Hall, the management of the Bird Cage Theatre was without cultural pretensions. It had a pretty clear idea of what miners, cowboys, and assorted outlaws liked, and it did a pretty good job of giving them what they wanted.

The lobby contained a bar, and there were girls for waitresses and other purposes. The usual program consisted of leg shows, bawdy skits, and the more boisterous type of variety acts. "Healey Bros.," announces a surviving handbill advertising one of these acts. "Engaged and will surely appear. Grotesque Dancing, Leg Mania and Contortion Feats in which they stand positively alone. In their specialty The Happy Hottentots. P.S. These gentlemen are the highest kickers in the universe — bar none."

To repeat, the customers were predominantly male, and so was the entire population of Tombstone in its great days. To house and feed this horde of bachelors was a business which didn't rank far behind silver mining and bar tending. For such of them who didn't spend all they made there were the local branches of two Tucson banks, the Safford and Hudson and the Pima County. Other services were taken care of by the Wells Fargo Express company, which undertook to transport bullion through a countryside swarming with holdup men, real estate companies, and mining agencies like the one Parsons opened. The undertakers offered their services, too.

Dead citizens were lodged a short ways from the northwest corner of town. Boot Hill is a generic term for the burying ground of all lawless western towns, and the Tombstone one is likewise thus referred to nowadays. Sometimes it may have been so styled then, but there is no evidence to that effect. In existing references it is called the Tombstone Cemetery, which, aside from not being a bad name for a burying ground, is descriptive. It is not and never has been a green place for flowers to bloom. Even cactus finds it difficult to take root there, although a few specimens manage it. Mainly the cemetery is a patch of land, peculiarly bleak and covered with stones. These, incidentally, were the only tombstones in a strict sense that most of the corpses had. The original grave markers were boards.

As for the live citizenry, the Southwest has never been a region where there was a tradition for big homes. The capacious three-story houses which were being thrown up by the thousands in other parts of the country at this time were not built even by very prosperous men in Arizona. Most family residences were

one-story structures of wood or adobe, big enough to be comfortable but without excess space. Parsons told what the quarters of a bachelor were like. He put up a twelve by fifteen foot wooden shanty at a total cost of $160 and rented it to man for $15 a month.

If a man tired of baching in such a place he could eat out for a flat price of $8 per week, or he could buy a single meal for fifty cents. If he wanted to put on the dog, he could pay a little more at the Cosmopolitan Hotel, at the corner of Fifth and Allen, or its rival, the Grand. Both were excellent hostelries, though neither was as imposing as the court house, complete with county jail. At first an adobe building on Fremont Street, it was rebuilt in 1882 as a three-story brick edifice which still stands on the south side of Tough Nut at Third.

The big red building on Tough Nut is no longer the court house for Cochise County, whose seat is now Bisbee. But nobody would have believed that could happen when Tombstone was in its pride. Who that drank on Allen Street could doubt the permanence of the city's glory? The dirty-shirt bartenders had given way to white jacketed attendants who could cater to any taste in mixed drinks. Their surroundings were in kind, for the ramshackle joints had been replaced by saloons decorated with all the magnificence of late nineteenth-century rococo.

Moving forces in the civic face lifting which transformed the business section of Tombstone were a couple of costly fires. They are worth noticing not only for what they indirectly accomplished but for the vote of confidence in the town they drew from its citizens.

The first of the two broke out on June 22, 1881. Its cause was ascertained to be a barrel of whiskey with whose quality an Allen Street saloon keeper was dissatisfied. He thrust in a gauge in order to determine the amount of liquor he was turning back to the distributor and lost the instrument down the bung hole. The bartender who tried to help him retrieve the gauge was said to have had a lighted cigar in his mouth.

The resulting blaze was out of control from the beginning.

The Last Chance

Miraculously no one was killed when it raced from one match stick building to another. The most seriously injured person seems to have been George Parsons, who was badly burned while fighting the fire. An inadequate water supply made this an ineffectual effort, and the flames ended by consuming four complete blocks in the heart of town.

Tombstone's response was to shrug and get to work. "With the dawn of Thursday's sun," *The Epitaph* reported, "men, women and children were astir, looking about to see what had been left them out of the ruins of the evening before. There was little but desolation, the few goods they had left being badly damaged. Nothing dismayed, the business portion of the community set about them to make ready for the new stocks that had been ordered by telegraph the night before — figuratively speaking, the dispatches being written by the light of their burning goods."

"We have not heard of a single case," *The Epitaph* exulted in another article, "where a sufferer has thrown up the sponge, to use a sporting phrase, and is going to close out his business. . . . As before stated, several commenced to clean off the debris yesterday, and had lumber on the ground before night with carpenters at work."

William Bishop, a professional tourist who was there later in the year, published a statement to the effect that the business section was rebuilt in two weeks. Although a great improvement on the shanty town carpentry it supplanted the construction was hasty rather than solid. The penalty was paid within a year, for on May 25, 1882 a second fire burned out almost the same area. It was on the third building, evidently as confidently undertaken as the second, that brick replaced wood to give Tombstone a metropolitan front.

Still the most significant fact about the city was its location. Cities are normally nourished by their commerce with one another, and are apt to sprout in clusters. The solitude of Tombstone was just short of being all encompassing. Today the ruins of Ninevah look neither more lonely nor more unexpected when

pictured against the emptiness of its setting. Then most cities reach their estate because of their importance in point of service to a considerable region. That had a bearing in only a limited sense in Tombstone. Its cause of being was a local phenomenon, and the attention of its citizens was focused on that phenomenon and the social and political conditions which developed from it. The city was for some years in the United States only by the imposition of geography.

One aspect of the wildness which surrounded its urbanity was that the Apaches continued to be a menace. No actual raid by the Indians on the town itself was threatened, or even feared; but the district was visited by war parties time and again. Parsons made repeated references to the danger. "Another Indian scare on hand people somewhat excited. Victorio is a ubiquitous piece of humanity." "Indian scare increasing. Dragoon people coming in. Several Tombstoners killed by Indians recently." "Fight reported in Mule Mountains. . . . Indians not far from town. In fact seen from here so it is said. Two poor fellows killed by them at south pass and bro't in today."

At that the Apaches were not more wild and certainly no more sinister than many who regularly walked the streets of Tombstone. That statement is applicable to women, in some instances, as well as men, including not a few who rode the range adjacent to the city.

CHAPTER FIVE

SOME WHO WENT THERE

I<small>F</small> <small>THERE</small> were ten to fifteen thousand people in Tombstone, the names of only a few dozen are preserved by history. Who were the others, and what were they doing while the six shooters were being fired and the roulette wheels spun?

A large percentage of them were professional miners attracted by a town that paid top wages. They drilled and blasted, took their four bucks a day, lived the life of the average untrammeled bachelor with plenty of money to spend, and let it go at that. Many of these were "Cornish Jacks," who had learned their trade in the mines of England and Wales. Many more were part of the western spearheads of the great Irish and German migrations. The only other foreign groups of a size to be noticeable were the Chinese and the Mexicans.

The genuine prospectors, of the class to which Schieffelin himself had belonged, did not stay around in numbers after the initial scramble for claims. It was the amateurs rather, men who were earnestly looking for a steady source of income if they couldn't find wealth, that remained to leave their mark upon the town. These were men like Parsons. They were not ones to bet a grand on the turn of a card in a gaudy saloon, nor would they have done so, if they had had that kind of money. These were the men who played whist and euchre to the accompaniment of beer and cheese in their shanties. Or they played chess, read the latest novels, like Tourgee's *A Fool's Errand*, took part in amateur theatricals, and ate ice cream at church socials.

If they had one thing in common, except those pastimes, it was that they had come to the West too late to be thoroughly acclimated. To bona fide prospectors home was where they happened to be. To the gamblers and gunmen Tombstone was just another room in their big home. To the miners it also represented normalcy in that mining towns weren't expected to be orderly residential communities. Parsons and his cronies, however, were living in Tombstone for the future rather than in the present.

Viewed broadly the metamorphosis of the West from lawlessness to law-abiding was a process of inevitable conformity to the rest of the country. In its workings, however, the process owed much to men like Parsons and his fellows, who were too much a part of the civilized East to accept rough country standards in their entirety.

Still they became partially moulded to the Tombstone pattern in spite of themselves. At first it is evident that Parsons carried a pistol as a boy would, self-consciously proud of being an armed man. Everybody did it, and it added to the fun. The time came when he went looking for his enemy, fully prepared, he stated, to kill him if circumstances made that appropriate. It was this toughening of attitude which qualified him to become a member of the vigilantes, or as they called themselves in Tombstone, "The Citizens' Safety Committee."

Others who walked Allen Street were shapers of Arizona's new economy, like Governor Safford and John S. Vosburg. The former, a banker and financial catalyst for the entire Tombstone enterprise, now made his headquarters in the city. Some of the men who actually furnished the capital were in town from time to time, such as the Corbin brothers of Connecticut, who bought the Schieffelins out for $600,000. Another visiting tycoon was Senator George Hearst of California. Yet although he caused great excitement in Tombstone by inspecting its mines, he apparently invested no money. The mining fortune later invested in a journalistic empire was made elsewhere.

A politician on a humbler scale than Senator Hearst, but one of far greater importance to Tombstone, was Marcus Aurelius Smith. At one time he represented Arizona Territory in Washington, but both before and after that his shingle was one of a good many on Rotten Row. This was Fourth Street north of Tough Nut, a roost for lawyers just around the corner from the Cochise County Courthouse.

There were also a good few doctors in the city; and a need for their services, what with hard bitten miners, gun fighters from both in and out of town, and the Apaches. The most notable local ornament of this profession was Dr. George Goodfellow. A graduate of Annapolis who oddly turned up as an Army surgeon, he was co-owner of a San Pedro Valley ranch with Captain Leonard Wood. The latter, who later came close to being given command of the AEF in World War I, was well known in Tombstone. There he was only a secondary figure compared to his partner, however. Dr. Goodfellow was not only one of the town's leading citizens but one of the few coroners in history whose reports were cherished for their entertainment value. In particular his decision in the case of Tombstone's most celebrated lynching made him a small but secure place in the annals of the West.

The cloth was ably represented by a man who made his reputation in another region of the nation. The Rev. Endicott Peabody, later to be headmaster of Groton, a Massachusetts school for sons of the wealthy, attended by Franklin D. Roosevelt among others, was the first rector of Tombstone's St. Paul's Church. He also supplied the initiative which built this edifice. An adobe structure still in use, it is claimed to be the first Protestant Church ever erected in Arizona.

At Groton Peabody established a national reputation as a disciplinarian. The boys who walked chalk under his rule might have been interested to read Parsons' report of a trip to Ft. Huachuca he took in company with the minister. Parsons was shocked by the free and easy conduct of the then young Mr. Peabody who evidently got squiffled with some of the garrison's junior officers. However that may be, Tombstone took to the rector, and not one class of people only. When certain gamblers heard that Peabody had failed to raise the necessary funds for his church from his bona fide parishioners, they pooled enough

Some Who Went There

of their winnings to make up the deficit. To the rector's honor be it said, he didn't turn up his nose at this offering.

In the world of journalism the most interesting citizen of the town was John P. Clum. A few years before he came to the San Pedro Valley this young man from New York State had been the first captor of Geronimo, nipping that redoubtable renegade's first insurrection in the bud. Years later he was to go to Alaska to set up the postal system for that territory during the last of the great gold rushes of this continent. In Tombstone his permanent contribution to the town was to found *The Epitaph*. There have been conflicting stories as to how the sheet came by this lugubrious name. Clum himself is authority for the statement that he thought of it himself and insisted on it over the objections of his partners.

A lesser figure of Tombstone's fourth estate was Bucky O'Neil, Arizona's preux chevalier. The career as a sheriff and ranger which was to end in Cuba, when a bullet finally caught up with Captain William O'Neil of Roosevelt's Rough Riders, had not yet begun. The adventurous youngster who crossed the San Pedro fancied himself as a reporter and became one of Clum's hired hands of the city room.

Still a fifth profession, fully accorded that status in the old West, had numerous practitioners on Allen Street. The men who ran the gambling concessions in the big saloons were men of mark who paid their operatives $25.00 for a single six hour shift. Sometimes they leased the entire saloon in which they worked, as was the case with Lou Rickabaugh of the Oriental and his partner Dick Clark, who subsequently purchased the Alhambra.

An aspirant to a like standing among dealers was only an apprentice, and a not too successful one, in his Tombstone days. This was the fabulous William C. Greene, who came to achieve the gambler's ultimate triumph, swapping in his faro box for one that ran ticker tape. But the days when he was to own the Cananea copper mines in Sonora, to beat Wall Street, and, in the end, to be beaten by it, were still far ahead of him. He had not then thought of manufacturing a colonelcy for himself. All Bill Greene wanted when he spent half his time in the Tombstone mines swinging a sledge to make a stake was to be able to wear the richly sober clothes which marked the established dealer.

Yet none of the figures so far listed, with the exception of Clum and O'Neil, were of the West to the degree that they had careers which could not be duplicated, though possibly to the tune of less excitement, elsewhere in the nation. Associated with the story of Tombstone, however, were quite a few who were Westerners in the classic sense.

One of the characteristics of the important western towns, whether it was mining or cattle that made them important, was that the names of the same crew of adventurers pop up in their histories as regularly as the names of a certain limited group of knights appear in tale after tale of the Arthurian cycle. They came to Tombstone, too, although by then their numbers had been sensibly diminished.

It requires some investigation to decide just which ones were actually present, and at which time. Tombstone was famous, and so were they. In the absence of any contradictory documents, at least such as were matters of public knowledge, some of them came to be associated with the town without license. In the memoirs of a man calling himself Arizona Bill the statement appears that he often saw Wild Bill Hickok in Tombstone. This took good eyes as Hickok had been shot to death before Schieffelin led his mules across the San Pedro. For another instance of inaccurate reporting an old timer named Hughes included in his autobiography the remark that Bat Masterson was mixed up in a gun battle which took place months after that notable sheriff had left town. To make an action take on stature one or more of the men in question had to participate, so a narrator who wanted his reminiscences to attract attention stuck in as many of them as he could think of offhand.

Many of the others had already joined Hickok in the collective underworld of Boot Hill, while still others had quieted at the

command of age or consented to being museum pieces in the
East like Buffalo Bill Cody. Some were missing who might have
appeared; but on the whole the roster of those who lived in or who
came to inspect Tombstone is a list of the survivors.

These were not the elder heroes — the mountain men and
scouts from the great days of exploration. These were celebrated
men from the era of transition. They had one foot in the old days
in that they had seen the buffalo and had all done a reasonable
amount of Indian fighting. But they were townsmen, too, so their
other foot was in the new West they had helped to bring into being.

The background of all might differ, but their actual careers had
the curious similarity of so many tramp newspapermen. They all
knew each other and had, if not in all cases a liking, a respect
for each other's prowess. They had been to the same places —
Dodge City and Wichita, the Kansas cow capitals, Leadville in
Colorado, Deadwood, the gold town of South Dakota, and so
on — before coming to Arizona.

Wyatt Earp was the dominant figure among them as far as
Tombstone was concerned. The peculiarities of his character
belong to a later place in this chronicle. Aside from the fact that
he had taken some time off for education his experiences were
typical of the order to which he belonged. His Virginia parents
had moved westward in a series of journeys, their progress marked
by the birth places of their considerable progeny. Wyatt himself
was born in Illinois, in Monmouth, and raised in Kansas. As a
boy of fifteen he made the journey to the West Coast, much of it
through Indian territory, and from then on he was a plainsman
in good standing. As a youngster just out of his teens he was one
of the buffalo hunters who cleared the range for the cattle to
come. Later, with that strange parlay so popular with his kind,
he was either by turns or simultaneously a gambler and a peace
officer. To follow these callings in that time and place it was
necessary to be able and willing to shoot before you were shot.
Wyatt was both.

Chroniclers are in the habit of claiming that such and such a one was "the quickest on the draw and the surest shot in the old West." Sometimes that accolade is given to Wyatt Earp, though with what justice it is impossible to tell. The argument that has raged among biographers has often led them to discredit the prowess of certain gunmen, Wyatt included, the better to build up their their own particular subject. But this is all opinion substituting for fact. In terms of reality the discussion is as futile as the one about which was the greatest ball player, Hans Wagner or Babe Ruth. Yet the same thing can certainly be claimed for Wyatt Earp that was true of them. Contemporary big leaguers, the men in the best position to know, held him to be better than very good.

With Wyatt, or soon after his arrival, came a whole string of his brothers. James, a half brother older than the rest, had been incapacitated in the War between the States, and Warren, the youngest, was a secondary figure. On the other hand Virgil and Morgan, the one a couple of years older and the other that much younger than Wyatt, just missed being hall of fame gunmen themselves.

Dr. John Holliday, Wyatt's dentist friend whom tuberculosis drove west and ruined for his profession, did not miss it. He still pulled or filled a tooth occasionally, but the source of his livelihood was gambling. Fortunately for his success at this trade his frailty had extended neither to his hands nor his nerves. Of him much more will have to be said in this chronicle.

A more orthodox member of the coterie was that other good friend of Wyatt's, Bat Masterson. One of the youngest buffalo hunters, he was a survivor of the renowned Adobe Walls fight when some twenty hunters holding a rendezvous in the northern end of the Texas Panhandle successfully repelled the assaults of hundreds of Indians, enraged at the slaughter which was depriving them of a livelihood. Like Wyatt Bat had made his big reputation as a peace officer in the lively Kansas towns at the end of the long cattle trails. Like Wyatt, too, he was at times a professional gambler.

Some Who Went There

So was Luke Short, sometimes called "the undertaker's friend," because of a penchant for shooting a man between the eyes, thus simplifying the business of dressing the corpse. He left Tombstone comparatively early, though not without first getting his man, who happened to be a distinguished member of his own fraternity. This was Charlie Storms, whom Wyatt cited to his biographer as one of the three handiest men with a pistol in Deadwood.

Another Deadwood alumnus was Turkey Creek Jack Johnson. His confidence in his shooting skill was such that he once agreed to fight two men at once in South Dakota. The terms were that the antagonists, each armed with two pistols, could advance on signal from points marked off on the street. The chosen spot for the combat was in front of the cemetery, as Johnson, according to Earp, thought that it was a consideration owing to volunteer sextons. Of his two enemies one fired seven shots and the other nine. Johnson, the lone survivor, proceeded until he thought he was near enough and then fired two.

Such were the men. The gambling which was one of their chief means of livelihood might take the form of poker; but by choice they dealt faro, which was the real big money game of the West. Faro has probably sponsored more words and phrases which have won a permanent place in American speech than any pastime other than baseball. The name was derived from the picture of an Egyptian ruler which used to be on the backs of the cards with which it was played. Notwithstanding a complicated system of counters, the game was singularly simple. Thirteen spades were painted on the layout, and the object was to guess which number or face card would match the winning or losing cards. They were dealt in series of two, called "turns," the betting recommencing after each turn. As the first card or soda could not count because the deck was exhibited face up, neither could the last one, or hock. By the time hock was left alone in its box the others were all displayed on the layout, which was commonly ornamented by the head of a tiger. Originally the cards were dealt by hand, but by the time faro reached the West the temptation to manipulate them had been removed by a mechanical device which thrust them out a slit in the side of the box containing them. It was thus a game in which by nature the chances were even on both sides of the board. The house owed its percentage to the arbitrary ruling that when a turn constituted a pair the winner split with the dealer.

But even so there were choleric losers whom the dealer had to be equipped to handle. These were so equipped, and they had additional weapons which qualified them for their other calling of peace officer.

Their chosen revolvers were .45 and .44 calibre guns with seven and a half inch barrels. The Smith and Wesson had to be broken for reloading, while the cylinder of the Colt swung out on a crane, as it does now. Both were usually single-action weapons, although the double action was beginning to come into fashion. The cylinder held six cartridges, but for safety's sake the hammer was universally set to rest on an empty chamber.

Afield they carried carbines or rifles, usually the latter, because of its greater range. Such guns were of very large bore by modern standards; and the comparative weakness of the far from smokeless powder necessitated a huge charge. Winchester was the first to manufacture repeaters suitable for the Western trade. In fact they were so successful in giving satisfaction that the name became interchangeable with rifle. A favorite was a lever action, calibre .45-70. Its effective range was limited by its simple sights as well as by the powder in the cartridges it fired to three or four hundred yards.

For certain conditions the sawed-off shotgun of the double-barrel variety was preferred. When riding forth on a manhunt all three kinds of weapons might be taken. "When mounted on a horse," Wyatt said in describing just such a state of affairs, "and, 'armed to the teeth,' as the saying goes, a man's rifle was slung in a boot just ahead of his right stirrup, his shotgun carried on the left by a thong looped over the saddle-horn. With the adoption of breech-loading weapons, a rider equipped with two pistols, rifle, and shotgun customarily had one of the belts to which his pistol holsters were attached filled with pistol ammunition, the other with rifle cartridges, while a heavier, wider belt filled with shotgun shells was looped around the saddle-horn underneath the thong which held the weapon. . . . Bowie knives were worn largely for utility's sake in a belt sheath back of the hip; when I came on the scene their popularity for purposes of offense was on the wane. . . ."

Arms and famous men to wield them there undoubtedly were in Tombstone. But there were other men of weapons of equal note whose avowed presence is not an absurdity, although the issue is clouded. The redoubtable Tom Horn, for one, asserts in his autobiography that he was in Tombstone at two different periods. Chronology and geography allow the first, but the attendant circumstances cited by Horn are so contradictory to established facts that he cannot be taken seriously. His biographer allows him the second visit, apparently on the theory that Tom didn't lie all the time. There is nothing to substantiate it.

Later Horn was to be hanged, charged with being the hired assassin — and an expert one — of cattlemen bent on driving out nesters. At the time when he came to Tombstone, if he did, in 1883 he was a young man well launched on the scouting career which was to win him distinction and promotion in the war against the Apaches. With him at the time was supposedly a far greater scout, Horn's hero and mentor, Al Sieber. According to Tom the two went on a heroic bender in Tombstone, before a renewed outbreak on the part of the Apaches called them back to duty and the rigors of sobriety.

Then there is the interesting question about Greek George. Many crannies of American history are reserved for comic romance, and George was part and parcel of such a lode. He was one of the drivers picked up on the docks of Smyrna when Secretary of War Jefferson Davis decided that the military solution to maneuvering on the Western deserts would be a camel corps.

The Last Chance

C. L. Lummis, who tried to get a pension for him when he was an old man, recorded that George — whose full name, according to him, was Georges Xaralampo — had forgotten Greek and had never mastered English. It was in Mexican Spanish that he told Lummis that when the Army got tired of the experimental camels he had stayed on as a civilian scout. In a fight against the Mohaves an Indian let drive at him, but the redskin failed to reckon with a Greek beard. The arrow got bogged down in the heroic chin growth and barely scratched the jaw.

Such an anecdote is to be doubted with regret, but either Lummis or Billy King, quondam deputy sheriff of Cochise County as well as Allen Street bartender and gambler, was a victim of mistaken identity. King stated that Greek George shot a man in Tombstone and committed suicide to avoid vigilante reprisal.

But if some of the dramatic figures attached to the Tombstone story are subject to challenge, there remain many more men whose ghosts have an unquestioned right to parade down Allen Street. Quite a few of them will be discussed at appropriate points in this chronicle. Meanwhile it should be remembered that all of the interesting citizens of the town were not men.

CHAPTER SIX

SOME WERE WOMEN

IT IS A truism rather than a pun or a paradox that the gold diggers always followed the miners. By ordinary the first women to hit a new boom town were the dance hall girls — and some others that didn't bother to dance. They played the Western circuit as alertly as the gamblers and mule team merchants. All they needed to hear was that a strike was big enough to draw men and money.

In reviewing the life of such girls the only conclusion you can come to is that they must have thrived on the change and excitement, exactly as the merchants and gamblers did. There must have been easier ways of making a living, in a region where women were as scarce as they were in the Old West, than being a frontier whore.

When they left one town they often had to travel hundreds of miles by stage or horseback to the next one. It was no primrose path over alkali, but they took their chances with weather and the Indians along with the other hazards of their calling. And when they reached a new town it was even rougher. A boom town is like an Army camp: it's either all dust or all mud, or an incredible combination of the two. The dance halls and saloons were tents or worse. Whorehouses were equally primitive. When gun fights started the girls could only duck and hope for the best. They had to rustle their own food. How, if anyhow, they avoided pregnancy is anybody's guess. If they didn't, there might be no doctors in town. To cap it all their clients were apt to be as savage, untrammeled, bristly, dusty, and muddy as the surrounding country. Taking it all for all, the chippies earned their pay.

A. H. Noon, a Chicago reporter who visited Tombstone as early as 1879 drew a disapproving and thoroughly unromantic picture of sin in that city when it was in its uncouth infancy. "The atmosphere is dirty and abominable, but they dance away never- theless — the men inanely grinning, the women evidently dancing as a matter of business. . . . Two are white and two are Mexican. One of the white women looks old and worn, dancing with evi- dent effort. All are homely; and with the evidence of worthless- ness and probable disease stamped on their faces, they form a ghastly picture of Low Type of Immorality."

But the money was just beginning to flow when Mr. Noon passed through town. Parsons, who was equally disapproving of commercialized sex, implied that the whores were both far more numerous and far more gay when he arrived a few months later. Then as the male population steadily increased in numbers and wealth, so also did the prostitutes.

In the foregoing paragraphs they have been all bunched togeth- er, but they themselves made no such mistake. Rather they rec- ognized themselves as belonging to several classes. These, how- ever, were less distinguishable in the early days of a mining camp than when it developed into a full-fledged town.

In Tombstone the girls favored to double as waitresses and chorus girls, for the small troupes which came to the Bird Cage variety theatre were rated at the top. The men who hired the curtained boxes suspended from the roof of this house had to be good spenders. Before the show started the girls were given ample time to encourage the buying of expensive liquors, from which they got a cut, and to make their assignations. Prior to keeping them, they danced, sang or played some supporting role in the entertainment of the evening.

A detailed description of a night at the Bird Cage has not been passed down, but a good idea of what went on can be gathered from an account of a similar house of the period made by a shocked reporter for *The Arizona Star* of Tucson in 1884. As far as the stage activities are concerned, the routine is recognizable to anyone who has ever seen a burlesque show.

". . . At an elevation of fifteen feet above and around the audi-

torium runs a row of "private" boxes. . . . Access to them is had by
means of stairways, one leading thereto from the ground floor and
another from the dressing or wine room at the west end of the
stage. The boxes are all heavily curtained, and in and behind
these the girls ply their trade. . . .

"The curtain rises about nine P.M. and falls on a climax of
obscenity about one o'clock in the morning following. Prior to the
opening of the theatre its patrons . . . are worked for all they are
worth by . . . girls, some young some old, in tight fitting abbreviated dresses. To drink with them is an esteemed favor, not to be
enjoyed by the impecunious. The man of money . . . is their
delight. If he be coy and bashful, he is coddled until he gives
down to his last nickel. In the curtained boxes the game is successfully played. Here screened from the observation of the
curious, men . . . yield readily to the wheedling caresses, naked
bosoms, bare arms, shapely legs and would-be winsome smiles
of the fair professionals. . . .

"To begin business with the girls . . . are supplied with a number of tickets . . . having certain money valuation which is charged
against them by the proprietor. These are, of course, taken up
and redeemed in accordance with the amount of money they
pay in. Of the proceeds of their particular sales, they, the girls,
realize from ten to twenty per cent. This together with the price
of their charms yields them a no inconsiderable income.

"Treat! Treat! Treat! and pay a double or treble, and sometimes
both together, price without any possible return of change for
the privilege, is an advantage offered to the habitues. . . . A bottle
of beer that retails at the bar for fifty cents is worth a dollar in a
box. The price of wine is even more disproportionate. . . . Call for
a bottle of beer for yourself and partner and immediately you are
beset by a half dozen others who demand of you a similar favor.
One bottle of wine soon grows into half a dozen and fifty dollars
vanishes as easily as five dollars.

"At the appointed hour . . . the curtain rose and disclosed a
meeting of two friends, one of whom declared he had made a

The Last Chance

mash at a ball. They were interrupted in conversation by the abrupt appearance of a negro who was apparently passing in haste and holding his hands at a given distance apart. He was seized and detained by the masher, who offered him a sum of money to carry a letter to the mashed Lucy Black. The negro protested and declared his intentions to proceed and buy a pane of glass, the measurements of which he claimed to have known by the position of his hands. He, however, consented to carry the message. He agrees to deliver a like message for masher number two, both missives went to the same girl.

"Scene second reveals Miss Black, a young woman previously in the pit soliciting beer, seated at a table with the negro messenger who delivers one letter to her but reads the other himself. He climbs over the table and makes himself generally obnoxious. Finally he goes to the door, then jumps back and in an affrighted voice says: "A man." "What does he want?" modestly inquires the lady. "He wants something," the darky innocently replied. The man designated as Masher No. 1 is at last shown in, states he has important news to communicate, says that he is going to take a bath, talks horses and diamonds. He is finally kissed by the darky and kicked out of the house by the same individual. Masher No. 2 appears, makes a like talk. The darky borrows his handkerchief, uses it, and returns it, kisses him and kicks him out in like manner to his predecessor. The young lady then proposes to the darky to play woman, to this he readily consents and at once begins to don a pair of woman's undergarments; but complains at the same time that they are almost cut in two. A bustle was the next thing offered, this in spite of her protestations, he tied in front of himself then putting on a dress he looked somewhat proud at his corpulency and said: 'In August'. He then paraded about the stage and with elevated dress would stoop down repeatedly with his back to the audience. Thus giving them an opportunity to admire the aforesaid garments even to the waistband thereof. In this brief synopsis the vulgarities and indecencies of the piece have been rigidly suppressed.

Some Were Women

"Here the entertainment was varied. A young woman, Miss Sallie Clinetop, dressed in slate colored tights created quite a hit by dancing around the stage on her toes. . . . She was followed by the Stanley sisters, two comely young women in short dresses and pink stockings. They sang several duets and were repeatedly applauded. They were succeeded by Miss Trixie Vernon similarly attired. She sang one or two plantation melodies and then retired to give place to another young woman in a Mother Hubbard dress, accompanied by a voluble darky in striped tights, who recounted the mishaps which befell a certain young lady when sliding down a bannister upon which her brother had placed a piece of barbed wire. Similar absurdities were kept up for the next hour.

"Shortly after midnight, however, the curtain rang up and the can-can came on in all its glory. First three young women in pink tights with dresses not of sufficient length to cover the hips danced the can-can through with barbaric vigor. As they retired amid the plaudits of an admiring crowd, three men blackened like negroes, clad in tights, with women's undergarments over them, sprang on the stage and vied with each other in the obscenity of their actions. Three times this performance was repeated by the women and a like number of times by the men, and at each repetition they strove to outdo if possible the filthiness of their previous actions, and to cap the climax both men and women joined in the debasing exhibition together. . . ."

Below the variety hall aristocracy, such as the harlots of the Bird Cage — talent always being at a premium — ranked the piano players of the various dance halls and saloons. Below these again were the dance hall girls, whose source of income, aside from prostitution, was also based on the number of drinks they could persuade a man to buy. Whenever her masculine partner ordered, she was handed a white check, which could be redeemed for a bit, or twelve and a half cents.

Lowest on the scale of whoredom were the street walkers or those who merely sat waiting at the door of their cribs to entice passers-by inside. Their earnings were not only not supplemented by other undertakings, but they didn't make as much at the basic occupation.

As has been the case everywhere and at all times most of the girls had to split their revenue with a procuress, a professional pimp, or merely some man who saw a way to augment his own earnings by appointing himself her "protector." His duties chiefly consisted of seeing that she paid off to him instead of to some other predator. In the West of the day they were commonly referred to as "macs."

The names of some of the well-known whores and madames have been passed down in various memoirs, although the form written down in most cases suggests that it was not the one given out on christening day. The photographs of some have likewise been preserved, for Tombstone boasted at least one portrait studio.

Among the noteworthy bats of the town was Crazy Horse Lil, who looked as formidable, if not more so, as the desperate Oglalla Sioux chief after whom she was nicknamed. A glance at her portrait makes a man shake his head at the intrepidity of the men who went before him. The Indians simply didn't have a chance with the sort who were game to take on anything like Lil in amorous embrace. A veteran of countless boom town redlight districts, she was in her rugged prime when she came to Tombstone with her pandar consort, Con O'Shea.

It should not be inferred, however, that Crazy Horse Lil tolerated or needed a "protector." That was Con, according to Billy King, who furnished much of the information about the city's night life. During periods of nervous stress, such as sometimes afflict even the most indomitable of women, Lil used to relieve the tension by giving Con a going over.

A more popular character was Dutch Annie, sometimes referred to as "queen of the redlight district." If she actually was and why that was so are subjects on which exact information is lacking. Her head board in Boot Hill does not give her last name,

Some Were Women

either. It is probable that none of her fellow citizens ever knew it.

Most of the prostitutes found it necessary to use a distinguishing nickname only; surnames were no more popular than they were with certain drifting gunmen. An exception was Big Minnie, who seems to have been legally married to Joe Bignon. After a successful career with houses and dance halls they stepped up in the world by purchasing the Bird Cage.

Yet the business of supplying whores was not left entirely to the initiative of individual operators. Tombstone became too big and too prosperous for the syndicates to leave it alone. At least two which made a specialty of importing French prostitutes set up relay points there. Big firms such as these found that they did more trade by changing the stock every now and then. Tombstone usually got its syndicate girls directly from San Francisco, which in turn got them from New York. They customarily stayed in town only a few months.

One madame who served as the local manager for one of these whore trusts was Blonde Marie, a plump faced woman who may or may not have owed her light hair to some bleaching process. The preserved photograph keeps the secret, if there was one to keep; but the camera was less kind to her rival, who was accurately if ungallantly known as Frenchy Moustache.

The names of a few lesser nighthawks have come down. There was Lizette, who came to Tombstone with a road show, billed as the Flying Nymph. Presumably better at nymphing than flying, she rose to be a madame in her own right. Rowdy Kate had a consort whose name, believe it or not, was Joe Lowe. Irish May invested her earnings in grub-staking a prospector, and picked one who actually found a mine that amounted to something. Then there are two others, commemorated by one of the epitaphs that make a tour of the Tombstone cemetery a lesson in the dramatic effectiveness of brevity. This one reads: "Margarita Stabbed by Gold Dollar."

The latter was the trade name of a hustler remembered in print by more than one old timer. Billy King gives the additional information that she was known as "Little Gertie, the Gold Dollar." To catch the appropriateness of the monicker it is necessary to bear in mind that at the time the United States was still minting a coin, quite a bit smaller than a dime, of that metal and value. Gertie is described as blonde, pretty and petite. Possibly the implication was also that she must be assessed strictly in monetary terms.

But the appropriateness of her nickname doesn't explain why she stabbed Margarita. For that the only authority is the autobiography of Dan de Lara Hughes, who was a boy at the time. On other points he is found to be no more reliable than anyone else who tries to make a factual record out of the dim and tangled memories of childhood. Still the only authority is bound to get a respect he might not otherwise receive, and in this case the account is circumstantial enough to be credible.

If Hughes is to be believed, he spent his time in all the places a child should not be found, including certain whore houses during the daytime, when the girls had the leisure to pamper a small boy. One of those he got to know was Gold Dollar, who was shacking up with, when her duties gave her time for it, a dance hall sheik named Billy Milgreen. At that point a Mexican chippie called Margarita entered this redlight idyll and turned it into a triangle. She stole Billy from Little Gertie and made the error of getting rough when the outraged Gertie ordered her to stop cutting in. Hughes claims to have been present when Gold Dollar drew a knife from some unspecified portion of her clothing and let Margarita have it.

A person with a larger range of interests than any of the foregoing was Mrs. Ah Chum, commonly known as China Mary. To repeat, Dutch Annie is often said to have been the queen of the redlight district. There is nothing to prove it one way or the other, though with so many contestants it may be doubted. There is better proof that China Mary was dictator of Tombstone's Hop Town.

King, who was at one time a member of the sheriff's staff, and therefore had some claim to knowing what he was talking about, stated his belief that she had tong affiliations. Certainly she controlled the gambling and opium houses of the Chinese settlement. She herself ran a store dealing in oriental goods. As a sideline she placed her people in employment. The girls she farmed out as prostitutes, the men as servants. Moreover, she underwrote them. "Him steal — me pay," was her reputed guarantee. Today the most imposing of the few stone monuments of Boot Hill is over the grave of this enterprising matriarch.

The fancy women, the feminine counterpart of the outlaw gunmen, inevitably steal the foreground in the history of a bachelor metropolis like a mining town on the boom. Even men who were married advisedly left their families behind until the dust of the claim rush had settled a bit. In the case of Tombstone, Parsons makes it clear, the wives and children didn't start arriving in any numbers until the fall of 1880.

There were, however, a few pioneer business women of the Old West to whom the excitement of a new boom town called as irresistably as it did to the dance hall girls. Usually they kept restaurants or boarding houses, both profitable in places where money was plentiful and men homeless. Tombstone's famous personage in this category was Nellie Cashman, frequently called "the miner's angel."

There is a picture of her, too, and a good story to go with it. A cook in her employ asked her for leave of absence so that he could make a visit to his native Hong Kong. When it was granted, he requested a photograph of Miss Cashman, insisting he was going to have a portrait painted from it by a Chinese artist of his acquaintance. Some months later he not only returned but had the portrait as promised. It is said to be an excellent likeness, and if so Miss Cashman was something worth looking at. The picture shows a lovely face, by parts strong and spiritual.

A curious combination of a taste for adventure and a quest for new fields for charity had led her all over other parts of the West before she came to Arizona. Because Clum later took thought to publish a biographical sketch of her, the general facts about her life are available. Born in Ireland, she came to America as a young girl, drifted west, and found where she belonged. Before going to Tombstone she had run a boarding house in Cassiar, British Columbia, when the first big Canadian gold rush drew men there. Years later, when men flocked to the Yukon and then Alaska, she was in the sub-arctic again, still seeking to keep home-starved men comfortable and well fed.

In Tombstone she kept the Russ House in an adobe building which still stands at the corner of Tough Nut and Fifth Streets. That was merely her official activity, however. "Her principal business," Clum wrote, "was to feed the hungry and shelter the homeless, and her chief divertisement was to relieve those in distress and to care for the sick and afflicted. . . .

"She was inclined to associate more generally with men than with members of her own sex, and on several occasions she joined in stampedes with men, tramping with them over rugged trails and sharing the vicissitudes and discomforts of their rude camps. Nevertheless, she maintained an unimpeachable reputation, and her character and conduct commanded the universal respect and admiration of every camp in which she lived. . . .

"There was no hospital in Tombstone, so there were many opportunities for generous, self-sacrificing, willing hands to help in these cases of illness or accident or pressing need, and we soon found that Nellie was prompt and persistent and effective with plans for relief. . . . If she asked for a contribution — we contributed. If she had tickets to sell — we bought tickets. If she needed actors for a play — we volunteered to act."

As a case in point, one prospector fell down the shaft of his mine and broke both legs. Two days later Nellie had raised $500 for him. According to Clum she also built Tombstone's Catholic church, adding what she could raise from others to her own generous donations.

What of the other women, who were neither renowned nor notorious? They had homes to make and children to raise, and

Some Were Women

Tombstone was held the toughest town in the nation. Yet they came and did those things within a few blocks of the wildest section of the city. They were within easy ear shot of the nightly shooting scrapes, the shouts, and the shrieks, but that didn't stand in their way. Instead of holding indignation meetings or wailing that they couldn't bear such a place, they coolly ignored the part of it they disliked. The whores might prance, and the outlaws might fire away; but they were going to build themselves a society to match that of any other prosperous American town, and they proceeded to do so. They were all right.

The identities of these determined ladies who shopped on one side of Allen Street while the hustlers switched along the other, and who gave piano recitals as opposition music to that of the dance halls, are not preserved in any of the memoirs. That's a pity, because the juxtaposition of the two phases of life gives the story of Tombstone a touch of comedy in the best and richest sense. What could be more exquisite than a bitter war between two groups whose attack and defense, strategy, and materiel consisted in denying each other's existence?

The names of some of Tombstone's home makers are found in the old newspapers, but there individuality is subordinated to the social event described. Parsons isn't much more helpful on this point — when, indeed, he gives anything except an initial. In his pages the amateur theatricals, the "at homes," the benefit suppers, etc., become alive again — but not the female participants. There are exceptions, for once in a while, witness the following example, Parsons could achieve a terse poignancy worthy of Pepys. "There was a full house. Miss B. sang — and very miserably, too."

But it was not to hear Miss B., or even some more accomplished performer, sing at a church concert that the riders of the San Pedro and Sulphur Springs valley ranges came to Tombstone. And they did come there, adding another explosive element to the combustible throngs on Allen Street.

CHAPTER SEVEN

CATTLEMEN AND OTHERS

ONE of the great facts about Tombstone in its capacity of the last chance city of the Old West was that both of the significant economic factors of the region impinged upon each other there. Usually the history of an early western town was conditioned by either mining or beef growing. Here there were both.

There were no cattle ranging that section of the San Pedro Valley when Schieffelin entered it. For this there were several reasons, of which the imminence of the Apaches was at once the most obvious and of least consequence in the long run. American cattlemen had repeatedly shown their indifference to danger when it came to locating on a good range; but it had to be worth their while.

Cattle had been introduced into Arizona at the instance of Father Eusebio Kino, the Jesuit founder of the territory's only two permanent Spanish missions. These were the ones at Tubac and Tucson, both in the Santa Cruz Valley, which parallels at the remove of some sixty miles to the West, that of the San Pedro. Mission Indians, mostly Pimas, had joined the colonials in taking to the industry, but it remained fairly local up to the time of United States annexation.

The American pioneers, aided by the Army, succeeded in taking the territory, then one with that of New Mexico, from the Apaches who largely controlled it. But, as earlier rehearsed, things then got worse instead of better. The pioneers lost out during the War between the States, which caused both the removal of the garrisons and a drain on civilian man power — limited at best.

The edict which made Arizona a separate territory in 1863 still failed to convince the Apaches that the United States owned the land. When they did eventually capitulate elsewhere, they remained free, which is to say rapacious, agents in the southeastern corner, with its easy access to Mexico.

Still, and granting the peculiar ability of the Apache to inspire terror, the presence of blanket Indians was only one obstacle to the expansion of the cattle raising industry in Arizona. Two others were decisive. The first was the huge distance to any rail heads, not to mention the rough and barren character of the intervening country. The second, which was especially operative in the district in question, was the absence of any sizeable local market.

The establishment of reservations for the Apaches served to make the ranges safer for man, if not for beast. The Indians still ate the cattle, but now the government paid for them. Cattlemen began to come into the territory in quantity, but the canceling of the reservation in the Dragoons after Cochise's death automatically ended the market. So the situation in the upper San Pedro Valley was again one that offered danger without compensation.

The Tombstone boom did three things for Arizona beef raisers. Locally, it drew so many men into the district that ranches became relatively safe from Indian attack. Locally also, the town's hungry citizens furnished a good sales outlet. Territorially, the boom induced the Southern Pacific to push east from California and make a junction with the Santa Fe. With transcontinental service established, the great markets of the nation were open to the Southwest. Cattle growing joined mining as a major Arizona enterprise.

The quality of the range in the southeastern corner of the territory drew cattlemen in steadily increasing numbers. Some appraisers have claimed that grazing conditions there were unmatched in Arizona and unsurpassed anywhere in the West. A certain species of grass was a particular source of pride. "This gramma grass," it was remarked in an anonymous survey of the territory published in 1884, "is beyond all comparison the most nutritious herbage ever cropped by quadrupeds."

The Last Chance

Some that attempted the region early in the '70s never lived to see better times. A few who could afford to hire enough fighting hands to keep the Apaches more or less at a distance held on in the northern part of the Sulphur Springs Valley until the Tombstone boom opened the country — and brought them new troubles.

The first large scale operator was Henry C. Hooker, sometimes called colonel and at others promoted to general. Whatever his true military rank, he was a cattleman of the first water. No catch as catch can rancher, he was a trained stock grower, familiar with the best known procedures and capable of devising improvements of his own. A New Englander who came to Arizona by way of Hangtown and other points of interest, he is supposed to have been the first to introduce shorthorns and then Herefords into the territory. Actually his ranch at Sierra Bonita Springs was in Graham rather than in Cochise County; but he was well known in Tombstone and took his part in its story.

John Slaughter was another early arrival. Already famous throughout the Southwest both as a fighter and a cattle baron, he was forty at the time he reached the region where he was to win a permanent place in history and folk lore. This emigrant from Louisiana via Texas was to epitomize his own name when he became Cochise County's greatest sheriff. He was a sheriff, incidentally, who seldom used the services of a posse or a jail, let alone a jury; but that was to come later. He was a cattle rancher when he brought his second wife and a considerable body of retainers into the periphery of Tombstone.

Among others of importance in the field was B. A. Packard, who was to become the partner of Bill Greene when the latter built his copper mining empire in Mexico. The money to back this mighty, and for a time very successful, gamble was made by the cows which grazed in the vicinity of his ranch in the upper San Pedro Valley.

Still another was John A. Rockfellow, who first came to Tombstone as a prospector and later established a ranch in Cochise's Stronghold in the Dragoons. Although he wrote that he had to move out a couple of times when the Apaches chose to return, he survived to produce a valuable little book of pioneer reminiscences.

Those so far listed were all legitimate practitioners of the beef producing trade. Others were not.

If cattle had not long been raised in southeastern Arizona, the business had flourished across the border in Mexico for quite a few generations. Many cowmen who had not troubled to bring large herds with them took note of the fact that this border was poorly guarded by representatives of either nation. This state of affairs offered two possibilities. Sometimes the cows, indifferent to the nationality of the range they grazed, would stray north, where they could easily be herded to an American market. If this did not happen, it was relatively easy to go south after them. The holdings of the wealthy Mexican stock growers were too vast to be closely watched.

There is seldom such a thing as an impartial morality. Stealing from Mexicans didn't carry the stigma that it might have. But, inevitably, the rustlers didn't stop there. Although it was more dangerous, a quicker way to make money was to change the brand of the original Arizona owner.

This did not always entail anything so difficult as a cattle raid. In the days of the open range cows strayed anywhere that food looked good to them. Even under the best of conditions a Western cow has to be athletic and industrious. The leisure for stationery cud chewing, so dear to the pampered bovines from regions of lusher forage, is unknown to it. The order of the day is hike or starve. Without fences to limit the grazing area there was no telling where a cow would turn up except that it was bound to seek a water hole from time to time. The approved practice then was to camp by water holes and wait for the neighbor's beef to appear.

At first the men who engaged in these pursuits were, if not amateurs, small scale operators working independently. Soon they were to be given support and leadership by men who had been, criminally speaking, in the big time.

The Last Chance

There were plenty of reasons why outlaws should have gravitated to southeastern Arizona, but one will suffice for a starter. Organized society was moving not only steadily westward from the Mississippi but also steadily eastward from the West Coast. Of the intervening territory Arizona was geographically the most remote from the pressure points of this implacable force. In Arizona, itself without organization, Cochise County was in the antipodes of law and order. Such a district was the inevitable refuge and natural locus for the Western felons of an elder day, the "bad men."

The first wave of these to come to the Tombstone country were men who had been moulded to toughness on the long cattle drives and the wild towns at the end of them. Many had been hired gunmen; but the conditions which had made them useful had passed farther east. Not being able to stomach the matter of fact hard work and modest pay of cow hands, they turned to rustling. The days of fencing hadn't yet arrived in Texas, say, but the days of organized efforts to stamp out rustling had. Southeastern Arizona, so newly opened that the law hadn't yet found a footing there, looked good to men whose way of business was crooked. The region became widely known as a stock thieves' Utopia, and that brought in the second echelon of rustlers.

Their activities might not have had too much effect upon the town, if they hadn't branched out. As it happened, Tombstone came into being not long after the breaking up of the Sam Bass gang and the first of the two James mobs. Refugees from these and lesser crews of hold-up men were attracted to the San Pedro Valley by tales of Tombstone's riches. When they found the atmosphere of Cochise County a congenial one, others of their stamp followed. Before long most of the outlaws were pooling their energies in a mutual profit organization.

Recognized as their chief until death disqualified him was N. H. Clanton, known even on the headboard of his grave simply as Old Man Clanton. This was to distinguish him from his get of three sons, Joseph Isaac, Phineas, and William. The tribe had gone to

California from Texas before beating a forced retreat to Arizona Territory. After first establishing headquarters farther north, they built a ranch house near Lewis Springs, itself only a few miles from Charleston. This became a recognized rendezvous not only for rustlers and horse thieves but for men engaged in unrelated crimes.

A subsidiary stronghold for gangsters was, also under the guise of an honest ranchman's house, owned by the McLowry brothers, Frank and Tom. Both were born in Mississippi but probably learned their trades in Texas. Their place was across the Mules in the Sulphur Springs Valley.

In time the adherents of these two outfits straddled the majority of the water holes in both the Sulphur Springs and the upper San Pedro Valleys. Only men like Hooker and Slaughter, able to hire small armies of gunmen on their own account, were able to hold their own at all. And even these fighters suffered a steady loss of stock.

The boldest sought to make headway by organizing under the aegis of the Arizona Cattlemen's Association. They were up against a more efficient organization; one which, as shall be seen, got more support from what law there was than the legitimate ranchers could find. This organization was strengthened by some of the most capable outlaws operating in the United States at that time.

Like Earp, Masterson, and Short the big wheels among these were veterans of Abilene, Wichita, and Dodge City. A few of them were gunmen good enough to get into the same paragraph with swift killers like John Wesley Hardin, Clay Allison, and Ben Thompson.

It seems to be a matter of opinion who was chief among them, yet Curly Bill Brocius, born — probably in Missouri — William Brocius Graham, is most often given the nod. At first a lieutenant of the elder Clanton, he came either to have or to share the leadership of the entire gang. Parsons, who met him once, describes him both as the chieftain of the crew and "the most famous outlaw of Arizona." Under his command the rustlers generally made their headquarters at Charleston or Galeyville rather than at a ranch.

Sometimes described as sharing the consulship of the mob with him was John Ringgold, nicknamed Johnny Ringo. He was a cousin of the Younger brothers, who rode with Quantrill before they teamed up with their kinsmen, the James boys, who in turn were related by marriage to the Daltons. A Missourian like the others, he seems to have come to Arizona after Texas got too hot for him. In certain accounts he is called the real brains of the gang. By general agreement he was the most dangerous man among the outlaws.

Russian Bill is somewhat harder to peg down. His existence as a prominent rustler rather than the burlesque figure fabricated by Burns is authenticated. As early a visitor to Tombstone as Bishop bracketed him with Curly Bill Brocius when listing some of the region's desperate characters. The story that he was actually a Russian count, ex-officer of the Imperial Army, etc., although persistent enough to exact notice, is insufficiently documented.

Sometimes operating independently but always on call for Old Man Clanton and his successors was a swarm of lesser mobsters. It is said that Curly Bill sometimes rode with a hundred men at his back. Among those of note were Pony Deal, Joe Hill, Frank Stilwell, who spent some of his spare time being a deputy sheriff, Johnny Barnes and Pete Spence.

The region also drew or developed outlaws only partially connected with the rustlers, as well as those who seem to have played a lone hand. In the first class was William Claiborne, who had come west with John Slaughter. A year or so sufficed to change him from a clean cut youngster to a trigger-happy killer.

A more enigmatical figure was that of Buckskin Frank Leslie. In his account of his first visit to Tombstone, the visit he probably never made, Tom Horn lists Frank Leslie among the recently demobilized scouts who accompanied Sieber and himself. As Leslie had a considerable reputation as a tracker, he may have had such a background. Most accounts, however, represent him as riding into town by himself, a man without previous existence or antecedents so far as anybody else in Tombstone was aware. In the years which followed only a couple of facts were established to a historian's satisfaction. One was that he was among the best gunmen in the district, which is more than high praise. The other was that he was a lady's man in a land where there weren't enough women to go around.

More famous nationally, if less of a figure locally, was Frank Jackson. What made him a man of mark in a region where outlaws were as common as spines on a cactus was the fact that he had ridden with the renowned Sam Bass. Better than that, he was not only with him at the fight at Round Rock where Texas Rangers gave Sam his death wound, but he was the man who had taken the dying Bass up on his horse and escaped with him from the conflict.

Jackson thus won ballad immortality for himself, yet just what he did around Tombstone is hard to determine. Some old timers mentioned in their memoirs what they knew but never told in Tombstone, *i.e.* that Frank Jackson was one and the same with William Downing, later a Cochise County train robber. Others have denied this on the score of chronology; and there is another point to be taken into consideration. Jackson's identity could not have been the deep, dark secret sometimes implied, for in 1882 *The Epitaph* named him as an accomplice of the late Sam Bass, nor was any alias noted.

The presence in Tombstone of still a different sort of criminal was asserted in the memoirs of Maj. Frederick R. Burnham. This veteran of various African campaigns, who came to be chief of scouts under Field Marshal Lord Roberts, was first schooled in the rigors of his profession while a youth in Arizona. He was the associate of such exploiters of South Africa as Cecil Rhodes, General Sir Robert Baden-Powell and John Hays Hammond, who wrote the preface to Burnham's autobiography. There is likewise an extant picture which shows him in a group with the then young adventurer, Winston Churchill. But before those days he was in Tombstone.

The Last Chance

Major Burnham, moreover, gives information about felonious enterprises, which are described by no other memorialist of Tombstone. As his accounts of his experiences in Africa have documentary backing, it seems reasonable that his stories about his Arizona days should also be examined with respect. Unfortunately, possibly because he wrote at a day when many of the pioneer residents of Cochise County were still alive, he largely used initials when referring to the characters involved.

In any case his report ran that while on the way to Tombstone he assisted and in so doing made himself the friend of a man he identified only by the name of McLeod. "I learned later that he was the most noted and successful smuggler along the Arizona frontier. . . . His agents reached from Mexico City to San Francisco. He had silent partnerships in several stores in Tombstone and Tucson, as well as interests in livery stables, stage lines, mail contracts, and mines. . . ."

According to Burnham, Tombstone was McLeod's principal base of operations in the early 1880's. In addition to that his book contains the inference that the activities of the smugglers and rustlers were integrated. "Curly Bill found here a market for his stolen stock, as did the smugglers for the goods they brought in from Mexico. The merchants, in turn, vied with the ancient and honourable pueblo of Tucson in supplying such smuggled goods as Mexico might require."

To return to the rustlers themselves, the shift of headquarters from the range to a town or so was significant of a broadening of interests. Horse and cattle thieving were still major occupations, but the wealth of Tombstone inspired other enterprises.

When the first bullion was produced from Gird's ore stamping mill at Charleston in the summer of 1879, the partners were still handling many details personally. The silver bars were placed in the same little wagon which had carried their supplies while they prospected. Ed Schieffelin himself went along as guard on the long trips to Tucson.

By fall that simple set-up was replaced. The increase of pro-

Cattlemen and Others

duction from the Charleston mill was only one cause. Other mills were being built, and Tombstone itself was growing. Stage lines, which had begun offering regular service, bid for the bullion carrying concession.

This proved to be as dangerous as it was lucrative. The Schieffelins had had no trouble, but the thieves had not gathered in force then. It wasn't until the tail end of '79 that the rustlers had the strength and organization they needed for complete effectiveness. When they were ready, they went in for stage robbing and the general pursuits of highwaymen. Robbery was added to manslaying as one of the regularities of Tombstone life.

The theft of bullion was a threat to the entire economy of the town. The concession of seeing it safely through was given to the pioneer express firm of Wells, Fargo and Company, which had dealt with similar situations in other parts of the West. Even then the depredations continued; and the United States mail was also rifled with impunity. This at least would seemingly have drawn retribution in the form of a Federal investigation. It did not.

The reasons why are geographical and statistical as much as political. Soon after his arrival in Tombstone Parsons observed in his journal that he was in the part of the nation which was the farthest away from his old home in New York, and the most difficult to reach. If he wasn't exactly correct in the matter of distance, he could hardly be argued with as to the question of accessibility. The upper San Pedro wasn't quite as far from the East as portions of California, say; but the state of communications made the journey days longer.

Arizona was a territory, not a state, and as such had only a skeleton government. Its charter gave it the right to enforce the law of the land, but as yet it had no organization with which to do so. The primitive communications made it easy to have any sort of jurisdiction only over the counties adjacent to Prescott, the capital. It also made it easy, be it added, for the territorial government to ignore what was going on in sundry counties if that's the way the government felt. All in all, distant ones like Cochise

were practically in the case of being separate territories themselves.

As for the Federal government, it is probable that Washington
had not the slightest idea of what was going on in southeastern
Arizona. Apparently the official attitude was that responsibility
stopped when an effort had been made to suppress the Apaches.
This laissez-faire policy was followed until the state of lawlessness
in and around Tombstone became such a national scandal that
the President himself was forced to take notice.

It required several years for that to happen, however. In the
meanwhile the citizens of Tombstone, or that group of them who
happened to be interested, found themselves pinched between
the cogwheels of circumstance. Item, their prosperity and geographical position drew outlaws. Item, they were on their own as
far as doing anything about it was concerned.

One more thing must be mentioned when considering their
plight. That was the difficulty of telling the malefactors for profit
from the men who simply raised hell and shot people because
they were ornery ruffians living in a district where they were free
to express themselves. For of the many crimes of violence committed on Allen Street and the sixty-four radiating points of the
compass only a minority were motivated by any desire for financial
gain. At the same time they created an atmosphere in which
calculated grand larceny could move while drawing a minimum
of attention.

CHAPTER EIGHT

THOSE MEN FOR BREAKFAST

THERE is seldom a statement made about anything that someone does not deny. It is generally claimed that Tombstone was one of the toughest towns in the Old West. Many have declared that it was the toughest of them all. Yet it has been said also that it was a relatively law abiding place, where murder was relatively unknown.

The principal person to offer this opinion was Mayor John P. Clum. It should be borne in mind, though, that he did so while defending the effectiveness of his administration. It should also be borne in mind that his administration lasted only for the year of 1881.

Clum pointed out, and correctly, that many acts of violence which actually took place elsewhere were credited to Tombstone. He added with equal correctness that many of the corpses brought to Boot Hill were actually shot in other towns which lacked the services of an undertaker. These are geographical truths of limited bearing. Tombstone was the focus of action for the entire cast of characters. The activities in certain other places of Cochise County were so interlocked with that of the county seat that all were like different facets of the same scene.

At the best it could be said that if murders were not of frequent occurrence in Tombstone, its streets were frequented by chronic murderers. However, it is not necessary to be content with generalizations, or to accept partisan opinions. The evidence doesn't stymie investigation.

At the same time the record is far from perfect due to three causes. One was the loss to fire of early newspaper files. A second was the fact that Tombstone was in Pima County prior to 1881, and there was little official knowledge of what went on there. The third factor was the attitude of the Tombstone citizenry.

This can best be studied in the brief statements incorporated in the earliest criminal record journal of Cochise County. The charge listed against such and such a man is "Murder." Shifting his eyes to seek the disposition of the cast, the reader finds the superb notation "Ignored by grand jury." Why or on what legal grounds deponent saith not. Who was murdered or under what circumstances? Impossible to find out in many cases.

But "Charge — Murder" and "Ignored by grand jury!" The assumption is that the citizenry held that personal business had reached a final settlement under circumstances which made legal investigation an impertinence. This is not an assumption only, for in certain of the coroners' reports the attitude is explicitly defined.

As clear a case as most is that of Prairie Jack, primarily so called in the coroner's report, which also gave his alternate name of J. B. Berry. A resident of Galeyville, Prairie Jack was anxious to clear the town of three Irishmen, notably one Pat O'Day. Carrying a loaded rifle, he entered a Galeyville store where the unarmed O'Day was lounging with eight or ten others. His finger on the trigger, Prairie Jack jammed the muzzle of the weapon against his enemy's ribs and threatened to kill him if he didn't leave town. At this point a bystander deflected the barrel, giving O'Day a chance to grab it and putting the contest on a man to man basis. Up to this point all the men present were in agreement as to the action — and then nobody knew what happened. Prairie Jack was found outside the store a few minutes later, his head bashed in with a rock, but the testimony shows that nobody had seen any violence. The coroner's verdict: Prairie Jack had met death from unknown causes.

There were other times when nobody troubled to convoke a coroner's jury, or at least no record is available in the case of known murders. Probably it was sometimes held that it was futile to make a coroner's report when all the circumstances were known to everybody anyhow.

Those Men for Breakfast

But if much cannot be discovered, an abundance of testimony remains. The first man to have the distinction of meeting death by violence after the Tombstone silver rush began was seemingly John Hicks in the fall of 1878. The town itself had not been started then, so the card game over which he was shot took place in the scratch mining settlement of Watervale. That deaths by violence became a commonplace of the Tombstone region then and for years afterward cannot be doubted. The pages of Parsons' journal are full of references to such demises.

Repeatedly he noted that the firing of pistols in the town was of such frequent occurrence that everyone took it for granted. Nor was this firing without effect, witness the ensuing jottings. "Men killed every few days." "Tombstone is getting a pretty hard name." "Men, killed, shot, stabbed, suiciding . . . every day or two."

Occasionally he named the parties involved. "Boynton shot." "One armed Kelly shot by McAllister." "Albert Bilicke shot a man." "Captain Malgan shot dead at Ritchie's Hall."

More rarely he cited some of the attendant circumstances. A man called Bradshaw killed his partner, by the name of Waters, because the latter struck him upon being kidded about a gaudy shirt he was wearing. One Carleton shot a fellow called Diss for paying too much attention to the former's wife.

Similar fatal encounters were listed by Billy King and Wyatt Earp. Finding that Tom Harper was making a jaunt to Fort Huachuca, John Tolliday requested the former to collect a bill for him there. Furthermore he requested the money after the other returned. Evidently injured in his tenderest feelings, Harper shot him. Roger King met Johnnie Wilson in a six-gun duel in the middle of Allen Street. The agreed distance was twenty feet apart. Wilson favored the cross draw. King survived.

If there was any legal action taken in most instances, Parsons does not mention it. An exception was a case in which he himself was called as a witness. An acquaintance of his, a Lieutenant Lester Perrine stationed at Fort Huachuca, had shot a man called Killen. Apparently resenting this activity on the part of an outsider, some prospectors talked of lynching Perrine if Killen died. The latter did, but the trial which took place instead of the lynching bee left the lieutenant a free and untainted citizen and officer.

Other manslayers were even less annoyed by the attentions of the law, either because nobody brought any charge against them or, as the Cochise County records report in certain instances, their cases were "settled out of court." One reason for the lenience no doubt was that in a community where everybody went armed it was difficult to prove that the shooter was not in fact doing so before he got shot. A morality conditioned the attitude toward this business. Shooting from behind or shooting an unarmed man in theory brought legal vengeance, and frequently did so. Anybody else who got into serious trouble for killing a man just didn't have any friends.

There was apparently no limit to tolerance, as long as the slain man was armed and received his bullets in front. One of Allen Street's famous shootings was that of Louis Hancock by his host, Johnny Ringo. The cause, according to Earp, was that Ringo was annoyed because Hancock had insisted upon drinking beer, whereas Johnny had invited him to have whiskey. Too much hospitality was as perilous as diffidence in accepting it. William Claiborne shot Jim Hickey in Charleston because the latter kept following him around, insisting upon buying Billy a drink.

There were other killings whose details have come down because of the fame of the parties involved. Of these the most renowned was the encounter between Luke Short and Charlie Storms on February 25, 1881, in front of the Oriental Saloon at Fifth and Allen Streets. As a gambler and a gunman Short was in the upper brackets — firmly enough entrenched to have earned a permanent niche in the records of a good few of the West's liveliest towns — and Storms had, if anything, a higher rating. Up until their mortal duel, that is. What the cause of the ill feeling between them was, and why it came to a boil in Tombstone are missing points. Wyatt Earp, who had known them both in other towns, and who was a good friend of Short's, at least, strangely ignored the incident. Those who did refer to it, including Breakenridge and Parsons, rendered a uniform report. Storms was the aggressor.

Short was dealing faro at the Oriental when Storms appeared with a loaded gun, and loaded himself. After an exchange of words he called Short out in the street with the statement that he was going to kill him. His words fell short of prophecy. He shot often enough but not straight enough, although he kept on trying even after he was down with a fatal wound. Parsons gave him aces for gameness, though he gave it as his opinion that Storms was in the wrong. Short fired twice, departing from his advertised practice of shooting for the head on both occasions. Unwounded himself, he left others to look after the corpse and carried on with the interrupted faro game.

Buckskin Frank Leslie first made his mark in Tombstone when he was courting the estranged wife of Mike Killeen, a fellow bartender and not to be confused with Killen, the victim of Lieutenant Perrine. Although not living with Mrs. Killeen himself, Mike still considered himself vested with the rights of chaperonage. Not finding his wife in her room at the Commercial Hotel late one evening, he waited on the balcony outside it. She was with Buckskin Frank when she finally returned, and Killeen showed his resentment by shooting at Leslie. He missed. Frank did not, and soon thereafter gave Tombstone a romance which pleased it by marrying the widow.

Just where Curly Bill shot Dick Lloyd is debatable. Most accounts say Ft. Thomas, though there's a minority vote for Galeyville. All agree that he was buried outside of the town in which he was slain. His headboard is in Tombstone's cemetery.

Nevertheless, all the accounts agree as to the general course of the action. Apparently there were no hard feelings in this instance. Curly Bill and some of his associates were playing poker. Lloyd, an old Charleston acquaintance, got drunk and decided he was under obligation to shoot up the saloon in which the game took place. He rode his horse into the tavern in the approved fashion, but it went out with an empty saddle. The available accounts say that several men were responsible, but Lloyd's headboard gives all the credit to Curly Bill.

The narratives go on to say that in the opinion of his executioners Lloyd was a chuckle head who couldn't hold his liquor, but that aside from that he was a pretty good old boy. They therefore decided that they owed him a funeral. After planting him, they drank to him at the grave-side, fired salutes in his honor, and returned to their poker game.

In none of the cases listed above was any legal penalty exacted; and Lieutenant Perrine seems to have been the only instance where action was carried as far as a trial. There were, however, limits to what the community would stand.

Consider the career of Jerry Barton, Charleston constable and bartender. Barton's name appears in the early criminal records of Cochise County twice for that of his nearest competitor in the matter of being charged with the most felonies. He had shot men to death, among other things. In so doing he had enjoyed the impunity granted other denizens of the Tombstone area; but one day he killed a man with a blow of his fist. That was bad. Jerry was dragged before a shocked jury and was sentenced to the territorial prison at Yuma.

Stabbing was also frowned upon, for the prestige once accorded the adept wielder of the Bowie knife had been transferred to the man skillful with a revolver. Some discussion of how this weapon was carried and handled is pertinent to the Tombstone chronicle.

The method of carrying the six-gun naturally depended on whether secrecy was desirable as well as on individual choice. Wyatt Earp, in recounting how, as a youngster, he was schooled in weapons by seasoned warriors of the vintage of Wild Bill Hickok said: "Jack Gallagher's advice summed up what others had to say, to wear weapons in the handiest position — in my case, as far as pistols were concerned, in open holsters, one on each hip if I was carrying two, hung rather low as my arms were long, and with the muzzles a little forward on my thighs. Some men wore their guns belted high on the waist; a few, butts forward, army style, for a cross-draw; others carried one gun directly in front of the stomach, either inside or outside the waistband, and another gun in a holster slung below the left armpit; still others wore two of these shoulder holsters. . . ."

Eugene Cunningham, who made an exhaustive study of gun play in the old West, has one or two things to add to the foregoing. By ordinary the shoulder holster was in the nature of a sketchy sling, equipped with a spring which increased the speed with which the gun could be unlimbered. Other hideaways were carried in reinforced pockets, in boot tops, or in the waistband at the back, under cover of a loosely hanging coat.

Some gunmen preferred to carry their revolvers hanging from plates riveted to their belts. Buckskin Frank Leslie was of that school. He had a stud welded to his weapon. This stud fitted into a groove in a silver plate fastened to his belt. Thus the revolver could be freed with a minimum of motion, or it could be pivoted and fired in place.

Now as to the matter of putting the guns into action. The thing stressed by the formidable William Barclay (Bat) Masterson when counselling a young fellow named Fred Sutton was that a true gunman never tried to bluff an armed man, for fear of being taken seriously and shot. No experienced westerner put his hand near his revolver unless he was fully prepared to slay or disable his opponent.

The other primary point always stressed by the old time experts was — granted the desperate need for speed — the necessity of a modicum of deliberation. "The most important lesson I learned from those proficient gun fighters," Earp said, still speaking of Hickok, Gallagher, *et al*, "was that the winner of a gunplay usually was the man who took his time. . . . When I say I learned to take my time in a gunfight, I do not wish to be misunderstood, for the time to be taken was only that split-fraction of a second that means the difference between deadly accuracy with a six-gun and a miss. . . . Perhaps I can best describe such time-taking as going into action with the greatest speed of which a man's muscles are capable, but mentally unflustered by an urge to hurry or the need for complicated nervous and muscular actions which trick shooting involves."

Trick shooting was, legend to the contrary, for exhibitions, for winning bets, and for damned fools. Hear Cunningham. "Well, in the first place fanning is a pistol stunt so rarely practiced in real life that some old time Rangers and peace officers of my acquaintance — veterans of dozens of duels; men who could notch their guns if they were the ostentatious sort — have never seen it used in a fight."

Wyatt Earp concurred. "In all my life as a frontier peace officer, I did not know a really proficient gun-fighter who had anything but contempt for the gun-fanner or the man who literally shot from the hip. . . . Cocking and firing mechanisms on new revolvers were almost invariably altered by their purchasers in the interests of smoother, effortless handling, usually by filing the dog which controlled the hammer, some going so far as to remove triggers entirely or lash them against the guard, in which cases the guns were fired by thumbing the hammer. This is not to be confused with fanning, in which the triggerless gun was held in one hand while the other was brushed rapidly across the hammer fanwise to cock the gun, and firing it by the weight of the hammer itself. A skillful gun fanner could fire five shots from a forty-five so rapidly that the individual reports were indistinguishable, but what could happen to him in a gunfight was pretty close to murder."

Wyatt also had remarks to make about the two-gun fighter. "That two-gun business is another matter that can stand some truth before the last of the old time gun-fighters has gone on. They wore two guns, most of the six-gun-toters did, and when the time came for action went after them with both hands. But they didn't shoot them that way. Primarily, two guns made the threat of something in reserve; they were useful as a display of force when a lone man stacked up against a crowd. Some men could shoot equally well with either hand, and in a gunplay might alternate their fire; others exhausted the loads from the gun in the right hand or left, as the case might be, then shifted the reserve weapon to the natural shooting hand if that was necessary and possible. Such a move — the border shift — could be made faster than the eye could follow a topnotch gunthrower. . . ."

There were tricks of the trade for those cool enough to use them. Luke Short, as an old gun fighter called Pink Simmons remembered to Cunningham, always crowded in close. "That way he got the effect of the muzzle blast. It knocked the other man off balance. The .45 burned terribly at close range. It was impossible to face it — as I once discovered for myself! It will even set your clothes on fire. So, the man who got to shooting first when only a few feet away, he had a big advantage, even if he missed his first shot."

The calculated risk of such a practice was representative of the qualities which made the expert gunman. It was a combination of physical and psychological attributes which produced the specimen. Cunningham stressed the fact that there were probably several antagonists of that phenomenal killer, John Wesley Hardin, who were his match mechanically. What they lacked was his sure knowledge of just what he was going to do, and his refusal to be rattled and diverted from his purpose by any sort of circumstances.

Here again Luke Short must have incarnated the necessary make-up. Fast as he was, he wore the scalps of at least two gunmen who were supposed to be swifter and more deadly. After he left Charlie Storms dead in his impetuosity and blood on Allen Street, he incurred the wrath of Longhaired Jim Courtright in Fort Worth. Everybody in Fort Worth but Luke was breathless about Courtright's skill. Short refused to be disturbed by it. When Courtright came to slay him, Luke's coolness made Longhaired Jim so furious that Short, although taken at a disadvantage, got to shoot first and finally.

The physical make-up of these men deserves special consideration. The immediate effect of a hit from a .45 is a paralyzing shock where most men are concerned. The gunfighter had to be able to disregard shock in favor of immediate action. Bat Masterson, for instance, was once shot in the leg and collapsed. By the time he hit the floor he had drawn. He survived, and his enemy, for all he had him apparently at his mercy, did not.

To turn back from generalities about gunmen to their specific activities in Tombstone, all the manslayings so far noted in this chapter were, even when perpetrated by professionals, in the non-commercial class. They do not include the deliberate assaults on the peace which formed an even grimmer side of Tombstone's social history.

The murdering of those who resisted stage and other hold-up operations was but one activity in this direction. The rustlers wanted to dominate the city itself and killed repeatedly in their effort to do so. They began by making open raids and ended by assassinating from ambush. At the climax of that phase Parsons was able to observe in his journal: "Calky times very. 14 murders and assassinations in ten days."

Meanwhile causes were insisting on having their effects. In a town where everyone went armed — at first in Tombstone itself, and later whenever they moved outside of it — the citizens who honestly wished a reasonable amount of law and order were included. Inevitably they were conditioned by their environment and its customs. They shared, or came to share, the attitude that a man had the right to kill to avoid being crowded. It took a while, though, for these to develop an awareness of what they were up against in the form of organized oppression. They got their first orientation through local politics.

A San Pedro Valley prospector photographed with his tools in the early '80s. (Chapter 5)

Wyatt Earp and a redoubtable group of friends, at Dodge City,
Kansas. Wyatt himself is seated, second from the left.
Standing are Luke Short, in the middle, and Bat
Masterson, at the right. The burly man at
Earp's right is the famous Charley Bassett.
(Chapter 9)

CHAPTER NINE

POLITICS AND PEACE OFFICERS

THE political situation which permitted Tombstonians to work out their problems independently cannot be drawn in detail at this remove. Still its outlines are reasonably clear.

General John C. Fremont, Governor of Arizona, was a man who thought his brilliant services as an explorer had been ill rewarded by his country. His temperament didn't qualify him for statesmanship, but that was neither here nor there as far as his attitude was concerned. He felt that his achievements entitled him to the national spotlight, and he was not at all appeased by being appointed the chief executive of a frontier territory. Feeling that way, he should not have accepted. He took the worse course, accepting the post but sulking at what he regarded as exile.

The evidence indicates that he did not make the necessary effort to handle the obligations of his office. He left administration to whomsoever felt it was worth his while to use the dangling opportunity. It is only a lucky accident if those who choose to take over unclaimed administrative powers are both conscientious and capable. More often than not self-seeking rather than a sense of duty is the prompter. It was so in this instance.

Documentary evidence leaves plenty of holes here. What was not done is clearer than proofs of positive malfeasance. Yet malfeasance was present as an extensive infection.

To take the two up in order. It can be granted that a territory does not have the sovereign resources of a state to control lawlessness within its borders. At the same time a territorial government, boasting its own elected legislature, did have the power to ask the

101

authority of the Federal government to take such steps as might seem necessary. It was not done. Not until Fremont resigned was there any appeal for Federal interference. Cochise County derived no benefits from being a part of the territory except the right to be represented by men who had originally been elected to represent Pima County. As far as Cochise was concerned, the government at Prescott seems to have been without agencies there.

That is to say it was without official agencies. Positive malfeasance is easy to examine locally. Beyond the borders of the county the trail is largely inferential, although accusations that political corruption stemmed from the territorial government are in print. Wyatt Earp flatly stated as much to his biographer. If Clum and *The Epitaph* only hinted at it, Burnham declared that the entire government at Prescott during this period was corrupt and in active collusion with criminals.

Earp's outline of the situation is brief, but it sounds startlingly like an analysis of the political set-up of Missouri's Pendergast, New Jersey's Hague, and so on. The name of the dominating figure in this case is absent, but all the other elements of a political machine milking a region in collaboration with racketeers are present.

The prime essential is always the cover of a crooked or negligent top officialdom. Here it was the latter in the person of the sulking Fremont. The second necessity is some easily negotiable article of contraband for the racketeers who actually collect the revenues which support the political machine in return for a hands off policy on the part of government representatives. During the '80s in Arizona stolen cattle played exactly the part that illicit liquor did during the prohibition era. Other rackets could and did develop, but untaxed whiskey on one hand and rebranded cows on the other remained the basic support of crime. The third essential is the aggressiveness of a group of men, ready to kill in order to carry on the illegal trade in question. Here the counterpart of the booze-running hood was the quick-drawing rustler.

The method of operation on a broad scale was to control county offices either by putting organizational henchmen in charge, or by

buying up the incumbent. County agencies could then see to it
that the racketeers were not interfered with. Their further function was to keep the racketeers mindful of the fact that continuing
to pay off was the price of immunity.

So much for the substance of Earp's accusation. Its justice has
been denied by William Breakenridge, who was a deputy sheriff
and therefore an operative of a county office during Tombstone's
liveliest days. Whether Earp was correct or not, as far as the Territory of Arizona was concerned, the political picture he drew is not
one to shock anybody into incredulity. Its territorial workings will
not be investigated at length here, even if they could be. To what
extent such a politico-criminal pattern can be found in the Cochise
County of the day is, however, a legitimate problem for this
chronicle.

In the vicinity of Tombstone two of the three requisite elements,
the contraband cattle and the organized group of rustlers, were
uncontestably present. The only point in dispute is the evidence of
collusion between gangsters and officialdom, i. e. the extent of protection given to rustlers, hi-jackers, hold-up men, and murderers by
officers sworn to suppress these activities.

A secondary point of inquiry is — granted, for the sake of argument, that protection was given to malefactors by peace officers —
which of two accused groups of peace officers making their headquarters in Tombstone was in fact the guilty party. To decide that
a discussion of the various offices and incumbent officers is in
order.

Examination must begin before Cochise County was formed, or
at a time when the territory from the San Pedro Valley to the border of New Mexico was only the eastern sector of Pima County.
When Wyatt Earp passed through Tucson, the county seat of Pima,
in the fall of 1879, he was, he said, given a deputy sheriff's badge
and the authority to take charge of the Tombstone region. Previously there had been no representative of the sheriff's office east
of the San Pedro, and the reason why one was then in demand was
not, as specifically stated, to keep the peace. There had been no-

body there to collect the revenues which made the sheriff's office a financial as well as a political prize, and Sheriff Charles Shibell wanted the taxes from the rich Tombstone district.

Earp, then, was seemingly the first officer of recognized standing to operate in Tombstone. He went there as a deputy sheriff, not as a deputy U. S. Marshal, as is frequently stated, and his primary duty was not law enforcement. Sheriff Shibell was not interested in that phase of his duties.

Dissatisfied with Shibell's attitude, citizens interested in law and order ran a man called Bob Paul in opposition to him. In spite of the fact that he had been appointed by Shibell, Earp supported Paul. Inevitably he resigned, to be replaced by one John Behan. The assumption is that Behan was a man whom Shibell felt he could count upon to carry out his policies of acute attention to financial matters and negligence where law enforcement was concerned. Whether Behan's practice jibed with that assumption is something best left to the testimony of the record.

Before that record became plain enough to read, the new county of Cochise had been formed. The act became effective January 31, 1881, but the county's citizens were not permitted to hold an election for county officers until November of the following year. Until that date all offices were to be filled by appointees of the territorial government.

John Behan was an avowed applicant. Many have claimed that Wyatt Earp was also. He himself insisted that he was not, as he had other lucrative duties which he would have had to give up in order to be sheriff. His declaration was that he would have accepted the appointment as an obligation only. He therefore agreed to a proposal by Behan that he should announce his intention of stepping aside in consideration for being appointed a deputy. This job would bring him a considerable sum in fees while not taking up so much of his time that it would interfere with his other pursuits.

For this tale to make sense a division in the government must be recognized. As the party in power nationally was Republican, it was a Republican — John C. Fremont — who was awarded the post

Politics and Peace Officers

of territorial governor. But the dominant political party of Arizona Territory was Democratic. So when Fremont scamped his job, it was the Democrats, not members of his own party, who took over the power. If a well-known Republican like Earp sought an appointive office, Fremont might bestir himself to see that he got it. But in the absence of a Republican candidate, the men who really ran the government could pick whomever they liked; and Behan was a Democrat.

That is Earp's side of the story. Behan has left none. The version generally recorded in memoirs was that Earp did try for the post and lost out. At all events Earp did not get to be sheriff, nor did Behan appoint him deputy. His accusation was that Behan double-crossed him after having made him a definite promise. Supporters of Behan declared that Wyatt was enraged because John beat him out. Whichever was true, the incident serves as a marker for one thing. From that point on a degree of personal enmity aggravated the contest between peace officers which was an unusual feature of Tombstone's shooting times.

Meanwhile Earp already held a second position as peace officer, his forfeited job of deputy sheriff being the first. The robbing of the bullion stages had become a regular event. Finally Wells-Fargo countered by hiring Wyatt to ride along as guard. This was one of the financially profitable jobs which he would have had to give up in order to be sheriff. Then Crawley P. Dake, United States Marshal for Arizona, appointed Earp Deputy U. S. Marshal for the Tombstone district. That, in addition to carrying certain prerequisites with it, gave him the authority to carry the war to the bandits. For if stealing bars of silver was a state and not a national concern, interference with the U. S. Mail and interstate express — and stages carried both — was very much the business of a Federal officer.

Taking that as his cue, Wyatt announced his policy, not in a manifesto but in personal conversations with individual members of the rustlers' gang. The sheriff's office had done nothing to interfere with the activities of the hold-up men, but the Deputy U. S.

105

Marshal was not going to play ball with them. Offenders could expect to be hunted down, and killed if they resisted arrest. This was an open challenge to an organization which previously had not been threatened.

Whether he meant what he said is again a matter for the record to say. He was later accused of covering up for the very crimes he professed to be anxious to suppress. According to some testimony it was his office rather than that of the sheriff which was guilty of profiting from lawlessness. It was not, however, the established gang of rustlers that he was accused of favoring. Rather it was certain cronies, previously known to him in Deadwood, Dodge City, etc., whom he had invited to Tombstone to abet his own vicious schemes.

As law enforcing agencies, it should be pointed out, the offices of the county sheriff and the deputy U. S. marshal theoretically did not have overlapping responsibilities. The sheriff was supposed to deal with local breaches of the peace and the ordinary range of misdemeanors and felonies on the way up to the cardinal offenses of horse thievery and murder. The marshal was supposed to step in only where there was an infringement of Federal law. It didn't work out that way in many cases. For instance, where murder accompanied the rifling of the mail both offices claimed jurisdiction.

To complicate the tangled situation further there was a third agency in the field. This was the office of the town marshal of Tombstone. Its history is not only interlocked with the story of the other two offices but is bound up with the development of the municipal government and the feuds which raged about civic graft.

Although Tombstone was formally laid out in the spring of 1879, it was not until the fall of 1880 that a patent for a town site was granted by officials of Pima County. Its town charter did not become operative until January of 1881. During the intervening twenty-two months the place had no standing as a political entity and could have no legal government. Yet some sort of organization was necessary for the booming community, and one was formed.

Politics and Peace Officers

There was a mayor, town council, and so forth, all strictly without credentials but recognized locally as in authority.

This reads like a fine example of pioneers working out their problems in the democratic tradition until you reach the point where you find that the chief activity of the provisional government was fraudulent dealings in real estate.

The mayor's name was Alder Randall. A peculiarity of the town's constitution — and one, incidentally, which was retained when the charter became official, and which remains in effect to this day — is that the mayor was given the power to dispose of town land at his discretion. Mayor Randall's discretion took the form of profiting by this circumstance.

In chief he operated through the real estate firm of Clark and Gray. The latter was a justice of the peace, mentioned in that capacity by *The Nugget* as early as October, 1879. "Our Justice of the Peace Mike Gray has been kept quite busy since his appointment, but has not had as much criminal business as he ought, only for the reason that the parties have not been brought before him." Anyhow Clark and Gray apparently formed themselves into a real estate corporation which was given a monopoly on disposing of lots in Tombstone. A brief later filed by lawyers fighting for a redistribution of property stated: "On the ninth day of November, 1880, Alder Randall, then Mayor of Tombstone, without being directed thereto by the Council and without consideration, by deed duly executed, conveyed said town-site to said Town-site Co."

That was the act of criminal arrogance which roused the citizens who cared to the realization that they must unite, using violence if necessary, in order to prevent their town from being gobbled up. But the high handed dealings of Alder and the two others can be traced in Parsons' journal from much earlier in the year. Take this item of May 5, 1880. "Quite a row in town this A.M. Gray — the justice — endeavored with several armed assistants to eject Hatch from the lot opposite the P.O. . . . . A crowd gathered and sided with Hatch when Gray and party after a flourish of pistols retired. Nice work for a justice. Gray offered the lot to

The Last Chance

Milton the day before. Having no patent he can't give good titles to property."

But determined malfeasance always has the drop on honesty when it is content with disorganized protests. In time this was recognized, and that recognition was the origin of the Law and Order League in Tombstone. Once formed, it commenced carrying the war to the others. For this development Parsons is again the star witness.

Nov. 7. "Mayor was summoned to a meeting this day and gave his solemn promise that he would not deed until the patent was in his hands and not then until meeting of the Council was called when he would be guided by their wishes. . . . Another meeting of the Council was held . . . when Councilman Jones made a complete expose of the frauds attempted and perpetrated by the Mayor and his crowd. . . . One instance of the Mayor's act will illustrate. Attachments issued against him of nearly $1,000 and his saloon property was seized. He claimed it wasn't his and defrauded his creditors or has thus far. He deeded the property to Clark, Gray & Co. as Mayor who in turn deeded to a friend of Randall's who is to redeem to the Mayor when the right time comes. The mayor's own words to Jones were 'there's more sugar in the other crowd' — meaning Clark, Gray & Co. Randall was to make $2500 and Jones $500."

But those highbinders were plainly not the men to be intimidated by public indignation. Only action in kind made them pull in their horns. See Parsons, Dec.4: "Clarke & Gray with a force of working and reputed fighting men or man — 'Texas' — at the head pulled down Reilley's fence and moved house part way into the street, where at last Lowery, it's only occupant, in R's absence asked help of the Marshal and he stopped proceedings, being compelled though to take off his coat and show he meant business. Looked like a grand row at one time. A few of us . . . cried 'put her back' but no words were needed. A lot of men seized the timbers and 'put her back' some distance. Much artillery was on hand and I expected shooting at one time but nothing serious to date —

none. 24 hours is allowed and then C & G will be arrested probably for obstructing street. I've not been wholly in favor of this movement as Reilley jumped improved property, but the precedent is a bad one.... Lowery sent word for me ... so I visited him when he requested me to stay the night with him ... as threats were made to finish the house during the night. I agreed provided everything was legalized, so that resistance would be entirely proper. I then saw Eccleston who called a meeting of the League at my suggestion.... Everything was made right. A police whistle was given me, revolvers and shot gun in place and I took over blanket and after smoking a while — Lowery on the cot ... and I on a broken down sofa, and all on our shooters, retired to sleep as best we could.... I thought perhaps an attempt might be made to blow the house up but ... the night was passed comfortably enough."

The item for Dec. 5 followed in calendar order. "Great acitivity this A.M. . . . a general report that C,G & Co. would attempt to move the corner house in the rear of R's and thus prevent the latter's being moved back to place. Vickers and I had a consultation and then set off to get men to move house back before the other idea was consummated. We didn't have much trouble in raising a crowd and at the word, we all made a rush and in a very few minutes had the house back where it belonged. There was much enthusiasm, Clark was present at the commencement, speedily left and with Gray kept away — a very prudent idea . . . Eccleston, Clum and others prominent in business took a hand. Few words and quick action. . . . Redfern said that at the theatre last night there were ten more who had shot guns loaded and ready in case the signal for help came and that they had brought some rope to stretch C & G's neck with in case they were not shot — so at last it would look as though the people would assert their rights."

Mayor Randall, for one, did not like, as Parsons expressed it, "the smell of hemp" and became convinced that he should not be a candidate when the first of Tombstone's authorized elections was held in January of 1881. To all intents and purposes the career of the provisional administration ended a few weeks earlier. Yet before dismissing it, two points must be dealt with.

What, if any, was the relation of these shifty operators to other political machines of the territory? Not easy to answer, but there is a clue. The unconscionable number of months of delay before the town-site patent was granted gave Randall and his associates so much time to dig in and get their grip that the issue was still being argued as late as 1883. For if Randall was willing to backwater, he had already made considerable profits from the sale of lots to men who were not willing to concede that their titles were no good. The delay in legalizing matters which gave the real estate jugglers their advantage of time was allowed by politicians of Pima County, many of whose associates had shifted their headquarters to Tombstone.

Secondly, to complete the circuit to the opening passages of this chapter, what was the relation of the office of town marshal to Mayor Randall's government? Gray, it has been shown via a passage from *The Nugget*, was a town official at least as early as October 2, 1879. The office of marshal was apparently an afterthought. Wyatt Earp stated that the first town marshal, Fred White, was appointed by a committee of citizens on January 6, 1880. If, therefore, the marshal theoretically acted under the authority of the provisional administration, he did not owe a henchman's allegiance to it.

That was to be an important factor in the story of Tombstone. Fred White took his responsibilities to his true employers, the citizens, so seriously that he was killed before the year was out while attempting to arrest Curly Bill. To fill out his term Virgil Earp, Wyatt's older brother, was appointed.

John Clum makes the duties of the town marshal clear to the modern reader. In writing of his Tombstone days he referred to the incumbent as "my chief of police." Yet his responsibilities were not as well defined as that sounds. There was a definite overlapping of authority with that of the sheriff's office, for the sheriff was sworn to enforce the law throughout Cochise County. If the law was broken in Tombstone, a part of that county, the sheriff might or might not decide to take the matter out of the marshal's hand. Moreover, the sheriff had a practical advantage of a crucial nature. He controlled the county jail, and so, in important cases, the marshal's prisoners had to be turned over to him eventually.

To reduce the offices from their impersonal possibilities to their personal actualities, John Behan, hostile to Wyatt Earp, was the sheriff. Virgil Earp, devoted to his brother and soon inimical to Behan on his own account, came to be town marshal on two different occasions. Officially as well as personally he was in alliance with Deputy U. S. Marshall Earp, whose feud with the sheriff grew progressively more bitter. In the end the three officers came to stand for two factions striving for control of the town.

CHAPTER TEN

SOME PRINCIPALS OF ACTION

WYATT EARP is a subject dealt with in any number of reminiscences. This does not simplify the problem of weighing the man's character, for the opinions handed down by his contemporaries are contradictory. Much of this writing is of a passionate nature. Wyatt seemed to have had a genius for earning either unforgiving enmity or lasting loyalty.

In this instance the record of his life is open for inspection, even aside from his biography, long before he reached Tombstone. He was one of the best known characters of the West, in especial for his activities as town marshal for the dangerous cattle capitals of Kansas. There he held his own in opposition to such accredited killers as Clay Allison, Mannen Clements, and Ben Thompson. He had also, he stated, encountered Curly Bill and Johnny Ringo there, though under what circumstances he did not say. Above all, and characteristically, he won both admiration and hate there.

The one point of agreement is that he did enforce the law. It was his methods which caused argument. His enemies claimed that he indulged in promiscuous shooting, and for blood money. They claimed that he killed, maimed, and imprisoned for so much a head, taking advantage of drunken men in the process. The testimony of citizens whose businesses and homes he saved from the molestation of cow hands hankering to indulge in the time honored practice of shooting up a town was all in his favor, on the other hand. According to them he was an honest, diligent, and proficient peace officer.

An arm of the law or not, he had the reputation of being no more than a bad man in many quarters; yet it is difficult to answer the question as to just how it was earned. He was feared as a killer, but just whom had he killed? Many perhaps, but they aren't in the record. He himself mentioned only the slaying of one George Hoyt in Kansas to his biographer. On the other hand he referred to many instances when he had disabled a man. For what it is worth, his own contention is that, with the exception of one period in Tombstone, he never killed if he could get by with disabling, and never disabled if he could get by with disarming.

Much of the available evidence supports his assertion. Yet it wasn't a reputation for magnanimity that made wild-eyed murderers think twice when they came up against him. As far as can be judged at this distance the explanation lay not so much in what he had done as in what people thought he could do. Among speedy gunmen there was little to choose in the time it took to get a pistol into action. Granted two men the same amount of coolness, the advantage belonged to the one who was most confident, and that always seemed to be Wyatt. Gazing at his sureness, men questioned their own; and when that happened, it was no contest. The amazing fact is that this man whom so many expert gun sharks were anxious to kill died in his bed at 80 without ever having been wounded.

Men of supreme self-confidence are not always better liked for being able to back up their faith in themselves. Men whom Earp had never personally injured disliked him for his thoroughness and accused him of being a sadistic tyrant. With many the very fact that he was a peace officer was enough to mark him lousy.

Whether or not it is true of other countries, in the United States John Law seldom wins out in a popularity contest. He is an agency, the more distasteful for being impersonal, which limits that free wheeling of the individual which is the most basic of American concepts.

If that is true now, it was ten times more true in the old West. Those who liked it best prized its lack of prohibitions most. A peace officer was felt to be one who had gone over to the enemy.

Another instinctive feeling conditioned the attitude toward an officer who killed or maimed while enforcing the law. This was simply that he was taking pay for it. The fact that a man undertaking such a dangerous job was earning his pay had nothing to do with it. He was held to be slaying for hire, and drew less sympathy with many than did the outlaw whose murdering was an incidental necessity to the accomplishment of a robbery.

Wyatt's personality no doubt made a distrustful view of his gunmanship easy to entertain. His nature was called reserved by his friends and cold-blooded by others. He had a calculating mind that always figured percentage, usually with accuracy. For instance, when all other buffalo hunters were shooting from a stand while a whole crew of skinners waited to tackle the day's bag, he figured out that he would make a greater net profit by stalking the herds with a shotgun, trailed by one skinner who took care of the animals as they fell. He was right. When the gold town of Deadwood was snowed in during the first boom year, Wyatt was the only man who thought it worth while to invest in enough feed to see his team of horses through a bitter Black Hills winter. There was no prospecting in the deep drifts, but he cleared $7,000 on his wood hauling monopoly.

Until he was over forty he drank nothing but beer and light wine, another thing that branded him as an odd fish in a bachelor society of bottle punishers. He gave no reason for this himself, but it would fit in with what else is known of him to assert that he practiced abstemiousness for the advantage it gave him in gambling and fighting.

One fact ascertainable from his own statements is that he liked to win for the taste of victory. A man endowed with such a competitive temperament is forced to seek contests to satisfy it. In the Old West the chief forms of competition were gunplay and gambling. He himself has recorded that he got a kick out of being marshal of the cowtowns, because it gave him a chance to beat self-proclaimed bad men at their own game.

Other motives went shares with the foregoing, in all likelihood, to make him a chronic peace officer. One was that it gave him an unquestioned license to carry a gun when and where he wanted to. Then there is the possibility that he was influenced by family tradition and early training, He was the son and grandson of lawyers and had himself read for the law.

He was not without a sense of fun. His biography tells how he and Bat Masterson rigged the vote in a babies' beauty contest, sponsored by the social elite of Dodge City, so that the winner turned out to be a pickaninny of uncertain paternity. Yet in his dealings with most men he was aloof and dignified. That didn't help his popularity. The man who is hail-fellow-well-met between murders is often held to be basically all right where the quiet gunman is loathed and dreaded.

Earp's honesty has been called into account by Breakenridge and other old timers who sided with his enemies. If these accusations were just, they were not proved, nor does there seem to have been a serious effort to prove them. On the other hand the effort to make him pay by law for deliberate murder was several times made in Tombstone. This case will be tried in the action of the ensuing pages.

His brothers, Virgil, two years older, and Morgan, two years younger, belong to history chiefly by virtue of being Wyatt's allies. Both, however, were dangerous fighters in their own right. The three were supposed to have looked so much alike — all blond, slender men, six-feet-one in height, and all wearing drooping moustaches — that they were often mistaken for each other. One woman who remembered them put it on record that she thought the Earp brothers and Doc Holliday the handsomest men she had ever seen.

John H. Holliday of Valdosta, Georgia, is another controversial figure. A great deal has been written about him, but Wyatt's summation is a classic of thumbnail biography: "He was a dentist whom necessity had made a gambler; a gentleman whom disease had made a frontier vagabond; a philosopher whom life had made a caustic wit; a long, lean ash-blond fellow nearly dead with consumption and at the same time the most skillful gambler and the nerviest, speediest, deadliest man with a six-gun I ever knew."

After Holliday's death some journalist disgusted Wyatt by writing of the doctor as a "mad, merry scamp with a heart of gold and nerves of steel." "Doc was mad, well enough," Earp commented to his biographer, "but he was seldom merry. His humor ran in a sardonic vein, and as far as the world in general was concerned, there was nothing in his soul but iron. Under ordinary circumstances he might be irritable to the point of shakiness; only in a game or when a fight impended was there anything steely about his nerves. . . .

"Perhaps Doc's outstanding peculiarity was the enormous amount of whiskey he could punish. Two and three quarts of liquor a day was not unusual for him, yet I never saw him stagger with intoxication. At times when his tuberculosis was worse than ordinary, or he was under a long-continued physical strain, it would take a pint of whiskey to get him going in the morning, and more than once at the end of a long ride I've seen him swallow a tumbler of neat liquor without batting an eye and fifteen minutes later take a second tumbler of straight whiskey which had no more outward effect on him than the first one. Liquor never seemed to fog him in the slightest, and he was more inclined to fight when getting along on a slim ration than when he was drinking plenty, and was more comfortable physically."

Many of Wyatt's other friends couldn't understand his fondness for Holliday, and held the dentist a liability, except when it came to a fight. There seems to be no question that Doc was a killer who liked the act. He was an outlaw wanted for shooting in a variety of places. One headboard in Tombstone's cemetery carries his name as the executioner. Moreover, he openly lived with a dance hall girl called Big Nosed Kate Fisher — apparently not to be confused with Nosey Kate, whose picture appears in *Billy King's Tombstone* — and in general was an embarrassment to the Law and Order League, of which his friendship with Wyatt made him a prominent defender.

Why that friendship persisted was evidently a mystery to everybody but the two most concerned. Wyatt seems to have been the only person in the world whom Doc thoroughly respected. He would even stay out of a fight to oblige him. Wyatt on his part paid no attention to the criticism directed at Holliday. "With all of Doc's shortcomings and his undeniably poor disposition," he recorded, "I found him a loyal friend and good company."

The time he found his company particularly good was the incident that started the friendship. Two cowmen whom Earp had once buffaloed and jailed got the drop on Wyatt when he was entering a saloon in Dodge City. They were supported, moreover, by a gang of cowhands with whom they were currently engaged in shooting up the town. Earp thought he was a goner and that the only question was how many he could take along with him. He had just reached that desperate conclusion when Doc charged through a side door with a pair of guns and roared a general order to reach for it. The interruption gave Wyatt a chance to draw his own revolvers, and from then on the situation was under control.

Bat Masterson and Luke Short, who else would have been formidable supporters of Wyatt, went their separate ways before the trouble between the Earps and their enemies reached its lethal climax. At that point their backing in a larger sense took the form of moral support from the Citizen's Safety Committee. Actively behind the Earps were sundry friends of Wyatt's, of whom Turkey Creek Jack Johnson was the best known.

The faction against them was also composed of two elements — the rustlers and the politicians who ran Cochise County. To begin with the latter, John H. Behan, a Missourian born, was a congenital Arizona office holder before he came to Tombstone. If he actually did get the appointment to the shrievalty of the county over Wyatt's head, it should be a cause for no astonishment. He was a lodge member of the party really, if not nominally, in power. Earp was an outsider, whereas Behan had been mixed up in territorial politics for a decade. Twice he had held a seat in the legislature from Mohave County, and once from Yavapai. He had also been successively the county recorder and the sheriff of Yavapai County.

Behan did not leave a personal memoir. He seems to have been well liked by many in Tombstone, although developments made some of them change their minds. He does not appear to have been reckoned a gunman — though a headboard in Boot Hill testifies to the fact that he could use weapons — in the sense that he was especially dreaded. At the same time Burns' characterization of him as a sort of babe in the six-shooter woods is a rank injustice to one who was, on the record, a completely implacable enemy. He preferred indirect methods of carrying his point, but when that didn't work he was capable of a stubborn boldness that balked at almost nothing.

The nearest thing to an authoritative spokesman for Behan was William Breakenridge, one of his deputies. He was a native of Wisconsin who had tried about everything the West had to offer — Indian fighting, professional game hunting, surveying, railroading, etc. — before he came to Tombstone. Like Behan, he was not then virginal to Arizona politics, as he had previously been a deputy sheriff of Maricopa County.

In his autobiography he may be judged to reflect the policies of the sheriff's office, and if he is offhand in the discussion of these policies, he is revelatory. He is reasonably temperate in his remarks about the Earps — after all Behan's personal enmity need not have been his affair — usually contenting himself with implication rather than accusation. Where his own actions are concerned, he is more explicit, often surprisingly so.

By his accounting he got along very well with the rustlers, taking them by and large. He did them favors, in his official capacity, of an extraordinary sort, and reported that they reciprocated in a manner no less remarkable. These actions will be examined shortly. Here it is rather in order to deal with some of the leading figures among the outlaws with whom he exchanged these amenities.

Originally reckoned their chief was N. H. Clanton. The breadth of his activities was expounded by Breakenridge himself. "The Clantons looked after the rustlers' interests in the San Pedro. . . . The McLaurys looked after the stock brought up from Mexico into the Sulphur Springs Valley. The stage robbers, hold-up men, and other outlaws that made these places a refuge, included Frank Stilwell, Pete Spencer (sic), Zwing Hunt, Billy Grounds, Jim Crane, Harry Head, Billy Leonard, and their followers whose names I have forgotten."

The Clantons also, Breakenridge went on to say, made cattle forays into Mexico and preyed upon smugglers operating between the two nations. A well attested illustration is the fact that Old Man Clanton personally led the band which ambushed a train of silver-laden mules in Skeleton Canyon, near the Mexican border in the Guadaloupes. The rustlers killed nineteen mule drivers and guards in the course of this exploit, which netted them $75,000.

Oddly enough Old Man Clanton was finally shot for a crime of which he was only an accessory after the fact. A group of his followers on a raid into Sonora ambushed the guardians of a large herd, murdered fourteen vacqueros and amused themselves by torturing a captive or so. While they refreshed themselves at Galeyville in celebration of this feat Clanton took over the stolen steers, intent to drive them on to a market in Tombstone. But in Guadaloupe Canyon he was waylaid by a party of Mexican avengers.

It was then that Curly Bill Brocius became the leader of the outlaws. He is said to have been full of fun in a boisterous way — when he felt like it. "Curly Bill," Breakenridge wrote in describing his first meeting with the rustler, "was lying on a card table. . . . He was fully six feet tall, with black curly hair, freckled face and well built. Shorty brought in a bucket of water and filling a tin cup said, 'Here's how, boys,' and lifted the cup to drink from it. Curly who had raised up on his elbow, shot the cup out of his hand, saying, 'Don't drink that, Shorty, it's pison.'"

Several old timers included in their reminiscences the time when Curly Bill shot up a church in Charleston and made the minister go through a repertoire of tricks, including dancing. Parsons, who later met the minister in question, supplies the information that his name was McKane and that he did not like to discuss his meeting with Mr. Brocius.

Still Curly Bill had an eye for business as well as pleasure. He was with Old Man Clanton when the smugglers of Mexican silver were ambushed. He was also a participant, and probably the leader, of the murder and torture raid into Sonora which led to his ascendancy to the chieftanship of the rustlers. Two head-boards in Tombstone's Boot Hill prove that all his bullets were not for Mexicans. One of them is that of the town's first marshal.

Sharing his eminence after the demise of Old Man Clanton was the more complicated figure of Johnny Ringo. In contrast to the burly darkness of Curly Bill, he was slender with reddish brown hair atop well moulded features. He is supposed to have had, in addition to certain criminal connections, an aristocratic family background. Well, he shouldn't have been lonesome. If you can believe many writers about the Old West, the roster of outlaws was a sort of mustang Burke's Peerage.

"Ringo was a very mysterious man," Breakenridge observed. "He had a college education but was reserved and morose. He drank heavily as if to drown his troubles; he was a perfect gentleman when sober, but inclined to be quarrelsome when drinking. He was a good shot and afraid of nothing, and had great authority with the rustling element. Although he was the leader on their trips to Mexico and in their raids against the smugglers, he generally kept by himself after they returned to Galeyville. He read a great deal and had a small collection of standard books in his cabin."

There has been a strong tendency to romanticize Ringo in Tombstone tradition. What especially endeared him to the romantic heart was the story that he brooded over his fallen estate. Much is made of this, and it may well have been so. Also current is the tradition that he was a squire of dames, some tales building him up into a sort of Traveler's Aid Bureau dedicated to sending wayward girls home to their parents. That, too, may have been so, although it is not well documented. What cannot be doubted was his skill with a gun and his willingness to use one either face to face with his enemies or from hiding. Even his own associates are said to have feared him when he was drinking.

Thus the generals, thus the rank and file. How many of these there actually were is one of the disputed questions — some putting the figure very high and others correspondingly low. Those who take the latter position, however, point out that the registered outlaws, so to speak, could call upon the services of a large assortment of small ranchers and irresponsible drifters of one sort or another. At all events there were enough of them to overrun the county and to completely dominate every town in it with the exception of Tombstone.

Although their operations were as well known as their persons, the rustlers preferred to style themselves "cowboys," a term suggesting honest toil in those days, when it lacked the flavor of romantic dash it has since acquired. In this they were supported by the Tombstone *Nugget,* which professed to see nothing wrong with their activities. When the existence of crime was admitted, *The Nugget* found somebody else to blame, usually the Earps or some of their associates.

The feud split the fourth estate as it did other elements of the town, for the city's other important sheet, *The Epitaph,* took a different view of matters. It made no bones about stating its belief that in Cochise County "cowboy" was synonymous with stock thief, hold-up man, and murderer. As far as the Earps were concerned, *The Epitaph* reported their acts as those of peace officers loyal to their obligations.

The columns of the two journals were devoted to a rousing, name-calling newspaper war, but unfortunately — due to the fact that the rescued files do not synchronize — it has to be followed largely in one paper at a time. Nevertheless, it is evident that the difference between them was more than a matter of slanting the news. The facts reported about a given incident by the two papers often had nothing but the date and location to show kinship. The questions then are: which one was guilty of partisan journalism, or were both guilty; also was it a war between newspapers, each trying to corner the circulation, or was there a larger stake?

One of the founders of *The Nugget* was John Dunbar, who had received the appointment of county treasurer when Cochise County was organized. Previous to that organization he had been a Pima County delegate to the House, or lower chamber of the Territorial Legislature at Prescott. While a member of that body his chief function had been to have Pima split up to create the new county, of which the treasurer's post was promptly awarded him. He was also a partner of Sheriff John Behan in the ownership of the Dexter Corral and Livery Stable at Tombstone.

The Nugget's original publisher was one E. A. Fay, one of the owners of the paper. According to *The Epitaph*, at least, the later and sole owner was not a resident of Tombstone at all. "It is well known that *The Nugget* establishment is owned by Hugo Richards of Prescott, who allows the present publishers to have the use of it on the condition they support him as a candidate for Congress." Now Hugo Richards was one of the founders of the Bank of Arizona. Somewhat earlier he had been a member of the legislature and was credited with being one of the men who manipulated the transference of the territorial capital from Tucson to the seat of his own business interests, Prescott.

But whether or not *The Epitaph* was correct about the ownership of *The Nugget*, the paper's publisher in 1881 and 1882 was Harry M. Woods. Like Dunbar this man was a delegate to the body which created Cochise County. It was he, as the record of the Eleventh Legislature of the Territory of Arizona shows, who bulled the measure through the House over the opposition of delegates from Tucson, who didn't want Pima County divided. After his political victory he was appointed undersheriff by Behan.

So it is fair to state that *The Nugget* was the organ of county politics. It reflected the attitude of county politics when it professed to view the rustlers as ordinary rangehands. Two at any rate of the men connected with it were actively associated with Sheriff Behan, who was at odds with the Earps.

To turn from *The Nugget*. Although he had two partners, John P. Clum was known to be the editorial strength of *The Epitaph*. He was also the political force behind it.

He had stepped into national history before coming to Tombstone in a manner which deserves some notice. Clum had come West in 1871. Two years later he received an invitation to become the agent of the San Carlos Apache Reservation. For causes not easily investigated these particular Apaches had been turned over to the spiritual guidance of the Dutch Reformed Church, a small sect usually confined to its own narrow reservations in limited strips of New Jersey and New York. When a new agent was in order for the year old Indian preserve, it was considered imperative that the applicant must be a member of the Dutch Reformed faith. Of these mysteries are governments made. Howbeit, adherents of the sect were rare in the West, and diverse Rutgers classmates knew Clum was in New Mexico. He had no experience with Indians, but at the age of 23, after some study of the matter, he accepted this dangerous post in 1874.

A previous agent or so had been killed. The last one had been run off the premises. It goes without saying, therefore, that Clum brought courage to the job. He also brought imagination and a conviction. His examination of the record taught him that although the United States, through its Department of the Interior, was pledged to the conservation and education of the Apaches, through its War Department it was dedicated to their extermination. He chose to take the stand that he would not and could not operate a reservation unless troops were kept out of the picture.

Instead he organized a force of Apache police, who brought their prisoners before an Apache tribunal. The experiment was an over-all success, but eventually the Army moved in on him anyhow. After taking care to insult about half the people of importance in Washington, Clum resigned in the summer of 1877.

The Last Chance

He has been criticized, both at the time and since then, — perhaps rightly so — for arrogance and hotheadedness. Nobody, however, has challenged the sincerity of his motives or proved that his Indian policy was not on the whole a sound one. Certainly a man who made a business of telling his superiors where to get off could never be accused of being a time serving politician.

In Tombstone, after a heated debate, Clum was the candidate for mayor of that faction of the Law and Order League who wanted somebody with the guts to take an aggressive stand against political grafters of the Randall-Gray stripe. He won the election of January 4, 1881, against a Mark Shaffer, who had the support of *The Nugget*.

Parsons, who claimed responsibility for the nomination of Clum, and who served as his campaign manager, was able to rejoice to his journal in these words: "Election day and an exciting one. Polls crowded all day long. . . . First trick of opposition was to gobble our tickets. I saw Clum and he settled the point by keeping the presses running all day. So that didn't work. I got my men in — Mark as tally clerk and Dickerson at window to challenge. Seeing that the ticket would be stronger with Walker on it in place of Fuller as assessor I authorized the change in our ticket. Much scratching for Walker against Fuller. Learning that 20 or 30 Mexicans were to be run in about noon . . . I notified D who got the help of Moore the Spanish teacher. . . . About 2 o'clock I tho't I saw our ticket would win — about two to one. . . . Mark Shaffer made a poor exhibition of himself inside the polling enclosure in a desperate effort to retrieve the day. . . . Clum behaved himself with excellent taste. . . . About sun down the polls were closed and I requested Dickerson, Eccleston and Campbell to preside at the count and got them in without any opposition — Clum inside too. . . . Our victory certain in a very little while and Shaffer retired before long very much disturbed at the frequency of Clum's name. . . ."

Then on January 5 Parsons summed up the election results. "Our whole ticket gloriously elected by astonishing majorities.

124

A crushing defeat. I have done my best to defeat corruption and fraud and have won."

Let it be remarked again that Shaffer, who was beaten by Clum, had the support of *The Nugget*. Political geometry being as logical as the mathematical kind, Shaffer was allied with the County machine and Clum, together with his followers, opposed to it. The split between the county and town governments was thus a marked one, but it is questionable if any but the professional politicians of the county organization were aware of it. It is improbable that the factions came to strife on the government level during the early months of county and town organization. From the record it seems almost certain that the members of the town government did not realize the strength and extent of the forces against them until late in the game. In all likelihood the first to have had this unpleasant knowledge forced upon them were the Earps.

CHAPTER ELEVEN

THE GROWTH OF A FEUD

THERE were six strands of the feud which made Tombstone a battle ground. It took better than a year before they were all plaited together, however.

Wyatt Earp, for instance, originally was at odds with Sheriff Behan as a separate contest from his struggle with the rustlers. Ill feeling, as has been remarked, began over John Behan's appointment. Whether or not he had agreed to make Earp a deputy and had broken his word, the feeling in Tombstone was that it was John's round. Wyatt himself conceded that it was, in as much as he had allowed himself to be taken in. He cited other rounds, though, which went to him. When Behan opened a gambling concession Earp sat in with the purpose of breaking the bank. He did so. A girl whom Behan fancied turned up hanging on Wyatt's arm, and so on.

This was strictly personal stuff, distinct from acts in their official capacities. The clash of offices was not at first a clash at all. It took the form of non-cooperation rather than direct hostility.

Earp's trouble with the rustlers did not begin at once, either. Although he had come to Tombstone with a deputy sheriff's badge, he was not under orders to deal with outlaws. "There won't be much criminal work," he quoted Sheriff Charles Shibell of Pima County as asserting. "Tombstone's going to organize and will appoint a marshal to handle law and order. Get the county's money and you can suit yourself about the gunmen. . . . The sheriff is tax and fee collector as well as a peace officer. He gets

The Growth of a Feud

a percentage of collections plus mileage. We should get ten or twelve thousand dollars a month from Tombstone, but a lot of fellows in there figure they're too tough to pay taxes, and what little is collected never reaches us. I'm after a deputy who's man enough to collect what's due, and honest enough to make certain the county gets it. I'll guarantee you five hundred dollars a month, if you'll take the job."

In spite of that statement, Earp made the rustlers watch their manners while in Tombstone, even though open warfare apparently didn't break out until, as a deputy U. S. marshal, he tried to halt the robbing of stages. Anyhow Earp accepted Shibell's offer, but by the next fall disgust for the sheriff's attitude toward law enforcement drove him to endorse the candidacy of Robert Paul, the hope of the Law and Order Party of Pima County. The headquarters of that party was naturally at Tucson rather than Tombstone. Nevertheless there were important results of the Tombstone phase of the contest.

First of all and inevitably Wyatt resigned before Shibell could fire him as deputy. His badge was turned over to Behan. The change was so to the liking of the "cowboys" that they once more favored Tombstone as a place where they could do what they wanted.

A week before the election of November 2, 1880, Wyatt, who had been in Tucson, reached town to find that the rustlers had staked a claim to Allen Street. Earp saw Curly Bill, the McLowry brothers, Pony Deal, Frank Patterson, and Ike and Billy Clanton enter a saloon together. None of them had obeyed the ordinance about checking guns while in town.

This was not, strictly speaking, the concern of a Federal officer, and Earp did nothing about it until he was appealed to by Tombstone's town marshal, Fred White. White stated that the "cowboys" had been camping in town for two days, using their guns freely, and that Deputy Sheriff Behan had refused to help him do anything about it. Wyatt agreed to back White's effort to round the celebraters up.

127

The Last Chance

The cabin Wyatt shared with his brother, Morgan, and Fred Dodge, the secret Wells, Fargo agent who posed as a gambler, was in the rear of a vacant lot on which the Bird Cage Theatre was later built. It was from the shadow of this, his own home, that Wyatt heard a voice inviting all of Tombstone to come out and fight.

Splitting up, Earp and White closed in on the challenger from two sides and found that they had boxed Curly Bill himself. White rashly seized the barrel of the pistol Bill was waving and got a bullet in the brisket. Brocius dropped, too, when Wyatt buffaloed him by laying the length of his own weapon across Curly Bill's noggin.

Morgan Earp and Dodge turned up at that juncture to carry White to a resting place in their cabin and to take Curly Bill to jail. Meanwhile the rustlers were showing disapproval of the assault on their companion by shooting at his captors. Fortunately for the Earps the darkness interfered with accuracy.

"I'll get the others," Wyatt said; and this, by his account, he proceeded to do. Picking out the leaders, he soon had both Clanton brothers, both McLowry brothers, and Pony Deal in with Brocius. His method of subduing each was to buffalo him, which was at once the most humane and most dangerous method of handling armed, drunken killers. It was also the most humiliating for professional bad men. "They never forgave me that manhandling," Wyatt later remembered. "If I do say so myself, I was thorough."

There is little doubt that at least part of the appeal of buffaloing for Earp was the very fact that it was perilous, both at the time and afterwards, and demanded the utmost of nerve and precise timing. His favorite revolver was especially adapted to this practice, as it had a twelve inch barrel. In itself this "Buntline Special" was not without a history. The long weapon was made by Colt at the behest of Ned Buntline, the dime novelist who created the legend of Buffalo Bill. Buntline visited the cowtowns to get local color for his wild western tales and had five of the outsize pistols made for the peace officers who most impressed him. The list of these reads like a miniature Western who's who. Besides Wyatt the recipients were Bill Tilghman, Charlie Bassett, Neal Brown, and Bat Masterson.

Curly Bill and the others got no more than a headache from the Buntline Special, but Marshal White died several days later of the bullet from Bill's gun. Yet before doing so he cleared Brocius of intent to kill, declaring that his own awkward grab for the revolver had made Curly squeeze the trigger inadvertently. In this opinion he may have differed from Curly Bill himself. Breakenridge, who was on good terms with Brocius, cited the incident to Cunningham as a method whereby a seemingly helpless man could get the drop on his adversary. According to his description of what happened, Curly extended his weapon, barrel down and grip foremost. A twitch of his hand, however, pivoted the pistol around his trigger finger, so that what White caught at and pulled was the barrel. Thus with malice prepense but with no actual movement on his part, Brocius made the marshal shoot himself. To this day the ruse is known in the West as "the Curly Bill spin."

In the darkness this play must have escaped White and Earp. The latter didn't press charges either, although he later threatened to for a motive separate from wrath at the killing.

Curly Bill had not been released on bail long, pending a final decision, when the results of the election for Sheriff of Pima County came in from Tucson. The count showed that Wyatt's man, Paul, had been beaten by a margin of 47 votes. Analyzing the returns, Earp found that of the total for Shibell 103 votes had come from the rustlers' headquarters town of Galeyville. Later *The Epitaph* was to refer to the phenomenon as follows: "Not many moons ago, when Sheriff Shibell, a gallant Democrat for whom a half dozen San Simon cowboys voted 104 times. . . ." Having decided on his own account that such was the approximate situation, Earp set out to play poker with Curly Bill.

"Come through about the Galeyville votes," Wyatt quoted himself as saying, "and I won't dispute White's dying statement. Otherwise I'll swear you shot White as he reached for your gun. If the law doesn't hang you on that, Fred's friends will."

Brocius was not then the leader of the outlaws, who were themselves not as powerful as they soon became. Moreover, casual as the attitude toward killing was in most instances thereabouts, killing a peace officer for greens, as an adjunct of a spree, was bad business. Bill could have skipped the country, but the pickings were too good. He agreed instead to get confessions from the men who had stuffed the Galeyville ballot box. The result was that the election was contested. Shibell remained in office while the territorial government considered the matter; but in the end it was proved that the man who got the most votes was Bob Paul, the Law and Order candidate.

This was a political defeat for the rustlers, and one directly chargeable to Earp; but it didn't help Tombstone very long, because Cochise County was shortly formed. In place of Shibell the new county got his hand picked operative, John Behan.

A by-product of the incident was that Virgil Earp first came into the picture as a Tombstone peace officer, for he was appointed to fill out White's term. Breakenridge declared that Virgil lost the election in January of 1881 to a Ben Sippy; Wyatt claimed that his brother was not up for election. In either case Sippy got the post; but in the two months before the other took office Virgil put a lid on the town and screwed it down in a way that further antagonized the "cowboys." He also undoubtedly made enemies of a good many who were not fundamentally outlaws. Neither thieves nor killers, they preferred both of these types to people who interfered in any way with their personal freedom — a subject on which they held expansive notions.

Just what rules of conduct Virgil set up for Tombstone has not come down in the record, but Wyatt listed six ordinances that he posted and enforced in Dodge City. In all likelihood Virgil's code was of the same nature.

One which sounds highly reasonable but which was often

greatly resented barred horses from the sidewalks. A second, which sounds in the class of telling children not to put beans up their noses, forbade riding an animal into any store, saloon, dance hall, gambling house, or honky-tonk. A third prohibited the discharge of firearms in the corporate limits "except upon Fourth of July, Christmas and New Year's Days and the evenings immediately preceding these holidays." A fourth banned carrying firearms within the town limits except by men actually in the process of coming into or leaving the place. The fifth, allied to the foregoing, ordered that all visitors should check their firearms immediately upon arrival at racks to be provided by proprietors of saloons, hotels, stores, and corrals. The sixth covered unmanageable drunkeness and gave the marshal authority to arrest anyone who was making a nuisance of himself.

None of these sound like brutal assaults on the citadel of liberty. Yet without any question many felt Virgil was a tyrant interfering with the just pursuits of men and stymying them in their normal quest for happiness.

To some degree their attitude is comprehensible. When range riders came to town for a break in the rigorous monotony of their lives they brought with them the conviction that something dramatic was bound to happen. Anybody who has been a soldier on pass will understand the feeling. But for soldier and range rider alike the hoped for drama is usually missing. Still it can be simulated with some success, and often was in the old West. Taking a drink is routine refreshment, but riding a horse up to the bar added a fillip of deviltry. Racing up and down a street and firing to see the citizens scamper for cover could also furnish something to talk about and chuckle over when a cowhand returned to drudgery. At least it meant that a man had gone the whole rooster; but when he couldn't carry his gun or ride where he wanted to his vision of himself as cock of the walk wasn't very convincing. He had no wing spread, his spurs had been clipped, and there was no use shaking his comb or crowing.

Virgil's first tour of duty, however, lasted only for the two months between the death of White and Tombstone's initial election for city officers on January 4, 1881. He had been out of office ten days when the rustlers again swept into town in force.

One of the lesser gamblers of the region was John O'Rourke. Both because he considered himself one of the outlaws and because he wasn't good enough for the big time at Tombstone, he frequented joints in the rustler town of Charleston. His nickname was Johnny-behind-the-deuce, earned by the regularity with which he backed his faith in the two-spot as a pay-off card in faro.

It was because of a poker rather than a faro game that he won a place of sorts in history, though. After a session in which Henry Schneider, chief engineer of the Tombstone Mining and Milling Co., had lost his shirt, Johnny chose to rub it in by lowrating the engineer's gambling ability. During the resultant quarrel Schneider drew a knife which he never got around to using, for Johnny shot him.

The robust sense of humor of Curly Bill responded to this situation. He took it upon himself to stir up Schneider's associates and the millhands in the name of law and order and called for a retributive hanging. His appeal was so successful that he soon had a large mob of millhands and rustlers fired to lay hands on the gambler, then in the custody of Charleston's constable, George McKelvey.

Hearing of the impending trouble, McKelvey loaded his prisoner into a wagon drawn by a team of mules and made for the town jail in Tombstone. Hearing of their quarry's flight, the mob, led by Johnny Ringo and Curly Bill, started in pursuit.

Even though he had a good lead the odds were against the constable. It was a nine mile climb, with many steep grades from Charleston on the San Pedro to the city perched on Goose Flats. Horses can be expected to run down mules in any case, and these particular mules were burdened by a wagon. The riders behind came near enough for long range fire when Tombstone was still three miles away. When McKelvey reached the Last Chance

(Courtesy of the Bank of Douglas)

A typical six-horse stage of the era and region. When not being photographed better than half the passengers shown aloft would be in the carriage. (*Chapter 16*)

Nellie Cashman—A photograph made in Tombstone from a painting made in China, which was made from a photograph taken in Arizona. (Chapter 20)

Saloon, a half mile farther on, his lead had been cut down to three hundred yards.

The betting against Johnny-behind-the-deuce had thus piled up to better than a thousand to one when the gambler got a break. When McKelvey had forced his mules as far as The Last Chance — which must have seemed a gruesome name to O'Rourke under the circumstances — he encountered Virgil Earp riding a thoroughbred of Wyatt's called Dick Naylor.

"That gang's aiming to lynch this fellow!" the constable shouted.

Without wasting time asking questions Virgil worked his mount alongside the jolting wagon. "Jump on behind," Wyatt quoted him as yelling. Johnny did so, and Dick Naylor took off for Tombstone. He was carrying double, but he was a powerful animal and comparatively fresh. The cowponies pursuing him had been pushed at a run all the way uphill from Charleston. The fugitives reached town with a somewhat increased lead.

Virgil made for the Wells-Fargo Office, where somebody with a responsible feeling toward the law was usually on deck, and a second time Johnny-behind-the-deuce's luck was with him. Wyatt and Morgan Earp were both there.

According to Wyatt what then happened was as follows. He picked up a double-barreled, sawed-off shotgun and told Virgil and Morgan to take Johnny across Allen Street into Vogan's Bowling Alley, an adobe building solid enough to constitute something of a fortress against men equipped only with small arms. Wyatt himself waited for the lynchers on the sidewalk in front of Vogan's.

Before locating them, the mob had gathered new strength. Miners were just coming off shift from the Tough Nut series of diggings. As these were employees of the Tombstone Mining and Milling Co., too, they were easily recruited. Some of the company's executives also caught the infection. There were several hundred in the mob which finally swarmed along Allen Street, ready to do business.

133

Some surmised that Johnny was in the bowling alley and urged action to get him out. Wyatt stood firm.

"Boys," he reported himself as saying, "don't you make any fool play here; that little tinhorn isn't worth it."

Those in position to look directly into the barrels of his shotgun were inclined to think that maybe he wasn't; but — after the fashion of mobs — the men in the rear saw no cause for alarm. Shouting that Wyatt couldn't stop them, they pushed the front ranks forward.

The tableau is that of one man holding off hundreds, half of whom were also armed; but as usual there are contradictory statements. Some old timers who claimed that they were eye witnesses remembered that the lynchers did not have a weapon among them. On the face of it this is not a probability. If it was indeed an unarmed lynch mob, it established a record not touched before or equalled since in the United States. Then it stretches reason to believe that in a region where every man owned and used firearms habitually that these would be left behind when lynch law was being invoked.

But there is positive as well as negative evidence to support Earp's picture of the scene. Breakenridge, whose tendency elsewhere is to belittle Wyatt's pretensions as a stalwart of the law, gives a version of the action which checks with Earp's. So does Parsons, who not only witnessed the encounter but allowed no time for his memory to play tricks before recording what he saw. "Mr. Stanley and I . . . got into the midst of terrible excitement. A gambler called "Johnny-behind-the-deuce" his favorite way at faro rode into town followed by mounted men who chased him from Charleston he having shot and killed Schneider, engineer of T. M. & M. Co. The officers sought to protect him and swore in deputies — themselves gambling men — (the deputies that is) to help. Many of the miners armed themselves and tried to get at the murderer. Several times, yes a number of times rushes were made and rifles leveled causing Mr. Stanley and me to get behind the most available shelter. . . ."

The Growth of a Feud

Their precaution proved unnecessary, for in the event no shot was fired. Some of the miners, although bent on lawlessness at the moment, did not want to be a party to shooting down a peace officer who was certainly doing nothing less and something more than his duty. Among those who had let their emotions suck them into this bad situation was Schieffelin's old partner, and Tombstone's most influential citizen, Dick Gird. Finding him in the front rank, Wyatt picked him out and nominated him leader. This also marked him as scapegoat in case violence boiled over.

"If I have to get anyone, Mr. Gird," Wyatt told him, "you're first. . . . Your friends may get me, but there'll be my brothers. It'll cost good men to lynch that tinhorn."

Like Lars Porsena's army, those in the rear cried "forward," while Wyatt was putting it on the line. Again like the Etruscans, those in front cried "back!"

Sensing the turning point, Wyatt made a personal appeal to Gird. "Don't be a fool, Dick," he said.

Gird turned away, and the miners drifted after him, leaving only the rustlers who had fomented the trouble. Wyatt announced to these that he was taking the prisoner to the county jail at Tucson — Cochise County didn't become a fact until two or three weeks later — and forthwith did so. There Johnny-behind-the-deuce broke jail, but that has a bearing on a different part of the Tombstone story.

What is of immediate importance is this. While the Earps, with only a deputy U. S. marshal's badge between them, were in action to preserve the law, two who should have helped them did not. These were Deputy Sheriff Behan and Town Marshal Sippy. Both saw what was going on, according to Wyatt, and made no move. So in every way the incident served to emphasize the crucial point of the feud. The only ready to hand force which stood between the rustlers and license at all points was the Earp brotherhood.

CHAPTER TWELVE

THE SHERIFF vs. THE MARSHALS

It was Wyatt's claim that Behan neglected his duties as an officer whenever an important member of the rustler crew was implicated in a breach of the peace. It was Breakenridge's claim that Behan was a thoroughgoing public servant, while Earp was a gangster. Yet when it comes to matters of fact Breakenridge often supports the statements of Earp rather than contradicts them.

In the beginning Behan may or may not have been guilty of protecting law breakers, for there is nothing but Wyatt's word to support the charge. The breach between the offices of the sheriff and the deputy U. S. marshal first grew wide enough for public inspection when the driver of a bullion stage was killed in the course of an attempted hold-up. At this point there began a definite clash of authorities which grew more bitter with every movement that either party made.

While the contested election for the shrievalty of Pima County was being weighed by the territorial government, Bob Paul, the candidate of the Law and Order League, put in his time at the dangerous business of riding as guard for the bullion stages as an employee of Wells, Fargo & Co. He was so engaged on the night of March 15, 1881, traveling on a coach bound for the railhead at Benson, when three men intercepted the vehicle about six miles down the San Pedro Valley from Contention City. They had picked a spot where the grade forced the horses to slow down.

Each of the bandits, it could be seen in the moonlight, had a rifle at his shoulder when the command to halt was given. "We don't hold up for anybody!" Paul is supposed to have responded. He raised his own weapon, a shotgun, and ordered the driver, Bud Philpot, to go on.

When Philpot cracked his whip as a sign that he had no intention of stopping, the stage robbers opened fire. So did Bob Paul. One of the bandits yelled, advertising that he'd been shot, but Philpot received a direct hit in the heart. He pitched forward on the rear team of horses, already in a runaway state of terror. The panic stricken animals tore past the hold-up men, carrying $80,000 in bullion out of their reach. Vengefully shooting after the stage, the robbers killed a passenger, a man called Peter Roerig, riding in the exposed boot. Paul meanwhile had been unable to fire again. The death of the driver, who had carried the reins with him when he fell, had created a situation which kept the guard too busy. By the time he had recovered the reins the stage was well out of range.

Arrived at Benson, Paul wired Wyatt. As the bullion stage also carried mail, this was legitimately the business of a deputy U. S. marshal. Wyatt deputized Bat Masterson, Virgil and Morgan Earp, and Marshall Williams, the local Wells, Fargo agent. With that posse he left Tombstone for the scene of the hold-up, where Bob Paul joined them. That Wyatt acted over the opposition of Sheriff Behan, who claimed sole jurisdiction is his own statement. That Behan tagged along is attested by Breakenridge, who was with him.

Earp, who reached the site of the hold-up first, found seventeen empty rifle shells where the three bandits had fired. Nearby he located a spot where a fourth man had waited with four horses. He also found four crude masks, to which frayed rope had been affixed as a stand-in for long hair and whiskers.

Four Clanton followers named Bill Leonard, Jim Crane, Harry Head and Luther King had been billeted in an adobe shack near the road to Benson not far from where Philpot and Roerig had been killed. These were the men whom Wyatt suspected. After days of trailing, during which he was shadowed by Behan and Breakenridge, he ran down King, trying to sneak away on foot from the ranch house of another Clanton follower named Redfield.

When Wyatt and Paul accused King of murder the latter protested that he had only held the horses. Wilting completely, according to Earp, he bleated a complete confession in the presence of all there, including the sheriff. The latter claimed that as the most important crime involved was murder that the bandit was properly his prisoner. Earp agreed to the propriety of this but sent Williams along to keep an eye on Behan, who later rejoined the marshal's posse with Breakenridge and Buckskin Frank Leslie.

"What did you do with King?" Wyatt asked.

"Locked him up," he quotes the sheriff as replying.

In the ten day chase for the other three of the hold-up crew the bandits had the advantage of being in friendly territory. The four hundred mile trail led from one rustler holding to another, where fresh horses were on tap in every instance. As if this was not discouraging enough for the pursuit, Jim Hume, a detective for Wells, Fargo, caught up to report that King had escaped.

Behan, when cross-examined, admitted that this was so but stated that what went on in his office was none of Earp's business. He did, however, give an explanation whose details were subsequently printed in *The Nugget.* "Luther King, the man arrested at Redfield's ranch charged with being implicated in the Bud Philpot murder escaped from the sheriff's office by quickly stepping out the backdoor while Harry Jones, Esq., was drawing up a bill of sale for a horse the prisoner was disposing of to John Dunbar. Undersheriff Woods and Dunbar were present. He had been absent for a few seconds before he was missed. A confederate on the outside had a horse in readiness for him. . . ."

Hume is supposed to have claimed that the sheriff never actually took King to the sheriff's office; but no matter for that. Whether or not he was taken to a residence conveniently located on the outskirts of town, as charged, he was neither in durance nor under surveillance. It was merely one of a number of escapes from the custody of Behan's assistants. Some of the others will come up for notice, but King has precedence.

Wyatt and Hume returned to Tombstone to try to pick up his

trail, leaving Morgan, Virgil, and Paul to follow the other three bandits. Behan, Breakenridge, and Leslie, never helping but always watching, continued to tail these. Bat Masterson had already been forced to give up the chase and hitch a ride back when his horse folded.

Eventually Head, Crane, and Leonard slipped over the border into Mexico. Hesitation to follow them illegally was not the only thing which halted pursuit at the international boundary. The posse had run out of food, and their mounts were done. The sheriff's men had food but refused to share it. Moreover, when they were convinced the chase had been abandoned, they turned to hurry back to Tombstone. Starving, and forced to lead their two surviving horses, the Earps and Paul headed after them.

By the time they had all foregathered in Tombstone again the case had taken a new turn. The faction hostile to the Earps had operated to shift the suspicion of guilt so that Doc Holliday, Bob Paul, Marshall Williams, and the Earp brothers would share it with the known actual perpetrators. The burden of publicizing these charges was carried by *The Nugget*.

According to this paper Paul had known of the impending hold-up and so had changed places with the driver, who thus got shot in place of the guard. Doc Holliday had been belatedly identified as one of the bandits and was in fact the man who had fired the fatal shot at Philpot. The Earps and Williams had connived to help King escape to help their dentist ally. "It was a well planned job by an outsider," *The Nugget* said in commenting on the story about King slipping out of the Sheriff's office, "to get him away. He was an important witness against Holliday."

There were a couple of things *The Nugget* did not point out. It did not point out that County Treasurer John Dunbar, who was pictured as buying the bandit's horse for his livery stable, was a partner of Sheriff John Behan in the ownership of the same concern. Nor did the paper mention its own excellent reason for wanting to shift the blame for Luther King's disappearance. The publisher of *The Nugget* was Undersheriff Woods from whose custody the bandit had admittedly escaped while the officer was kibitzing on the horse deal.

Of all the accusations the only one which proved seriously embarrassing to the Earp faction was the one against Holliday. Here is the basis for the charges against him, as presented by *The Nugget*. "On the afternoon of the attempted robbery he engaged a horse at a Tombstone livery, stating that he might be gone for seven or eight days, or might return that night. He left town about four o'clock armed with a Henry rifle and a six-shooter. He started for Charleston, and about a mile below Tombstone cut across to Contention. When next seen it was between ten and one o'clock at night, riding back into the livery at Tombstone, his horse fagged out. He at once called for another horse which he hitched in the street for some hours, but he did not again leave town. Statements attributed to him, if true, look very bad, and, if proved, are most conclusive as to his guilt, either as a principal or an accessory after the fact."

Now Doc had known Bill Leonard when the latter had been a jeweler in Las Vegas, New Mexico, where Holliday had for a time practiced dentistry. Having offices in the same building, they had become friends, and the fact that Leonard had chosen to throw in with the rustlers after he came to Tombstone made no difference to Holliday. He continued to associate with him and had, indeed, visited him at the adobe shanty while he was bivouacking there with Head, King, and Crane. All this Doc freely admitted; but he insisted that on the day of the hold-up he had ridden up the valley to Charleston and not down it toward Contention City. As for the second horse which *The Nugget* had referred to, he claimed that he had kept it ready outside the saloon where he was dealing faro, in case Wyatt sent for him to join his posse.

The accusation did not disturb Doc as such, but it hurt his feelings to be connected with an unsuccessful crime. "If I had pulled that job," he declared, "I'd have got the eighty thousand. Whoever shot Philpot was a rank amateur. If he had downed a horse, he'd have got the bullion. As for riding out of town with my six-gun and rifle, I did go over to Charleston that afternoon, and, as it's the hangout of certain persons who dislike me intensely, I went prepared for any attentions they might offer." He also stated that he had returned to Tombstone about six o'clock, not ten as asserted by *The Nugget,* and had spent the evening gambling.

Being entirely unproved, the charges against Holliday remained as no more than town gossip when Doc had a falling out with his red light mistress, Big Nose Kate Fisher. Theirs had never been one of those relationships of quiet understanding. Miss Fisher had once shown her fondness for Doc by slipping him a gun at a critical point in his life, but she could be equally unfond of him when riled. She went on a bender for days after this latest quarrel, and her mood in the course of it was vengeful. The odds are that she made no effort to keep the fact that she was a wronged woman to herself. In any case some of Wyatt's enemies found out about her current feelings toward Holliday and saw a chance to embarrass the marshal. They got Kate to sign an affidavit swearing that Doc had participated in the fatal hold-up. Whereupon Behan promptly arrested Holliday for murder.

The Earps had to work fast, and they did. While Wyatt was getting his friend out on bail, Virgil gave Big Nose Kate the iron cure, so she'd be sober in time for the hearing. In that condition she testified, by Wyatt's account, that she had been drinking with Sheriff Behan himself when she signed the affidavit. She added that she didn't know what was written on the paper she had signed. The case against Doc was killed, and he was released.

The incident had two results. At Wyatt's request Doc gave Kate a thousand dollars to leave Tombstone and stay away. The other was more important as far as the history of the town was concerned. Up to then Behan had been merely non-cooperative or obstructive to the efforts of the deputy U. S. marshal. Now he was revealed as an agent actively engaged in trying to force the Earps to go elsewhere.

When it came to the rustlers, however, aggression on the part of the sheriff's office was not in evidence. For proof there is the direct testimony of William Breakenridge.

The sheriff had had difficulty in collecting taxes from many Cochise County cattlemen. Seeing that they got absolutely no legal protection in return for the money he wanted them to put in his pocket their stubborness was understandable. Nevertheless, Deputy Sheriff Breakenridge was detailed to get what he could; and in time he arrived at Galeyville, Curly Bill's headquarters and the capital city of rustlerdom. Inspiration had visited the deputy on the way. He got himself introduced to Curly Bill.

"I told him who I was and what I was, and said I wanted to hire him to go with me as a deputy assessor and help me collect taxes, and I was afraid I might be held up and my tax money taken from me if I went alone. The idea of my asking the chief of all the cattle rustlers in that part of the country to help me collect taxes from them struck him as a good joke. . . ."

Brocius agreed to the proposition, and the taxes were paid without argument. "I was treated fine by all of them," Breakenridge recalled, "and I never want to travel with a better companion than Curly was on that trip."

More than one old timer intimated that all the men shaken down in this fashion were not rustlers; but suppose the facts were just as Breakenridge gave them. The picture is that of a boss gangster making the small fry come across for the political machine which was giving him the benefit of its negligence. There is no hint that any taxes were collected from Brocius himself.

Breakenridge also knew the other outlaw leader. This relationship was evidently one which went beyond the call of duty. "I had met Ringo frequently on my trips to Galeyville . . . and we had many pleasant visits."

On no occasion was Breakenridge called upon to molest Curly Bill. Only once did he bother Ringo. That was after Johnny had played poker neither too well nor wisely. The ensuing events formed a convincing illustration of the extent to which the sheriff's office and the outlaws played ball with each other.

Ringo was supposed to have been a top notch poker player, but once when he sat down for a heavy session with some miners luck was against him. He lost a lot and took it hard. In the upshot his losses squeezed him out of the game. When he returned to it after some brooding his hand was filled with something that could beat a royal flush in spades. He held a revolver, called, and collected.

Thinking better of it some days later, he returned the money, according to Breakenridge, to everybody involved. Someone, however, either was not paid back or wasn't amused by the show of temperament. A warrant was sworn out for Ringo, and Breakenridge was sent to advise him to come in and answer the charge. Johnny consented to do so on two conditions: he would keep his weapons and nobody in Galeyville would be informed he was under arrest.

When they reached Tombstone a tender regard was still shown for his feelings. "I asked the jailer," Breakenridge wrote, "who I knew had an extra room, to let Ringo keep his arms and sleep in his house across from the jail, and I would be down early next morning and help him get his bail signed." In the morning he was on deck with a friend of Ringo's. Also in the party were County Treasurer John Dunbar and County Recorder Al Jones.

The money for bail was thus available, but the district court had not yet got around to approving the bond when word was passed around that the vigilantes were trying to catch Curly Bill in Charleston and arrest him on a charge of stage robbery. How anxious the sheriff was to see that Curly Bill was warned is related by Breakenridge.

"There was a law and order committee formed in Tombstone that stood in with the gang that was opposed to the sheriff, and it was reported that some of them had gone toward Charleston to arrest Curly Bill and a lot of cowboys and bring them to Tombstone. Ringo was anxious to get down there and be with his friends. While waiting for Judge Stillwell to approve the bond,

The Last Chance

Ringo's attorney came to the sheriff's office and said, 'All right Johnny, the bond is approved,' and Ringo got on his horse which I had brought to the office for him and went to Charleston. He got there before the law and order party did. . . ."

But the sheriff had overplayed his hand. The bond had not been approved, or even considered, and Judge William H. Stillwell startled Behan by saying that instead of making a routine matter of it he would have a hearing at which Ringo must be present. Even the most brazen of political organizations has to observe some of the formalities in order to stay in power, and the sheriff was worried. He sent a hurry call for Ringo to return. Johnny's mission of warning his associates accomplished, he dashed back to Tombstone, where Deputy Sheriff Breakenridge prepared a bed for him on the lounge in the sheriff's office. When the judge demanded the so-called prisoner, he was therefore produced by a relieved county official.

It was not merely that the sheriff made few arrests. When he did make the gesture of collaring somebody — if he was a rustler, that is — something always happened. Parsons reported a typical case. "The deputy sheriff who went for him, (meaning a stolen horse) was reported near Tombstone in wagon with prisoner, but falling asleep, prisoner escaped. Rather thin, I think."

Then there was the case of the Hicks brothers, Milt and Will. Contrary to the usual practice these cattle thieves were actually put behind bars. Yet before they could come to trial there was a jail break. That may have been an accident, but the history of the tenderness with which malefactors were treated by the sheriff's office makes all such incidents suspect.

A point not in the least in doubt is that sheriff Behan not only sheltered stock thieves and worse but hired them as deputies. The case of the notorious Frank Stilwell will be dealt with later; and there were others. *The Epitaph* was aware of the situation and never lost an opportunity to needle Behan about it. There was this item, for instance: "Charles Rodig . . . was in Galeyville looking after a horse which had been stolen a few days previous. Upon

144

inquiry he found that the horse had been there, but that the thief had skipped with it, being notified, as was reported, by the deputy sheriff that the owner was looking after his property. Mr. Rodig laid the case before several of the leading citizens, who held a meeting and investigated the matter, and gave the deputy sheriff three hours to leave town. . . . If this report is true it does not speak well for Sheriff Behan's judgment in the selection of his deputies."

It was to meet the emergency created to a considerable degree by the attitude of county officialdom that a vigilante organization was formed, teste Clum. "Virgil Earp was Chief of Police and Wyatt Earp Deputy United States Marshal, and the fact that the Citizens' Safety Committee was organized for the purpose of supporting them in maintaining law and order within the city limits evinces the confidence which the leading citizens of Tombstone entertained both toward Virgil and Wyatt in their respective capacities as dependable and efficient peace officers. . . ."

The fact that he spoke of Virgil Earp as chief of police rather than Ben Sippy, the man duly elected on the same ticket as Clum, requires a word of explanation which Clum himself has supplied. "The following day I learned that during my absence Ben Sippy, the city marshal, had decamped — leaving the city without a police head; that Virgil Earp with the approval of the city councilmen, had assumed the responsibility in the emergency and that he had rendered a most efficient and satisfactory service. The result was that Virgil was retained as Chief of Police. . . ."

It does not appear that Sippy was dishonest or in any way connected with the outlaws. To all appearances he simply decided that the town was too tough to handle and cleared out to look for an easier job. However that may have been, the historic effect was that the Earps again represented two peace offices as the various ingredients of the feud began to reach the right mixture for detonation.

CHAPTER THIRTEEN

AN INVOLVEMENT OF NINE

It is not on record that Old Man Clanton himself had any encounters with the Earps. He does not seem to have caused any disturbance in Tombstone; probably because by the time that city was built he was no longer of an age to yearn to shoot up a town. No memoir that has so far come to light contains much about this first chieftain of Cochise County's outlaws. Yet Tombstone's big war has always been known as the Earp-Clanton feud.

In part this was due to force of habit. The "cowboys" had originally been known as Clanton men. They continued to be so called, even though old N. H. Clanton's sons didn't have the force to keep the leadership in the family after their father was killed. In part it was due to the personal enmity which two of the younger Clantons conceived for Wyatt. Eventually the intensity of this hatred was to cause the most famous single incident in the history of Tombstone.

If the outlaws were, after the death of old N. H., Curly Bill men rather than Clanton men, the Clanton boys continued to be influential members of the gang. For one thing, they were prosperous ranchers whose large holdings formed a convenient base for rustling operations. If questioned as to his activities, a rustler could always claim he was a hand riding for the Clantons; and a good many outlaws did in fact bunk at the ranch up the San Pedro from Charleston.

Of the three Clanton boys Phineas, or Phin, remains a somewhat shadowy, if sufficiently nefarious figure. William, or Billy, was a hard-bitten youngster in his late teens. He was apparently the best liked of the lot, and certainly courageous. Joseph Isaac, or Ike, was a craven flannel mouth, a double-crosser whose genius lay in getting other people into trouble.

Allied to this trio in business as well as friendship were the McLowry brothers, whose relation to the rustlers was almost identical with that of the Clantons. Like the Clantons they were fences as well as thieves and killers. Another thing that came to strengthen their alliance with the Clantons was a hatred for Earp.

Wyatt had met many of the outlaws, in addition to Curly Bill and Ringo, before he came to Arizona. The McLowrys and the Clantons do not appear to have been among his former acquaintances, however, although he does not specifically say so. He seems to have run afoul of them first after his appointment as deputy U. S. marshal. The names of the holdup men who had been robbing the bullion stages were matters of common knowledge. Anybody interested in finding out could also make a roster of those with whom they associated. In addition to telling the thieves that he intended to maintain the law at the price of anybody's skin, Wyatt gave that information to ranchers known to be sheltering outlaws.

That was in 1880. The county organization had not yet been formed. In the absence of this legal buffer between them and direct retaliatory action, the rustlers were not as brazen as they later became. Earp's argumentum ad hominem did not effect a permanent reform, but the stage robberies stopped for a while. The other result was that Wyatt's favorite horse turned up missing and remained so for months.

Later on a much bolder theft of stock took place. Curly Bill, Tom and Frank McLowry, Billy Clanton and Frank Patterson ran off a bunch of mules from Camp Rucker. As the animals in question were Federal property, this crime was the business of the nearest deputy U.S. marshal. An army captain named Hurst rode into Tombstone to put the case into the hands of Wyatt Earp.

Summoning Virgil and Morgan to aid him, Wyatt set out with the captain and tracked the mules to the McLowry ranch near Soldier Holes in the Sulphur Springs Valley. The McLowrys sent word by Patterson that they would return the stolen animals only if the Earps withdrew. Wyatt saw no sense in that, but at the insistence of Captain Hurst he and his brothers returned to Tombstone. A few days later the captain did likewise. Not a single mule had been turned over to him.

"The McLowrys sent word," Wyatt reported the captain as saying, "that if you and your brothers interfere with them again, they'll shoot you on sight."

"Tell 'em they'll have their chance," Wyatt answered.

Three weeks later the marshal ran into the McLowry brothers in Charleston. "That army officer give you our message?" Tom is quoted as asking.

"He did," Wyatt told him, "but in case you didn't get my answer I'll repeat it."

The brothers did not at that time follow up the implied challenge. "If you ever follow us again," Frank said as he and Tom passed on, "your friends'll find what the coyotes leave of you in the sage brush."

Two things must be said about the foregoing passages. As the McLowrys left no known report of the occasions referred to, the conversations rest on the word of the sole remaining authority, Wyatt Earp. On the other hand the theft of Wyatt's horse and the government mules by the Clanton faction are attested by other evidence than that given by the marshal.

So in some measure is the story of the horse's recovery. See above in many places, Charleston was a rustler town. Sheriff Behan had appointed two deputies to be in charge of law enforcement there. Of these one was Frank Stilwell, generally credited with being the most accomplished stage robber in Cochise County. It was later said that Stilwell had held up the stages so often that veteran horses of the lines responded to his voice as well as they did to those of their drivers. His peace officer running mate, a fellow called Gates whose given name can't be located, was also a Clanton man.

The first news Wyatt got about his long missing horse was that it was being ridden by Deputy Sheriff Gates, who had been seen leaving it at the corral operated by Deputy Sheriff Stilwell. When Wyatt went down to Charleston to investigate, however, it happened that he found his animal between the legs of young Billy Clanton. The latter was just in the act of leaving Stilwell's corral.

An Involvement of Nine

According to Wyatt he discouraged Clanton's attempt to ride him down by putting his hand on his gun. He also took the precaution of disarming Billy, telling the latter where he could recover his weapons when he, Wyatt, had put his turned back comfortably out of range. Billy, like the McLowrys, was supposed to have retaliated with a threat.

"Next time it won't be your horse we'll get," he called after Earp, "it'll be you."

The exact sequence of events is not plain, but it seems probable that it was before the last of these encounters that Wyatt had occasion to manhandle Ike and Billy Clanton and both McLowrys. This was the time in the fall of 1880 when Marshal White was shot by Curly Bill. While rounding up other leaders of the gang overrunning Tombstone, Earp had walloped all four over the head with his Buntline Special before dragging them to the calaboose.

All four, then, had personal as well as general reasons for hating Wyatt. Three of them, at least by Earp's account, had threatened him with death as the penalty for further interference with their pursuits. It was not too long before the fourth was voicing a thirst for the marshal's blood.

For reasons easy to pick out Earp was particularly anxious to run down the men charged with the attempted stage hold-up during which Bud Philpot and Peter Roerig were killed. Doc Holliday, although officially cleared, was still suspected by some. The story that the U. S. marshal had acted in collusion with the bandits had not been entirely quashed. Wyatt wanted that case brought into court, if possible, but settled at all events.

Luther King had ridden off into Mexico, but Harry Head, Bill Leonard, and Jim Crane hadn't bothered to go very far away. Learning as much, Wyatt suggested that Wells, Fargo & Co., as the contractor for bullion deliveries, would do well to offer a reward of two thousand dollars for each of the three murderers. The suggestion was adopted, with delayed fuse results.

Earp's story of what happened will be given first. Ike Clanton had an entirely different explanation for his hostility toward

Wyatt. It will be taken up in its due place in the chronicle.

According to Wyatt's version, then, there were plenty to offer tips about the whereabouts of the bandits, but nothing really promising turned up until Ike Clanton came to town. Ike made several attempts to see Wyatt on unrevealed business, and Earp became convinced that the rustler was willing to turn squealer. Smelling this rat, the marshal avoided Clanton for a while.

"I let Ike itch a bit," he stated in retelling the incident.

When he thought the right time had come, he maneuvered to encounter Clanton on the street. "Ike," he said without preamble, "how'd you like to make six thousand dollars?" As a result of this query a meeting was arranged where the two could talk things over in private. "Ike," Wyatt offered, "you help me catch Leonard, Head, and Crane, and you can have every cent of the Wells, Fargo reward."

Clanton then discussed the project freely. A week later he returned to Tombstone with Frank McLowry and Joe Hill. "Any strings on your offer?" Hill asked.

"None," Earp told him.

"We can use the money," McLowry said, "but if the rest of the crowd ever learn who turned up these fellows, we won't live twenty-four hours."

"I won't give you away," Wyatt promised. "You get Leonard, Head, and Crane where I can grab them, then I'll collect the reward and turn it over to you in cash. You won't appear in the business."

"You'll never take them alive," McLowry said.

"How about that?" Clanton demanded. "The reward is offered for their arrest. Does that go dead or alive?"

As Wyatt wasn't prepared to answer that question, he asked Marshall Williams, the local Wells, Fargo agent, to query the home office in San Francisco by telegraph. The reply, which Earp had to request Williams to show to the three rustlers before they would believe it, read: "Yes, we will pay rewards for them dead or alive." The message was signed by L. F. Rowell, assistant to John

An Involvement of Nine

J. Valentine, who was president of Wells, Fargo & Co. It was dated June 7, 1881.

On the Fourth of July Ike and his associates were again in Tombstone to report progress. Leonard, Head, and Crane were in New Mexico, but they would be decoyed back into Arizona by a promised chance to rob the payroll of the Copper Queen Mine down in Bisbee.

Several things happened to wreck this scheme. Before it could be put into effect Old Man Clanton led his forces into Skeleton Canyon to slaughter the silver smugglers. Ike Clanton, Frank McLowry, and Joe Hill were all participants; and they also took part in the big drunk in Galeyville by which the bandits celebrated their coup. By the time they were ready for the saddle again Curly Bill made his murderous raid into Sonora and turned the bovine loot over to Old Man Clanton to fence off. As already related, avenging Mexicans killed Clanton and killed all but one of his helpers. Among the slain — a fact noted by Parsons in his journal — was Jim Crane.

The would-be traitors, as it turned out, were balked all along the line. When Joe Hill went into New Mexico to lure Harry Head and Bill Leonard into Wyatt's trap, he found that they, too, had been killed. Unluckily for them the Haslett brothers, who ran the store in Huachita the bandits were trying to rob, were better shots. The brothers were not good enough, however, to take care of Curly Bill and Johnny Ringo, who soon showed up to get even for the loss of their associates. That happened a little later. Just before this act of retaliation Morgan Earp had gone to Huachita to make certain that Head and Leonard actually had been killed. He was told that Leonard made a dying statement to the effect that only four men, counting Luther King, who had held the horses, had been involved in the attempted robbery. He said Crane had killed Philpot but that he could not say who had shot Roerig as Crane, Head, and he himself had fired after the runaway stage.

With all three of Philpot's and Roerig's murderers dead, the conspiracy against them looked like a closed deal. It opened again a couple of months later when Ike Clanton accused Wyatt of letting out word of his, Ike's, scheme to sell the since deceased bandits. Earp insisted that he hadn't mentioned the matter to anyone. Ike swore that he must have, because Marshal Williams had just told him that he knew what Clanton had planned to do. Williams, by Ike's admission, had been drinking. Seemingly he had figured out for himself what was going on when Clanton, McLowry, and Hill had demanded to see the telegram stating that the reward for Crane and the others would be paid whether they were dead or alive. Meeting Ike while in his cups, the Wells, Fargo agent hadn't been able to keep his suspicions to himself.

Ike was so fearful of being killed by his associates as a stool pigeon that he wasn't content with ignoring an unproved accusation. He insisted on denying it publicly, in the hearing, among others, of Doc Holliday.

In the view of some Doc's only virtue, aside from courage, was loyalty. Clanton's treachery outraged this feeling; and there was a personal issue involved. Holliday, as has been earlier remarked, was completely indifferent to public opinion. He liked whom he liked, and one of his chosen associates had been Bill Leonard, thief and murderer or not. It was all right with Doc for Wyatt to have hounded Leonard in the natural course of his duties as a peace officer, but it was not all right with Holliday for an avowed ally to have planned to double-cross him. As soon as Doc became convinced, through the very strength of Clanton's protestations that this is what Ike had been up to, he told him what he thought of him in a voice that all Allen Street could hear. On his part Ike announced that he would kill, not Holliday, but the next man who accused him of collusion with Wyatt. Thereafter he left Tombstone for the McLowry ranch so that he could apprise Frank of the disturbing development. That was about the middle of October, 1881.

On the 22nd of the same month Ike and Billy Clanton, together with the two McLowrys arrived in Charleston. There they obtained the release of Billy Claiborne, who had been held in mild durance for the shooting of James Hickey, the unwisely hospitable. Two days later Curly Bill, Johnny Ringo and a crowd of their mobsters swarmed along Allen Street, letting it be known in every bar that the Earps were to be run out of Tombstone.

As chief of police, it was Virgil rather than Wyatt who had the authority to control those threatening violence within the city limits. The Citizen's Safety Committee offered to support him with arms and men, but the Earps elected to handle the situation themselves. Accepting this decision, the committee deputized Wyatt, Morgan, and Doc Holliday to serve under Virgil as deputy town marshals.

By the afternoon of the next day, October 25, most of the rustlers had left town, as if following a prearranged plan. At about the same time Ike Clanton and Tom McLowry hit Tombstone. Frank McLowry, Billy Clanton, and Billy Claiborne remained in Charleston, where one of the saloons was kept by a man called J. B. Ayers. Actually he was a spy for Wells, Fargo & Co., whose duty it was to maintain liaison with that other local undercover agent of the concern, Fred Dodge of Tombstone. Through this hook-up Wyatt learned that Frank and the two Billys were standing by under arms.

Meanwhile Ike was making the rounds, talking louder with every drink. As several witnesses subsequently testified, he was promising everybody to kill not only Wyatt but Doc Holliday for good measure. He continued in this vein until Holliday himself found him in the Occidental Saloon.

"Ike," Holliday was quoted as saying, "I hear you're going to kill me. Get out your gun and commence."

"I haven't got a gun," Clanton answered, which happened to be true, for he had checked his revolver and rifle at the Grand.

While they were wrangling Wyatt and Virgil showed up and dragged Holliday off to his room. There Wyatt explained to him that if he, Doc, with his bad name for belligerence, started hostilities it would discredit the police department's avowed effort to handle the situation in a legal manner. Doc regretfully listened to reason, and Wyatt left, to run afoul of Ike and be threatened by him once more that evening.

"Go sleep it off, Ike," Wyatt advised, but the next morning Clanton was still at it. As the Earps were rising, they were warned that Ike was on the warpath, armed with two revolvers and a rifle. Soon afterwards word was brought that Frank McLowry, Billy Clanton, and Claiborne had ridden in from Charleston to join Ike and Tom. Meanwhile Holliday was not yet astir, and Wyatt voted to let him rest.

The order of the day was for the three Earps to begin by rounding up Ike Clanton, who, as a man unlawfully under arms, was actively disturbing the peace. Virgil was the one who eventually caught up with Clanton. As Ike swung around with a leveled rifle, the marshal conked him with the barrel of his revolver, and helped to drag him before a magistrate. The judge let him off with a twenty-five dollar fine, but Virgil confiscated his weapons.

The next two clashes involved the McLowrys. Wyatt literally bumped into Tom when leaving the courthouse, and after an exchange of words struck him. McLowry started to draw but wasn't fast enough to escape being buffaloed. Wyatt did not arrest him, however. It is reasonable to assume that he disarmed him, although he does not mention doing so. Then a little later four of the Clanton-McLowry group, Ike not included, were seen by Wyatt entering Spangenberg's gun shop. There Ike shortly joined them. Earp did not take exception to that, but Frank McLowry's horse was breaking a city ordinance by virtue of being on the sidewalk. There followed an altercation which ended by Wyatt moving the horse and Frank announcing his plan to get rid of Wyatt.

Having finished their shopping at the gun store, all five of the rustlers — all now armed in defiance of the law — repaired to the Dexter Corral, the one owned by Dunbar and Behan. There they were joined by a sixth man, a Clanton follower named Wesley Fuller.

An Involvement of Nine

News of this was brought to the Earps at Hafford's saloon at the corner of Fourth and Allen Streets. R. J. Coleman, the man who brought it, added that Sheriff Behan was also with the rustlers. The Clantons were making war talk for the benefit of anyone who wanted to listen, and Behan had not accepted suggestions that it was his duty to disarm them.

Subsequently Behan himself showed up at Hafford's to tell Virgil of the hostile intentions of the Clanton crowd. "You're Sheriff of Cochise county, Behan," Virgil is quoted as saying, "and I'm calling on you to go with me while I arrest them."

"That's your job, not mine," Behan is supposed to have replied. He left, and as it turned out, to rejoin the rustlers.

Yet it is not necessary to depend upon the Earps for evidence as to the sheriff's actions at this time. There are Behan's own words to go by. Clum, in recounting the events of the day, was to write: "Sheriff Behan's testimony . . . may be reduced to its lowest terms as follows: About half past one or two o'clock on the afternoon of October 26, 1881, Behan saw a crowd gathering at the corner of Fourth and Allen streets and heard talk of an impending clash between the Earps and the cowboys. Behan met Virgil Earp who told him the rustlers were in town looking for a fight. Behan told Virgil he better disarm them. . . ."

"When Sheriff Behan," Clum went on to comment, "saw a crowd gathering at Fourth and Allen streets and heard the talk of an impending combat he did not summon his deputies, nor a posse comitatus to aid him in enforcing his authority. . . . In fact, it appears that his final meeting with the cowboys served only as a last minute warning to them to be prepared for the anticipated coming of the city police."

After making sure that he would receive no assistance from the sheriff, Virgil went to the Wells, Fargo office to secure a double-barreled shotgun. By the time he had rejoined Wyatt and Morgan it had been learned that the rustlers had shifted their base of operations to the O. K. Corral. The party was reported to have been made up of the five principals, all armed with revolvers, and

Wes Fuller, who may or may not have been armed. They were leading two horses, those of Frank McLowry and Billy Clanton. In the boots attached to the saddles of each of these animals was a rifle.

The vigilantes made one more offer to overpower the Clantons by force of numbers. Yet it was unthinkable that the most dramatic moment of that stronghold of individuality should be settled by mass action, and — rest at ease — it was not. The Earps refused for reasons specified and unspecified.

In the first category was the fact that they had been given the job. In the second was the common conviction that a police force which asks for aid prematurely suffers a loss of prestige which it has to suffer for sooner or later. Then it was recognized by everyone that the issue was personal as well as civic. The outlaws were anxious to overwhelm the peace officers who kept them from dominating Tombstone — but they were also anxious to kill or cow the Earps as entities. Everybody in town who was abreast of affairs knew that. Elsewhere a man to man challenge might have been ignored by officers, but in that time and place it had to be answered in kind.

As the Earps saw it, they had two courses which were heads and tails of the same coin. They could wait for the rustlers, emboldened by the inactivity of the law, to try to make good their threats; or they could advance upon the enemy. As Clum reported the situation confronting them: "These well-known leaders of the rustlers came to Tombstone and defied our laws and the officers we had appointed to enforce those laws. Not only that, but Ike Clanton had actually appeared upon our streets that day carrying a rifle in his hands and had declared his intention of shooting our chief of police on sight. . . ."

In view of all the factors listed above, plus the native aggressiveness of the clan, it is not surprising that the Earps decided to attack. They stepped out of Hafford's and turned down Fourth Street on their way to the O. K. Corral.

CHAPTER FOURTEEN

THE GUNS GO OFF

THE O. K. Corral fronted on the north side of Allen Street midway between Fourth and Third, but the property ran all the way through the block to the south side of Fremont. Here, opposite the original courthouse of Cochise County, was an open yard. This could also be reached by an alley, which cut east through the block from Fourth to Third Street. On the west or Third Street side the yard was bounded by the office of an assaying concern. On the east side of it was the photographic studio of C. S. Fly.

It was in this yard that the rustlers had chosen to take their stand. In assessing the men they were going to meet, the Earps discounted Fuller as a tagalong. Ike they rated as a blowhard, who talked a better fight than he would ever be willing to make. The other four, though, were in a different category. Billy Clanton, if a youngster, was a veteran of many rustler excursions. From these he had emerged with the reputation of being as hard and full of sand as they come. Young Claiborne, two or three years older, aspired to be called Billy the Kid, now that Bonney no longer had any use for the name. He had killed three men in recent months and was considered a fast man with a gun. Tom McLowry was about in the same class. All three were swift killers, then, but none of them held a candle to Frank McLowry. Wyatt, a connoisseur in such matters, placed him with Curly Bill, Leslie, and Ringo — Tombstone's six-gun cream. Clum also picked him out from the rest. "Frank McLowry was reputed to be unerring in his aim with a six-shooter, and an exceedingly dangerous adversary in actual combat."

But the odds were not to be five against three. The Earps had just emerged from Hafford's when Doc Holliday caught up on the run, indignant at the thought that they had meant to leave him behind.

"This is our fight," Wyatt recalled explaining. "There's no call for you to mix in it."

"That's a hell of a thing for you to say to me," Holliday told him. So four men walked north along Fourth toward Fremont. At the corner ahead of them they saw Frank McLowry talking with John Behan. Catching sight of the Earp party in turn, the sheriff and the outlaw withdrew west toward the corral. Fuller, posted at the entrance to the alley halfway down the street, also ran back to the yard to give the rustlers warning.

The order of march was Wyatt and Virgil in the lead, Morgan and Holliday behind. Doc, who used a cane when his tuberculosis was bad, had brought one along, but at Virgil's suggestion he had given it up in favor of the Well, Fargo shotgun. Removing an arm from his sleeve, Doc held the weapon under his overcoat. Virgil took the cane as a sort of baton of office, and this was the only thing resembling a weapon which was in evidence as they advanced.

Presumably it was Doc's condition which prompted him to wear an overcoat — a black one to match his black sombrero — for mid-afternoon on the 26th of October is not normally cold in Arizona, even at 4500 feet. The three Earps were likewise all in black from the broad-brimmed, high-crowned hats, through frock coats to the trousers jammed into short boots, high-heeled in the fashion of the Southwest. The only alleviating note were the white shirts, for the string ties which dangled down the front of these were black, too.

All four were tall men, the Earps better than six feet, the doctor just under that. The brothers, so remarkable in their resemblance that strangers couldn't tell them apart, wore each what Clum called "a royal moustache." These were tawny, but dark compared to the blond one which bloomed on Doc's emaciated face. All four were blue-eyed and tanned by the thoroughgoing Arizona sun.

The Guns Go Off

According to Wyatt the only word spoken among them was Holliday's remark that they ought to have shot Fuller, just for luck. A half minute later they had reached Fremont Street, and there, lest they be caught in enfilade fire from ambush, they shifted formation. On Fourth they had been in a column of twos on the narrow sidewalk. As they swung left toward the O. K. Corral they deployed to walk four abreast down the middle of Fremont Street.

It is this tableau of four tall men in black striding to confront destiny which haunts Tombstone to this day. Men who saw them in the act declared that although the faces of the three Earps were set inflexibly, Holliday was whistling to himself.

Part way to the corral they were intercepted by Sheriff Behan. "It's all right, boys," he is said to have declared, "I've disarmed them."

"Did you arrest them?" Virgil demanded.

When it was discovered that the rustlers had not been arrested, the Earps brushed Behan aside. The sheriff beat a retreat into Fly's studio, and the four continued toward the O. K. Corral. A moment later they saw the men they had come to meet. They were standing with their backs to the wall of the assayer's office at the western side of the corral yard. The two horses were at the north end of the wall, so placed that the outlaws could not be outflanked.

The "cowboys" ranged in years from Billy Clanton, whose age is variously given as 17, 18, and 19, to Frank McLowry, who was about 30. Claiborne was around 21. Tom McLowry and Ike Clanton were in their middle or late twenties. They are remembered as a handsome lot, well set up and tough as only a life in open country can make men. The McLowrys and Ike wore slim moustaches, vacquero fashion. All were dressed in the manner of cowhands who have plenty of money to spend on boots, silk neckerchiefs and so on. Ike and Tom wore short jackets, the other three gay, sleeveless vests.

Fuller had disappeared. Nearest to Fremont Street and therefore the horses was Tom McLowry. Frank was at Tom's right.

The Last Chance

Next in order stood Billy Clanton, Ike, and Billy Claiborne. Unlike the Earps, their weapons were all in plain sight. Frank and the two Clantons each had a single revolver in a belt holster. Tom had a revolver shoved in the waistband of his trousers. This could be seen, because his jacket was opened. Claiborne wore two holstered guns. In addition to this armament, a rifle butt stood up above the saddle of each horse.

When they had passed Fly's, the three Earps did a left oblique into the corral. As they closed in, Virgil was in the lead on the inside, or more or less confronting Claiborne and Ike Clanton. Wyatt was in the middle, facing Billy Clanton and Frank McLowry, while Morgan was about vis a vis with Tom. Holliday remained in Fremont Street in a position to control that thoroughfare.

"You men are under arrest," Virgil is said to have told the rustlers. "Throw up your hands."

It is the consensus of witness opinion that the ensuing action took about fifteen seconds. Wyatt said it required about twice that, and even he was probably on the conservative side. Give it a minute, to be safe.

When Town Marshal Earp gave his order all the rustlers but Ike dropped their hands on or toward their revolvers. Virgil made the mistake of not dropping his cane. Instead he raised it in a commanding, if futile gesture, crying: "We don't want that!"

As sometimes happens, what he wanted and what he got were different. Frank and Billy Clanton drew and fired at Wyatt, the chief object of their enmity; but only sent bullets through his clothes. Wyatt on his part had his mind on getting one man — Frank McLowry. This was not a case of personal hostility but of self preservation, for Frank was the real big time gun slinger in the Clanton crowd. Wyatt's bullet caught Frank, as was later determined, just above the belt buckle.

Tom McLowry had also drawn, but he jumped behind one of the horses as he did so. From this cover he sent an ineffectual shot at Morgan. Meanwhile Billy Clanton exchanged shots with Wyatt, the former missing and the latter creasing the rustler's arm. As Frank was still doubled up over his abdominal wound, Wyatt turned to smoke out the other McLowry from behind the horses. To effect this he wounded the animal behind which Tom was crouched. As the beast bolted, Tom vainly grabbed for the rifle it was carrying away.

While all this was going on Virgil dropped his cane and went for his gun. Simultaneously Billy Claiborne arrived at the decision that the troubles of the Clantons and the McLowrys weren't his concern after all. He fired three shots at Virgil, but as he was on the run toward a side door of Fly's studio at the time, all his shots went wild.

After missing his try for the rifle Tom whirled to fire at Morgan Earp and scored. The bullet ripped along the base of Morgan's neck and plunged through his shoulder. At about the same time Virgil got his gun into action and threw a shot at Billy Clanton, which broke his right arm. Billy promptly made "the border shift," tossing his gun to his left hand so he could go on fighting.

When Morgan was hit, Wyatt told him to get behind him and lie doggo. Then he prepared to throw down on Tom, now left in the open by fleeing horses, for the second, although not hit, bolted in panic. In the mean time Ike Clanton was doing the same thing. His frenzied flight took him directly toward Wyatt. He had never drawn, and he wanted to be sure it was understood that he was a non-combatant. "Don't kill me!" he begged, grabbing Wyatt by his left arm. "I'm not shooting."

"This fight's commenced," Earp snarled, as he shook him off. "Get to fighting or get out!" Ike then made for Fly's in the wake of Claiborne. Behan opened the side door for each of them in turn.

While Wyatt was momentarily diverted by Ike, Tom leveled his gun at Wyatt. But by this time the horses had moved far enough to give Holliday a clear shot from his flanking position in Fremont Street. Tom got both barrel loads from the Wells, Fargo shotgun. McLowry ducked around the north corner of the building, heading toward Third Street, and Doc thought he had unaccountably missed. He tossed the shotgun away and drew his pistol.

Morgan had not obeyed Wyatt's injunction to make himself small. Seeing that Billy Clanton had not been put out of action, he sent a bullet through his abdomen. A second later Virgil shot the youngster in the chest. The latter was still game, but he started to retreat toward the corner of the building around which Tom McLowry lay dead. The latter had gone only about ten feet before collapsing.

Frank McLowry was as full of guts as Billy Clanton. He already had a mortal wound, but he threw off the shock of it to get back into the fight. He tried for both Morgan and Wyatt as he staggered toward Fremont Street. He missed, but the war wasn't over yet.

A gun barked twice behind the Earps, as somebody fired from the side window of Fly's. No opinions are in the record as to who fired these two shots, but probably it was Claiborne. Turning to face this new attack, the weakened Morgan fell. With his pistol now in his hand, Doc turned toward Fly's, too. He sent a couple of bullets through the window, drawing no answering fire, but smoking out Ike. The latter dashed out of the studio's rear door toward the stalls of the O. K. Corral, throwing away his revolver as he ran.

Doc snapped two shots at the vanishing Ike, then faced about to find that Frank McLowry was pulling himself together for one final effort. Holliday, only ten feet away, was the object of that effort. "I've got you," Frank announced.

"Think so?" Doc asked.

Aware of his friend's danger, Morgan shot from where he lay on the ground, as Holliday and McLowry fired at each other simultaneously. Doc winced, for a bullet had creased his back. Frank pitched forward with two more wounds, either of which would have killed him instantly. Morgan had shot him through the head and Holliday through the heart.

Of the rustlers only the dying Billy Clanton was still in the ring.

The Guns Go Off

In an exchange of shots with Virgil, the outlaw hit the marshal in the leg. Wyatt brought young Clanton down by putting a bullet through his hip, and Virgil's return fire gave him a scalp wound. Billy made one more try, but couldn't hold his gun. About then Claiborne fled from the photographic studio, taking the same route as Ike Clanton had used. Holliday fired at him, but the hammer fell on empty shells.

Claiborne's second flight signified the end of the Battle of the O. K. Corral. By Wyatt's count seventeen shots had been fired by each side. This included two shots from Fly's studio, but did not include any shots by Ike Clanton, the man who had really promoted the fight. The final score was: three peace officers wounded, three rustlers dead. Holliday's wound was not disabling, but those of Virgil and Morgan were much more serious. Frank McLowry, lying in Fremont Street, had three wounds, all of them mortal. Tom McLowry, crumpled in front of the assayer's office, had two fatal wounds. Billy Clanton, who survived the fracas for about thirty minutes, was hit six times, twice fatally.

"What in hell did you let Ike Clanton get away like that for, Wyatt?" Doc wanted to know.

"He wouldn't jerk his gun," Wyatt explained.

The matter had been settled, and he was then concerned in seeing that his brothers got prompt medical attention. But if the fighting at the O. K. Corral was over, the troubles of the Earps had just begun. If they themselves intended to take the affair in stride, they were about the only ones in town who felt that way. The lid was blown off Tombstone, not to settle again for quite a few months.

The first and most natural manifestation of the popular interest in the fight was that dozens of people rushed to the scene as soon as it seemed safe to do so. These self-appointed investigators represented both factions, as well as the idly curious, making for blood with the sure instinct of flies. Whatever their intentions, the mass accomplishment was to destroy evidence essential to reconstructing what had happened. In the absence of such evidence there were twenty stories, representing the two sides of the quarrel.

Of that quarrel the counter-offensive was not long in coming. The Earps had barely had time to realize that they had all come through alive when Behan emerged from Fly's and told Wyatt he was under arrest. The conversation which followed is given in different forms, though there is agreement as to the general purport. By one account a Mr. Comstock horned in when Behan spoke to Wyatt. "There's no hurry in arresting this man," Comstock said, "he done just right, and the people will uphold him."

At this Wyatt spoke up. "You bet we did just right, and you," turning to Behan at this point, "threw us. You told us they were disarmed." According to the version of another witness what Wyatt said was: "I won't be arrested, but I'll answer what I have done. You deceived us, Johnny, you told me they were unarmed."

There was no action taken against the Earps at the moment, because the Citizens' Safety Committee was on the job. Its members came marching down Fremont Street in a column of twos under the eyes, among many others, of Mayor Clum. "I distinctly remember," Clum wrote, "that the first set of twos was made up of Colonel William Herring, an attorney, and Milton Clapp, cashier of a local bank." This Milton Clapp was none other than the man who had come to Tombstone from California with Parsons. The latter would no doubt have been of the group, too, but unfortunately he was out of town on a prospecting trip at the time. Therefore the first hand account of proceedings which could normally be expected from him is missing.

The first move of the vigilantes was to carry Virgil and Morgan to their homes. Then they established a rotating system of guards so that no reprisal could be taken against the wounded men. After this demonstration the town was outwardly peaceful for the rest of the day. It wasn't until the next morning that the newspapers officially launched the quarrel which has divided Tombstone, Cochise County, and to a lesser degree all of Arizona, into two camps ever since.

The Guns Go Off

"The feeling of the better class of citizens," *The Epitaph* offered by way of editorial comment, "is that the marshal and his posse acted solely in the right in attempting to disarm the cowboys, and that it was a case of kill or get killed." *The Nugget,* on the other hand, had far different things to say. The paper charged the Earps with wanton assault and murder.

Wyatt and his brothers, described as a taciturn lot, probably had little previous knowledge of the power of propaganda warfare. They got a lesson from experts. Public opinion is always a soft touch for certain types of influences. None possible was overlooked.

The men who worked the problem out realized that the law officer who kills is on the spot if it can even be hinted that he shot with unnecessary haste. There was no hinting in the accusation against the Earps. Out of arrant viciousness they had fired upon men who had in no way provoked assault.

Everybody knew that the feud between the Earps and the Clantons had been building up to the danger point for weeks. Parsons, who returned to Tombstone the day after the fight, observed: "Bad blood has been brewing for some time and I was not surprised at the outbreak. It is only a wonder it has not happened before." This aspect of the case was ignored by the county-rustler-*Nugget* faction.

The Clantons, by their accounting, were not hard-bitten thieves and fences, they were cowboys — ranchers in town for business and pleasure only. The threats dozens of people had heard them make against the lives of the Earps were likewise ignored. The approach of the police officers was pictured as taking them totally by surprise.

So little did they understand what was afoot that when they were told to raise their arms, they did so. It was not until the Earps drew and fired without warning that they fired back. *But —* not all of them fired back, because only Frank McLowry and Billy Clanton were armed. Had not Ike's weapons been confiscated by Virgil Earp? As for Tom McLowry, he had checked his revolver

165

at a bar, where it still was. Claiborne was all but dismissed from the scene. He was just an innocent bystander.

Boiled down, the accusation was that four armed men had attacked four men who had already surrendered and of whom only two were armed to begin with. The motive for the brutal killing was not immediately given. That was to come later.

Meanwhile tear-jerking sidelights of the battle were bruited about. It was not enough that Billy Clanton, his age reduced to the minimum of credibility, was under twenty. His last thought had been for a pledge he made to his mother. This fast shooting stock thief, who had been taking part in raids, ambushes and hijacking expeditions for at least the past two years, had made a promise to his beloved mother that he would never die with his boots on. With his dying breath he remembered it, and asked for his boots to be removed.

That ought to have taken the prize for inspiration, but the boys came up with an even better one. Ike, good old Ike, had not rushed up to Wyatt to beg for his own life. His sole concern had been for the welfare of his young brother, Billy, and, unarmed though he was, he had dashed through the bullets to plead for him.

After that the preparation of three headboards for Billy, Tom, and Frank, all marked "Murdered on the Streets of Tombstone" was an anticlimax. The job had already been done, and words forced Wyatt to back up as guns had not succeeded in doing. Although the coroner's jury had attached no guilt to him, these were charges that a peace officer had to answer. Behan had deputized a bunch of rustlers to serve him with a warrant for murder, but Earp was thinking fast, too. He stole a march by going to Judge Wells Spicer and requesting that the court investigate the matter.

It has been stated by Breakenridge and others that Spicer abused his prerogatives by doing everything in his power to favor the Earps. There is still extant, however, a document which proves that the Earps did not find this to be the case.

The order of events seems to have been that the prosecution

opened the hearing by demanding a bail of $50,000 each for the defendants, Doc and Wyatt. The defense had scored an initial point by arranging that Virgil and Morgan would not have to appear in court. Safford, the former territorial governor and head of the Safford & Hudson Bank, offered to put up bonds in the amount requested, but Spicer, ruling it exorbitant, placed the sum at $10,000. Nevertheless, he must have changed his mind as the prosecution commenced building up its case, for the defense filed a petition for a writ of habeas corpus on behalf of Wyatt and Doc addressed to J. H. Lucas, probate judge of Cochise County. This petition shows that in spite of the fact that Holliday and Earp had been admitted to bail, the court had permitted the sheriff to put them in jail. It reads in part: "During examination of one of the witnesses for the prosecution . . . and long before the prosecution had closed their case on behalf of the Territory the said Wells Spicer, Esq. . . . on motion of counsel for the prosecution, made an order that the said defendants be remanded into the custody of the Sheriff of the County of Cochise, Arizona Territory, without bail."

The petition must have got results, for though it states that the defendants were arrested on October 29, Parsons' entry for October 31, proves that Earp was at liberty: "Met Wyatt Earp in hotel who took me in to see Virgil this evening. He's getting along well. Morgan too. Looks bad for them all thus far."

The hearing was closed to all but the parties involved and witnesses. The court also seems to have imposed limits as to what could be used by the press, for *The Epitaph* complained that silence was imposed on reporters regarding certain points. Why this was so, if it was a fact, is not now determinable; but the probable reason for the closed hearing was to prevent a demonstration in court by partisans of the Clantons. Tombstone was in an uproar, and rioting was apparently only prevented by action on the part of the vigilantes. "A raid is feared upon the town by the cowboys," Parsons observed after returning from his prospecting trip, "and measures have been taken to protect life and property. The 'stranglers' were out in force and showed sand."

But it still looked bad for the Earps. The prosecution began by presenting the spearhead of its offense in the form of John Behan, now in the role of a man whose sole interest was upholding law and order. Excerpts from his testimony follow: "Saw Marshal Earp standing there and asked him what was the excitement. He is Virgil Earp. He said there were a lot of s — of — in town looking for a fight. . . . I said to him, 'You had better disarm that crowd.' He said he would not; he would give them a chance to fight. I said to him, 'It is your duty as a peace officer to disarm them rather than encourage the fight.' He made no reply, but I said I was going down to disarm the boys. . . .

"I went down Fourth Street to the corner of Fremont and met Frank McLowry holding a horse. I told McLowry that I would have to disarm him as there was likely to be trouble in town. . . . He said he would not give up his arms, as he did not intend to have any trouble. . . . I said, 'Frank, come along with me. . . .' When I got down to where Ike was I found Tom McLowry, Billy Clanton, and Will Claybourn. I said to them, 'Boys, you have got to give up your arms.'

"Frank McLowry demurred. . . . Ike told me he did not have any arms. Tom McLowry showed me by pulling his coat open that he was not armed. Claybourn said he was not one of the party. . . . I saw the Earps and Holliday coming down the sidewalk. . . . I said to the Clantons, 'Wait here awhile, I will go up and stop them.'"

But the Earps would not heed the sheriff's plea for a peaceful settlement of the matter and launched a monstrous attack upon unprepared and inadequately armed men. And after Behan had finished several others came forward to support his story. Some, their connections and affiliations now unknown, may have been disinterested witnesses. At least two certainly were not. The testimony of Wes Fuller and even of Billy Claiborne was offered as that of spectators who had had nothing to do with the battle.

Then Ike Clanton fired the second big gun. What had not been offered was any explanation for the murders. Ike had such an explanation and gave it. Wyatt Earp's story — repeated in court — about having offered Ike the Wells, Fargo reward money for the capture of Head, Crane, and Leonard was just a blind. What had really taken place was that the Earps had themselves planned the holdup during which Philpot and Roerig had been killed, although Holliday was the only one who had joined Leonard, et al in the execution of the crime. Doc, in fact, had fired the shot which killed Philpot. Then when the robbery was bungled and the Earps had failed to catch Crane and the rest — presumably with the design of silencing them for good — Wyatt and the others had turned to Ike. What they asked him to do was to use his influence with the rustlers to keep Head and his associates from telling that the Earps had been involved with them in the holdup.

But after Head, Crane, and Leonard all died Ike was no longer useful to the Earps — and he knew too much. The O. K. Corral massacre, then, had been staged for one purpose: to get Ike Clanton out of the way, so he couldn't talk.

That was the plaintiff's case, and, as Parsons said, things didn't look good for the defendants. After producing all its witnesses, the prosecution demanded that the hearing should result in a decision which would make a formal trial for murder mandatory.

CHAPTER FIFTEEN

THE DEFENSE COUNTER PUNCHES

THE HEARING lasted for weeks. Notwithstanding the prosecution's anxiety to wrap the case up in a hurry, there were many points in its testimony which required examination.

Inexplicably, considering that they had planned so thoroughly in other respects, the anti-Earp faction had not coached its witnesses beforehand. After the hearing started Spicer apparently kept each in isolation until he had testified, for there were startling discrepancies in their stories.

Behan, as stated above, swore that he had ordered all five of the Clanton crowd to give up their arms. Yet Claiborne contradicted this, when he took the stand. He said he had been talking to Billy Clanton while Behan had been in conversation with the other three, and that therefore he didn't know what the sheriff had said. The two Billys, then, had not heard any request to give up their weapons, if such a request had been made.

Wes Fuller was even less of a help, leaving it in doubt as to whether he had stayed to see any of the action at all. For instance, although all other witnesses were in agreement that Holliday had carried the shotgun, Fuller placed it in the hands of Virgil Earp at the opposite end of the battle line. He also said that Tom McLowry had gone into Fly's, leaving it doubtful as to just why he had emerged to die in front of the assayer's office on the other side of the O. K. Corral.

Behan himself did not prove too good a witness because of the inherent weakness of his position. He was a peace officer who had not — even giving him the best of it — disarmed at least two of the rustlers for whom he was now appearing as an advocate. This was a fact he could not get around, and the defense made the most of it. Behan was asked point blank whether he had not put these men — openly wearing arms in town, contrary to the law he was sworn to uphold — under arrest. To this the sheriff replied that he had considered the men under arrest, but that he couldn't be sure that they themselves had felt that they were.

There was a thing Behan had done which he now had cause to regret. After Wyatt had announced before witnesses that the sheriff had tried to conceal the fact that the rustlers were still armed, Behan had temporarily lost his nerve. He and his backers had not yet cooked up their case against the Earps, and the sheriff thought he had better take some steps toward clearing himself of the charge of conspiring with outlaws. He had gone to the house of Virgil Earp and explained to the wounded marshal that in the excitement of the moment he hadn't made himself plain. What had happened was that he had tried his best to disarm the outlaws, but they had all defied him. Anxious to stop the fight at all costs, he had gone to the Earps, but not with the intent of deceiving them.

The defense did not depend on a statement by Virgil Earp for these admissions. This evidence was offered by W. S. Williams, newly appointed deputy district attorney for Cochise County, who had been with Virgil when Behan came to visit him.

The defense had other witnesses for which the prosecution wasn't prepared. Ike Clanton had been seen going into Spangenberg's gun shop, after he had been disarmed by Virgil, by others than Wyatt Earp. At least two men had seen Tom McLowry just before he joined his allies. Both testified that he had a pistol when they met him.

Then the sheriff and other witnesses for the prosecution were not the only ones who had seen any of the actual fighting. Judge Lucas, peering from his office on the second floor of the courthouse had seen, he said, Billy Clanton fire at least twice before he was hit. A Miss or Mrs. Addie Bourland, a window of whose millinery shop commanded a good view of the corral, declared that all the combatants had started shooting at once. She added that nobody had thrown up his hands before the fighting commenced.

Next Dr. George Goodfellow, experienced in such matters as a former army surgeon, showed conclusively that the location of the wounds on the arms of Billy Clanton could not have been received while his arms were held up in surrender. Rather their position indicated that the arm had been held as it naturally would have been if Clanton had been aiming a revolver.

There remained the point of whether the fracas was premeditated at all by the rustlers, or whether, as prosecution witnesses insisted, they hadn't dreamed of starting any trouble. A woman related how she had entered a butcher shop on Fremont Street and could not get waited upon because everybody was talking about the anticipated clash between the Clantons and the Earps. A man gave similar evidence. Plainly if the rustlers were not aware that a conflict was in order they were the only men in Tombstone who were so ignorant. But it wasn't left at that. There were witnesses who had personally heard the various members of the Clanton-McLowry crew threaten the Earps with death.

After due deliberation Judge Spicer wrote his opinion. That opinion and its author have been reviled every year since — in the main by people who have neither bothered to review the testimony nor to examine the judge's conclusions. They deserve examination.

He commenced by observing that the killings and the identities of the men who had done the slaying were not matters of debate. The primary issue was whether the killings were justified. It was implicit in the testimony of the prosecution that the Earps were flagrantly in the wrong for going to the O. K. Corral, whereas by avoiding the place they could have prevented the disturbance of that peace they were appointed to defend, not to break.

"Was it for Virgil Earp, as Chief of Police," Spicer wrote in comment, "to abandon his clear duty as an officer because his performance was likely to be fraught with danger? Or was it not his duty that, as such officer, he owed to the peaceable and law-abiding citizens of the city, who looked to him to preserve peace and order, and their protection and security, to at once call to his aid sufficient assistance and proceed to arrest and disarm these men? There can be but one answer to these questions, and that answer is such as will divert the subsequent approach of the defendants toward the deceased of all presumption of malice or illegality. When, therefore, the defendants, regularly or specially appointed officers, marched down Fremont Street to the scene of the subsequent homicide, they were armed, as it was their right and duty to be armed when approaching men whom they believed to be armed and contemplating resistance."

Behan had adduced in the course of his testimony that Frank McLowry had not definitely refused to give up his weapons but that before he considered it he had insisted that the sheriff must first disarm the Earps and Doc. In remarking on this point, Spicer said: "In view of the past history of the country and the generally believed existence at this time of desperately reckless and lawless men in our midst, banded together for mutual support and living by felonious and predatory pursuits, regarding neither life nor property in their career, and at this time for men to parade the streets armed with repeating rifles and six-shooters, and demand that the Chief of Police of the city and his associates should be disarmed is a proposition both monstrous and startling. This was said by one of the deceased only a few minutes before the arrival of the Earps."

The judge also took account of the accusation that one of the slain men, Tom McLowry, had been unarmed. "Certain it is that the Clantons and McLowrys had among themselves at least two six-shooters and two Winchester rifles on their horses, Therefore if Thos. McLowry was one of a party who were thus armed and were making felonious resistance to an arrest, and in the meleé that followed was shot, the fact of his being unarmed, if it be a fact, could not of itself criminate the defendants if they were not otherwise criminal. It is beyond doubt that William Clanton and Frank McLowry were armed, and made such quick and effective use of their arms as to seriously wound Morgan and Virgil Earp."

The matter of conflicting testimony on important points was also taken up. The prosecution had insisted that the evidence of mere spectators like Judge Lucas and the Bourland woman was less valid than that of participants, such as Ike Clanton and Billy Claiborne. Referring to the fact that the chief occupation of these last two had been to get out of the way, Spicer drily remarked: "I am of the opinion that those who observed the conflict from a short distance and from points of observation that gave them a good view of the scene, to say the least, were quite as likely to be accurate in their observation as those mingled up in or fleeing from the meleé."

The judge then disposed of the avowed reason for the alleged massacre. The prosecution had agreed with the defense that, with whatever motives to drive him, Ike had run directly up to Wyatt while the latter held a loaded revolver in his hand. It was also an established fact that Ike had not been injured, as Spicer noted: "The testimony of Isaac Clanton that this tragedy was a result of a scheme on the part of the Earps to assassinate him, and there-fore bury in oblivion the confessions the Earps had made to him about piping away the shipment of coins by Wells, Fargo & Co., falls short of being a sound theory because of the great fact most prominent in the matter, to wit: that Isaac Clanton was not injured at all, and could have been killed first and easiest."

As Chaucer said, although in another connection, "what nedeth wordes mo?" But Spicer added one thing as he exonerated Doc and Wyatt of the charges against them. He pointed out that the grand jury was then in session, and that if its members were dissatisfied with his findings they were, of course, free to indict Earp and Holliday.

The grand jury took no such action, but the case continued to be argued. "The sentiment of the community," *The Nugget* proclaimed in an editorial, "was that justice had not been done." The pro-rustler faction went on beating the propaganda drums,

and they persuaded many. Officialdom is always a fine target
for indignation; and if it can be sentimental indignation, so much
the better. What right did police officers, of all people, have to
participate in a street fight? And one of their victims was no
more than a boy, who had told his mother, etc. There are tears
still being shed about that one.

The city administration backed up the Earps, both officially
and in the columns of the Mayor's paper, *The Epitaph*. Nor had
Clum changed his position nearly fifty years later, witness excerpts
from an article he wrote in 1929. "There has been much discussion
as to who fired the first shot in this street battle. The question is
utterly unimportant to me, though I believe that the rustlers shot
first. . . . I do not think that an officer of the law should offer
himself as a target for the bullets of every thug and bandit and
desperado he may be called upon to apprehend, and to wait until
the criminal has missed him a couple of times — or has mortally
wounded him — before he joins in the shooting. . . .

"Some of the partisans of the rustlers have appealed to public
sentiment by emphasizing the fact that Billy Clanton was a mere
youth. . . . We are told that "Billy the Kid" was only twenty-one
years old when he was killed by Sheriff Pat Garrett, and that in
his brief career the "Kid" had killed twenty-one men. . . . Today
a majority of our bandits are mere youths. The police authorities
will tell you that a "mere youth" with a handy gun and a hostile
purpose may prove to be an exceedingly dangerous foe."

But the county-rustler-*Nugget* party, having no intention of
being convinced, had no patience with either facts or logic. "While
six witnesses," Breakenridge wrote, "swore that the McLaurys and
Clantons held up their hands as directed by the Earps, and three
swore that they did not see them throw up their hands, Spicer
still gave a verdict of not guilty." Breakenridge did not observe
that the six prosecution witnesses included Behan, Wes Fuller,
Ike Clanton and Claiborne, while the three defense witnesses did
not include Holliday, or Morgan and Virgil Earp. No, Spicer
could have come to his conclusion, against the evidence — cogent

parts of which Breakenridge was careful not to quote — because he was a venal magistrate.

Nor was Spicer the only one charged with conspiracy. Mayor Clum was accused because he defended the actions of the police; Thomas Fitch because he had acted as the officers' legal counsel. Dr. Goodfellow was put on the black books for having been a witness at the trial damaging to the rustler cause. E. B. Gage and James Vizina, prominent mining men, were among several leaders of the vigilantes held implicated because their organization supported the Earps. The outlaws and their backers had taken it upon themselves to indict Tombstone's leading citizens.

They soon went further than that. It began to be the talk of the town that the rustlers had made a death list of men who would not be allowed to leave Tombstone alive. The Earps, Holliday, and all the men mentioned in the above paragraph were said to be on it. Their names, so the story ran — and Tom Sawyer couldn't have bettered it — had been written in blood at a secret gathering in a canyon at the dead of night.

This was not taken as seriously as it might have been. "As for myself," Clum recalled, "I felt that if a fight should occur within the city, the rustler-clan would not overlook an opportunity to rub me out, but I did not believe — desperate as I knew them to be — that they would deliberately plan to murder me. I was mistaken."

But before he found out that he was wrong, certain residents of Tombstone whose funnybones had been tickled by the dramatic story had amused themselves. Everybody anyone didn't like or wanted to frighten began receiving threatening, unsigned missives. The result was that the whole city contracted a bad case of the jitters.

Even those who discounted the rumors and the bogus black-hand notes began to take precautions. Clum, who was post-master as well as mayor, had reinforced shutters made for the P. O. Bldg. so that he could not be shot in the back when he worked after dark.

The Defense Counter Punches

This only served its limited purpose of protecting him while he was in the city. But Clum's wife had died earlier in the year, with the result that he had sent his infant son to be cared for by his grandparents, who resided in Washington, D. C. At the approach of Christmas the Mayor made the decision to go east for the holidays. Accordingly he took the stage for the railroad town of Benson on December 14, 1881.

The next day *The Epitaph* announced that four men had attacked the coach for the purpose of assassinating the Mayor. They had come near enough to succeeding. Clum himself has supplied such details as could not have been known to the press.

Leaving at night, the coach had been ordered to halt by men standing in the road about five miles down the valley from Tombstone. The driver frankly admitted that he had tried to obey; but the horses got panicky, and the brakes wouldn't hold. The coach had rattled away to the tune of following gunfire. Camping teamsters had seen and heard shots, estimating fifteen or twenty. The most shocking fact of all, was that when the stage reached Contention the Mayor was mysteriously missing.

Now strangely enough there had been two stages on the scene instead of one. An empty coach, driven by Whistling Dick — a driver frequently mentioned in Tombstone annals — had just caught up when the first stage was ordered to halt. Whipping up his own animals, Dick was caught in the fire meant for the coach Clum was in. The casualties were a wound in the leg for Whistling Dick and one in the throat for a lead horse of the other team. This proved fatal, necessitating a halt while the horse was cut out.

Dismounting with the other passengers while he waited for this to be done, Clum thought things over. The stage had not carried mail, express, payroll money, or bullion — the things which normally made a holdup worth while. Adding that consideration to the repeated threats he had received, he was certain that his life was what the bandits had been after. Being dismounted, they had not offered immediate pursuit, but Clum felt sure that when they went for their horses they would make a short cut to intercept the stage at another point on the road. When the word came to resume places in the coach, he did not heed it, therefore. In the darkness this was not noticed. Those up top thought he was inside, and those in the carriage thought he was aloft.

When the others alighted for refreshment at Contention City and found that Clum was not among those present, everybody concluded that the outlaws had somehow nabbed him after all. Contention was shaken with an excitement which soon reached Tombstone. Telegraph messages caused friends of the Mayor to roust out Sheriff Behan, the officer with jurisdiction. A posse under his leadership discovered that the bandits had totaled five or six, counting a man or so to hold the horses. They found lots of blood, which turned out to belong to the slain horse, but no trace of the vanished city official.

He himself was, in the nature of things, the only authority for what happened before he turned up at Benson at eight o'clock the next morning. He had started out to make the remaining twenty miles to the railroad station afoot, traveling by the stars until he almost fell into two successive abandoned mine shafts. Deciding that it would be safer faring along the river, he followed a gully down to the San Pedro. There, by good luck, he found himself within earshot of the Grand Central Mining Company's stamping mill. After resting a couple of hours in a bunk furnished by the superintendent, he borrowed a horse and set out for Benson again about four A. M. As it was December, daylight was still several hours away.

Crossing the river, he set out to pick up the Benson road at Contention, which was on the west side of the San Pedro. Not far outside of the latter town he almost met disaster again. Before he knew it, he was right on a group of "cowboys," asleep in their bivouac. Clum was convinced that these were his would-be assassins. As he pictured the sequence, they had gone on to Contention City to make sure which of the two stages their intended victim was in before riding to head it off again. The discovery that the Mayor was not aboard either coach had upset their plans.

The Nugget, as an indignant editorial in The Epitaph survives to indicate, found the episode amusing, and had great fun with the Mayor in the role of fugitive. The Epitaph, of course, was in a fury about the attempted outrage. There could have been, its columns pointed out, no doubt of what the bandits had in mind, for passengers reported that one of the holdup men had yelled something about making sure of getting the bald headed old son of a bitch. Clum was not old, being only thirty, but he had been precociously bald for years.

The row made by The Epitaph was the nearest thing to any action being taken against the bandits. Sheriff Behan had gone to the scene of the crime under pressure from the Mayor's friends and business associates, but he made no effort to track the outlaws down. Although dispatches were sent to other papers, so that what had happened was well known in Arizona, there was no investigation by territorial officials.

Nothing could better illustrate the political isolation of Cochise County, or of Tombstone within it. The chief executive of Arizona's largest city was as fair game as a rabbit as soon as he passed outside of the municipal limits. His only recourse when attacked was furtive flight.

Nor did the outcry caused by this incident bring about any improvement in conditions. Things got worse, rather. Tombstone had seen much in the way of violence, but soon it was to be invaded by a new and peculiarly daunting variety.

CHAPTER SIXTEEN

STAGES AND AMBUSHES

JOHN CLUM, no doubt with reason, but at the same time not leaving that reason for the record, stated his conviction that one of the men who had tried to murder him was Jack Stilwell. But Clum wrote this name down forty-eight years after the event. It was evidently a mistake for Frank Stilwell, whose brother Jack, a well known Texas scout, does not seem to have come near Tombstone. Frank, on the other hand, was one of southeastern Arizona's best known characters. In addition to being one of Behan's deputies, he was recognized as being *dux et princeps* among its stage robbers.

The whole business of stage holdups in Cochise County, together with the reaction it drew from peace officers, deserves more attention than it has so far been given in this chronicle. It was the one point where the lines of duty of the sheriff and the deputy U. S. marshal were apt to cross. There was also a private agency involved.

This last was the powerful Wells, Fargo Express Co., whose stake in the matter was financially larger than that of the Federal government. The success of this company against bandits in other parts of the West had been, on the whole, excellent to phenomenal. Those stage robbers who weren't sent up for prison terms were shot by guards or hunted down by Wells, Fargo operatives acting in conjunction with local or Federal peace officers.

As the richest mining town in the nation, Tombstone was an object of special attention to the outfit which had undertaken to protect loads of bullion and payrolls in transit. As their losses grew, their concentration on the area increased. By 1881 they had an organization in the Tombstone district consisting of at least the following men. Marshall Williams was in charge of the office on Fremont Street. Under cover were two men, one in town and one in the outlaw stronghold of Charleston. Of these the first was Fred Dodge, identified by Clum as well as Wyatt Earp as the confidential representative of John J. Valentine, president of Wells, Fargo & Co. Ostensibly, though, he was a faro dealer for Hafford's Saloon. He lived with Wyatt and Morgan, but as they were both professional gamblers, too, he was apparently never suspected. The other, J. B. Ayers, kept the best known saloon in Charleston, whence he sent messages by telegraph to Tombstone. Aside from the Earps and Mayor Clum only certain leaders of the Citizens' Safety Committee knew what Dodge and Ayers were doing. Then in the open, in addition to Williams were special officers James B. Hume and John Thacker. They had operated all over the West as Wells, Fargo's prize trouble shooters.

Good as they were supposed to be, the special officers won no laurels in Cochise County. In other parts of Arizona many arrests were made, but in the Tombstone district the rustlers were too well organized. In 1885 Hume and Thacker addressed a report to Valentine, covering the years from 1870 on and dealing with punitive activities of the company in various parts of the West. Specifically, it covered positive action taken against bandits molesting stages carrying Wells, Fargo cargoes. That is to say, if the robbers were not incarcerated or killed, the case was not cited.

Now it is impossible to guess how many assaults were made on various stages going to and from Tombstone, although everyone connected with the town agreed that these were extremely numerous. *The Epitaph* files of 1881 are missing, and *The Nugget* had little to say on the subject. The criminal records of Cochise County are also of little help. But it *is* possible to tell how many times reprisal followed an attack on coaches in which Wells, Fargo & Co. were interested. Only once.

The case referred to was the holdup of March 15, 1881, when Eli Philpot and Peter Roerig were killed. Hume and Thacker were able to include it, because Head, Crane, and Leonard were all soon killed — a lucky accident. Of 206 convictions for robbery and attempted stage robbery listed in the report none was for a crime committed around Tombstone. Luther King was, of course, captured by the Earps, only to escape from the custody of the sheriff.

There was one other time when prisoners were actually taken. On September 8, 1881, the stage to Bisbee was stopped by two men. Their loot, taking the form of a Wells, Fargo box and a mail sack, was about $2500. The driver, Levi McDaniels, recognized the bandits and identified them as Pete Spence, whose real name was said to be Lark Ferguson, and Behan's deputy, Frank Stilwell. He also saw two men, presumptive horse holders, whom he could not identify in the dark.

There are two stories on what followed, offered by Wyatt Earp and Breakenridge, each of whom led rival posses. The Wells, Fargo men, Dodge and Williams, were with the deputy U. S. marshal. Each of the two peace officers claims to have tracked one of the bandits to Bisbee, there to identify him. Both, however, agreed that the man was Frank Stilwell.

Breakenridge stated, with no show of probability, inasmuch as he gave no reason for the strange conduct, that Williams refused to swear out a warrant for the thief he had ridden so far to help apprehend. The deputy sheriff therefore arrested him, and it was only when Stilwell was released on bail in Tombstone that Wyatt arrested him for robbing the mail. Earp's version was that although Behan tried to claim jurisdiction, he, Wyatt, took the outlaw on a Federal warrant to Tucson, where his bail was set at $5,000. With Stilwell went Spence, whom Wyatt and Morgan had located near Charleston. It was suspected that the other two members of the holdup foursome were Curly Bill and Pony Deal, but nothing was proved.

At all events, by the allowance of everyone, Stilwell was back on the old stand in short order. It was not proved that he took part in the attempt to murder Mayor Clum on December 14th, though his subsequent actions made that a tenable theory. If he was among those present, he could have fired the shot which wounded Whistling Dick, called Wright by some but listed as Richards by Hume and Thacker, whose report also noted all company employees who had become casualties in the line of duty. Whatever his surname, Dick had been on his way to pick up a load for Wells, Fargo at Benson.

The ensuing month there were two sensational robberies in adjoining columns of one issue of *The Epitaph*, the weekly, not the daily. On January 6, 1882, the Tombstone-Bisbee stage took off with a Wells, Fargo money box guarded by Charles A. Bartholomew. When bandits tried to halt the coach, Bartholomew's answer was to open fire. W. S. Waits, the driver, whipped up the horses, the holdup men caught up their mounts and gave chase, and for five miles there was a running fight in the best wild West show tradition.

The rustlers finally circled around to cut the stage off and to halt it by shooting a couple of the horses; but Bartholomew had plenty of moxy. He held the robbers off until the passengers, of whom one was a woman, finally persuaded him that he had no right to endanger their lives. The Wells, Fargo box was lifted by men whom the driver recognized, but, as he was threatened with death if he revealed any names, he kept silent.

That's about as far as *The Epitaph* story went. Wyatt Earp had more to say. According to him the five bandits were recognized as Frank Stilwell and Spence — thus putting in their time while they were out on bail, charged with the same offense — Curly Bill, Pony Deal, and Ike Clanton.

Wyatt had taken the field with a posse as soon as he was informed of what had happened. He was still arduously following signs from the scene of the Bisbee stage holdup when word was brought to him that money and mail had been taken from the Benson stage by Curly Bill and Pony Deal, two of the men he was after. This intelligence came from Hume, who probably took no pleasure in giving it. Caught literally napping when the coach was intercepted, the Wells, Fargo officer had been relieved of his ivory-handled, gold-mounted revolvers.

Brocius and Deal were pursued, but, supplied with horses by other rustlers whenever they needed them, they outdistanced the posse. Eventually the pair was heard of in Charleston. Wyatt, with a backing of vigilantes, was set to ride into Charleston at the very time that Johnny Ringo, as earlier described, was prematurely sprung by Behan. Ringo's warning sent Curly Bill and Pony on their way again.

And so it went. With Stilwell and Spence bailed out, and probably figuring on skipping bail, the score of peace and special officers was zero against stage robbers. Rustling was indulged in daily and with as much impunity. The outlaws evidently didn't try to take over mining claims, for that would have entailed work, but nothing else was safe. Clum was not the only one who felt that he was risking his life whenever he ventured out of Tombstone. Parsons remarked that "cowboy" and holdup man were one and the same. Whenever he saw one in the offing, he rode with his revolver in his hand.

In the whole county there was no fortress for law and order but Tombstone, shakily held, especially since the Battle of the O. K. Corral, by the Earps and the Citizens' Safety Committee. In the meantime the grip of this garrison had been dealt a blow aimed at its morale as well as its power. Two weeks after the abortive attack on Clum there was proof positive that the attempt was not something his imagination had manufactured out of a routine holdup. On December 28, 1881, Virgil Earp, once more on duty as town marshal, was shot from ambush as he emerged from the Oriental Saloon on Fifth and Allen Streets.

Parsons has left a vivid account of the moment. Ever since a balcony collapsed with him while he was fighting the big June fire, he had been having trouble with the crushed bones of his nose. These had been several times adjusted by Dr. Goodfellow, who had been letting his patient bunk in his office. One shot came through the window, just missing Parsons' head. He was fully

awake at the time, because, as he wrote, the doctor had just been
to see him.

"Tonight about 11:30 Doc G had just left and I tho't couldn't
have crossed the street — when four shots were fired in quick succession by heavily charged guns, making a terrible noise and I
tho't were fired under my window under which I quickly
dropped, keeping the adobe wall between me and the outside till
the fusilade was over. I immediately tho't Doc had been shot and
fired in return, remembering the late episode and knowing how
pronounced he was on the Earp-cow-boy question. He had
crossed though and passed Virgil Earp who crossed to the west
side of 5th and was fired upon when in range of my windows by
men — 2 or 3 concealed in the timbers of the new 2 story adobe
going up for the Huachuca Water Co. He did not fall, but re-
crossed to the Oriental and was taken from there to the Cosmopolitan being hit with buck shot and badly wounded in left arm
with flesh wound above left thigh. . . . Doc had a close shave.
Dan and I went to the hospital for Doc and got various things.
Hotel well guarded, so much so that I had hard trouble to get to
Earp's room. He was easy. Told him I was sorry. 'It's hell, isn't
it,' said he. His wife was troubled. 'Never mind. I've got one arm
left to hug you with,' he said."

Virgil's left arm was permanently crippled, as Parsons indicated in his entry for the ensuing day. "Longitudinal fracture,
so elbow joint had to be taken out. And we've got that and some
of the shattered bone in room."

Just who tried to kill Tombstone's chief of police was never
legally established. Wyatt accused Ike Clanton, Frank Stilwell
and a follower of theirs called Hank Swilling, all of whom had
been seen hastily leaving town not long after the crime. Parsons
suspected Ike and two different members of the rustler gang. His
words on the subject support the statement, elsewhere made, that
a brother of the slain Tom and Frank McLowry had come to
Cochise County from Texas after the Battle of the O. K. Corral.
"It is surmised that Ike Clanton, Curly Bill and McLowry did the

shooting." Anyhow, at Wyatt's request the Citizens' Safety Committee swore out warrants for Clanton, Stilwell, and Swilling, who promptly surrendered to Behan. At the hearing dozens of rustler witnesses supplied them with alibis, and they were dismissed.

As far as the history of Tombstone was concerned, the important result of the attack was to bring about a realignment of peace officers. Virgil was incapacitated as a candidate to succeed himself in the city election of January 3, 1882. Probably his enemies had this imminent election in mind, although he might not have won out in any case. Wyatt stated that John Carr, who followed Clum as mayor, had the backing of the Law and Order League. Yet he must have been a compromise candidate, for *The Epitaph,* the organ of that party, came out against him not long before election day. Clum, incidentally, was still absent in Washington, and so evidently not out to repeat.

However that may have been, Carr got the votes and David Neagle was elected Town Marshal. Wyatt seems to have shared a general liking for Neagle, for whom he claimed honesty in spite of his associates. These included Sheriff Behan, of whose deputies Neagle was one. He had ceased to be by the time he ran for chief of police, but the Law and Order League didn't get much good out of him. In spite of acknowledged bravery and good intentions, he didn't have the drive to be a force where one was so badly needed. In the struggle between the offices of the sheriff and the deputy U. S. marshal he appears to have been a harried neutral.

As the year 1882 opened therefore the Earps had been stripped of better than half of their official power. For it was the authority of the town marshal's office which had permitted them to control the rustlers in Tombstone. Except where a Federal law was broken a deputy U. S. marshal had no more to say in the management of local affairs than any other citizen.

Virgil's rules for conduct which had so galled the rustlers were no longer enforced. The outlaws came to town in a body and would have owned the town they had so long coveted but for the fact that the Earps, this time only with vigilante backing, were again in their way. If Virgil's dependable revolver was missing, Wyatt and Morgan had the support of such gunmen as Texas Jack Vermilion, Sherman McMasters and the redoubtable Turkey Creek Jack Johnson.

So Tombstone at this period was not like one armed camp, but two. "A bad time is expected again in town at any time," Parsons wrote in describing the situation. "Earps on one side of the street with their friends and Ike Clanton and Ringo with theirs on the other side — watching each other. Blood will surely come."

Wyatt and Morgan had early moved into the Cosmopolitan Hotel, taking rooms which sandwiched that of the disabled Virgil. The rustlers had responded by establishing headquarters at the Grand, just across Fifth Street. Shuttling groups of outlaws were on duty to keep an eye on the Earps and, as was with justification suspected, to watch for another opportunity to kill from ambush.

Curly Bill does not seem to have taken an active part in this phase of the campaign, but Ringo was much in Tombstone. On one occasion he came within an ace of dueling with Doc Holliday. This, we have Parsons' word for it, was on January 17. "Bad time expected with the cow-boy leader and D. H. I passed both not knowing blood was up. One with hand in breast pocket and the other probably ready. Earps just beyond. Crowded street and looked like another battle. Police vigilant for once and both disarmed."

Wyatt supplies the details of the encounter. Strolling down Allen Street, Doc met Ringo in front of the Cosmopolitan. After an exchange of unpleasantries, seemingly overheard by Parsons, they agreed to go to work on each other in the middle of the street. At this point a constable named Flynn grabbed Ringo from behind, and Wyatt dragged Doc away. Shots at that time would have, in all likelihood, provoked a free for all shooting scrap between the factions — the last thing desired by the Citizens' Safety Committee.

Breakenridge, who also recorded the almost-duel, asserted that Johnny Ringo was the aggressor — loaded for bear and out to bring things to a head. What action, if any, was taken about Holliday is lost from the record; but Ringo was brought to the sheriff's office, whither he was accompanied by Breakenridge himself. The outlaw leader had been deliberately trying to make Tombstone a battleground, but this, in the deputy sheriff's own words, was the treatment accorded him:

"When we got to the office, Behan told him he would have to give up his arms, as it was against the law to carry arms in town. Ringo handed him two pistols from his pockets, and Behan put them in a drawer in the desk, and walked out of the office." The master having given the cue, the man took it up, following an appeal from Ringo. "I told him that I could not help him being disarmed, and when he was ready to leave no doubt the sheriff would return him his pistols. I walked over to the drawer and pulled it out to see if the guns were still there, and, forgetting to close it, I walked out also." When Breakenridge returned to the office, the guns were gone, and so was Johnny.

The first move to break the stalemate was made by the vigilantes, who finally persuaded territorial and Federal officials to find out what was going on in the upper San Pedro Valley. Fremont had resigned and Acting Governor John J. Gosper not only realized what was happening but saw that the condition could only be cured by drastic measures. On the advice of Crawley P. Dake, U. S. Marshal for Arizona, Wyatt Earp was given the job which properly belonged to the sheriff — that of suppressing outlawry in the county. With him were deputized, Holliday, Morgan and Warren Earp, McMasters, Johnson, and Vermilion.

The plan called for a considerable appropriation of funds, presumably so that liberal rewards could be offered for information leading to the capture of certain outlaws, and so on. For this purpose territorial resources would be supplemented by Wells, Fargo, the Southern Pacific, and the long suffering cattle raisers of Cochise County. It was doubtless to this scheme that Parsons referred when he wrote on January 25: "At last national government is taking a hand in the matter of our troubles and by private information I know that no money or trouble will be spared to cower the lawless element."

As yet the lawless element was very far from being cowed. Its immunity from control had lasted so long that the threat of interference by the U. S. Marshal for Arizona didn't faze it.The territorial governor was taken even less seriously. So instead of yielding ground the outlaws and their political colleagues struck back at the agency created to suppress them.

How far the special U. S. Marshal's posse had been able to proceed is indeterminate; but the fact that a plan has been approved by a government does not mean that it is promptly implemented. Probably Wyatt and his associates were still waiting for their political, industrial, and private backers to pony up the necessary finances when Behan moved again.

What he had elected to do was to reopen the O. K. Corral case. No judge in Tombstone would oblige him, but the sheriff found a justice of the peace in Contention City who was willing to swear out warrants for the Earps and Holliday on the charge of having murdered Billy Clanton and the two McLowrys. The trial was set for February 14, 1882.

Wyatt, Doc, and Morgan did not ignore the summons, but they were wearing their Federal badges when they reported to the sheriff in Tombstone. "You men are under arrest," Behan is supposed to have said. "Give me your guns and get into the buckboard. One of you'll drive. We'll ride behind."

"And herd us down the road where your friends can shoot us in the back?" Wyatt recalled asking. "Not much."

At about this time Colonel Herring led a band of vigilantes up to join the Earps, and Behan ceased to argue the point. He and his deputies formed one of the armed bands which walked into the courtroom at Contention, the prisoners and the vigilantes another. Herring took the initiative before the flabbergasted justice of the peace could get his bearings. "We're here for justice or a fight and ready for either," the lawyer was quoted as telling the court. "You haven't any more jurisdiction over this case than a jackrabbit. If there's any hearing, it'll be in Tombstone." Deciding that the case was too rich for his blood, the judge agreed.

By March, certainly, the U. S. Marshal's special posse had begun to function in earnest. With the aid of Federal warrants Earp was able to attack rustling operations — the real structure which was supporting the outlaw organization. Most of those who were caught in the dragnet, or who fled the county to escape it, were small fry; but at least two were not. Frank Stilwell and Pete Spence were again arrested and were bound over for investigation by the Federal grand jury in Tucson on March 21.

Several days before that they rode into Tombstone with the ostensible purpose of securing legal counsel. The next night murder struck from hiding in an alley in back of Allen Street. This time the victim was not merely wounded.

"Another assassination last night about eleven o'clock," Parsons wrote as part of his entry for March 19. "I heard the shots two in number. . . . Poor Morgan Earp was shot through by an unknown party. Probably 2 or 3 in number in Campbell and Hatch's while playing pool with Hatch. The shots, 2, came through the ground window leading into alley running to Fremont Street. . . . Geo. Berry received the spent ball in his thigh, sustaining a flesh wound. The second shot was fired apparently at Wyatt Earp. Murderers got away, of course, but it was and is quite evident who committed the deed. The man was Stilwell in all probability. . . . Morg lived about 40 minutes after being shot and died without a murmur. Bad times ahead now."

That was an understatement.

CHAPTER SEVENTEEN

THE BIG BLOW OFF

WYATT, who saw his brother shot down, left an exact account of the events leading up to Morgan's death. On March 18 the two Earps had taken the precaution of checking up on Stilwell, who was known to have foregathered with several other rustlers. The officers learned that the outlaws had ridden out of town and toward Tucson. The inference was that the robber meant to keep his date with the Federal grand jury.

That night Lingard's *Stolen Kisses* was on the boards at Schieffelin Hall. Wyatt and Morgan were in the audience. After the final curtain the former returned to his hotel, but the latter said he had arranged to play billiards with Bob Hatch, co-owner of Campbell and Hatch's pool hall, on the north side of Allen Street between Fourth and Fifth. Continuing to the Cosmopolitan, Wyatt got as far as his room when a premonition changed his mind. He replaced the boot he had taken off and walked back down Allen to Campbell and Hatch's. There he seated himself in one of the chairs along the wall to watch the match between Morgan and Bob.

The pool hall must have been bounded on two sides by alleys. Parsons mentioned one running from Allen to Fremont, and Wyatt stated that the rear door opened on an alley running through the block from Fifth to Fourth. The upper half of this exit was largely made up of four panes of glass, of which the lower two were painted over. The upper two panes, however, made it possible for anyone to peer in from the unlighted alley with little danger of being seen.

Hatch was sighting along his cue while Morgan stood by when both of these panes were shattered. Two revolvers fired. Morgan whirled, trying to get his own weapon, and collapsed. The bullet went through him to wound George Berry, who, by Wyatt's account, died instantly from the shock. A second bullet hit the wall just above Wyatt's head. Leaping across the room, Wyatt returned the fire, but it was blind shooting. The door was bolted, and it was some seconds before it could be opened. By the time that was done the fugitives were clear of the alley. The sound of booted feet running gave way to the sound of running horses.

Morgan's back was broken. After diagnosing his injury, he looked at his opponent at billiards. "I guess I've run out my string, Bob," he said. There was little more than time for James and Warren Earp to assist the still ailing Virgil to the spot, before Morgan was gone.

The coroner's jury in this case had no hesitation about affixing the guilt. Wyatt said that Dr. H. M. Matthews, the coroner, was furnished with evidence by the wife of Pete Spence, who had made the mistake of socking her just before he left home. At all events the finger of accusation was pointed at five men. "The finding of said jury," the report runs in part, "was that his death was caused, as they believe, from the effect of a gun shot or pistol wound on the night of March 18, 1882, by Peter Spence, Frank Stilwell, one John Doe Freeze and an Indian called Charlie and another Indian, name unknown."

In addition to those named by the coroner, Wyatt had reason to believe that Curly Bill and a man called Hank Swilling had some connection with the murder. J. B. Ayers had sent word from Charleston that these two had been seen with Stilwell, Spence and Indian Charlie before dawn, or within five or six hours of the crime. The word was that Stilwell, Swilling, and Spence had gone to Tucson, while Curly Bill and Indian Charlie had ridden toward the Dragoons.

Meanwhile Wyatt had made a series of linked decisions. He was going hunting for the men who had got Morgan. His aim was to arrest them, if they didn't resist, but he went on record as hoping that they would put up a fight. His urge to retaliate was doubtless sixty per cent hot vengeance, but the other forty per cent was cold common sense. To stay inactive was to wait around until he, like his brothers, was shot from ambush.

But before he could take the trail something had to be done about Virgil. He told his brother that he had to leave town, a course whose necessity had now become obvious. No one bearing the name of Earp was safe from assassination in Tombstone, especially one whose helplessness made him a sitting bird for ruthless potshotters. Virgil and his wife headed west for Colton, California, where the senior Earps were then living. On the same train was the corpse of Morgan.

Just when James Earp, the half brother crocked during the War between the States, left Tombstone is an open question, but it must have been at about that time. Warren Earp, the youngest brother, kept his post as a member of the U. S. Marshal's posse. Wyatt meant to lead that posse; but, knowing the men he was up against, he escorted Virgil as far as Tucson, where the train halted an hour for supper in a day when there were no dining cars. Doc Holliday went with Wyatt.

Just east of Tucson the train was halted and boarded by the deputy U. S. Marshal who made his headquarters in that town. This colleague of Earp's, a Joseph Evans, gave Wyatt the information that Stilwell, Spence, and an unknown half-breed had been joined in Tucson by Ike Clanton. Moreover, the rustlers had been receiving telegrams from Tombstone. Evans was sure that they knew the Earps were on the train.

Doc and Wyatt stood guard while Virgil and his wife ate supper, then Wyatt put his brother on the train again. By that time it was almost dark. As he was peering from the platform, to take a last look around before alighting, he caught a glimpse of gleaming metal westward in the shadows. Looking closer, he could make out that light from a car window was reflected from two barrels. In all there were four men crouching behind a flatcar parked on a siding not far ahead of the car in which Virgil was traveling. As soon as the train started, Virgil would be on display for them.

Wyatt figured he had a good chance of potting all of them with his double barreled shotgun but to make the shot while keeping covered by a corner of the car whose platform he was on necessitated shooting from the left shoulder. While he was maneuvering to assume the unwonted position necessary, he banged the barrels against the platform railing. The would be assassins heard the noise, and perhaps spotted Earp, for they fled from their ambuscade. Wyatt jumped to the ground and began stalking them.

The first man he ran across was dressed like a Mexican or Indian laborer. Earp passed by him in the semi-darkness, to learn later that he had lost a chance to bag Hank Swilling. The latter had changed from his normal cowman's garb to that of a peon and was the "unknown half-breed" Joe Evans had mentioned.

But if the smaller fish got away a big one did not. Wyatt had been heading west along the tracks toward the engine, and he saw a man dash through the beam thrown by the headlight. One of the other outlaws must have seen Wyatt as he darted in pursuit, for there were two rifle shots, and he heard bullets whiz by him. He kept on, though, and finally stopped the fugitive by threatening to shoot him in the back. The man who then turned to walk toward Wyatt was Frank Stilwell.

What happened next is as dramatic for what was not done as for what did occur. Earp reported Stilwell's actions without interpretation; but there is a strong possibility that what caught up with the outlaw to wilt him in the clutch was the close resemblance Wyatt is said to have borne to the man Frank had just murdered.

"His guns were in plain sight and I figured he'd jerk them," Wyatt said in giving a play by play account of what took place to Mr. Lake, his biographer. "As I got closer, his right hand started down, but quit halfway and he stood as if he was paralyzed. I never said a word. About three feet from Stilwell I stopped and looked at him. Then he lunged for me.

"Stilwell caught the barrel of my Wells, Fargo gun with both hands, his left hand uppermost, almost covering the muzzles, and the right hand well down. I've never forgotten the look in Frank Stilwell's eyes, or the expression that came over his face as he struggled for that gun.

"I forced the gun down until the muzzle of the right barrel was just underneath Stilwell's heart. I had not spoken to him, and did not at any time. But Stilwell found his voice. You'd guess a million times wrong without guessing what he said. I'll tell you, and you can make what you care to out of it. 'Morg!' he said, and then a second time, 'Morg!' I've often wondered what made him say that."

"What happend then?" Mr. Lake asked.

"I let him have it," Wyatt answered. "The muzzle of one barrel, as I've told you, was just underneath his heart. He got the second before he hit the ground."

Holliday and Earp vainly looked for Ike Clanton, Spence, and Swilling before they caught one freight train east to Benson, and another south to Contention City. There they picked up the rest of their posse, consisting of Turkey Creek Jack Johnson, Warren Earp, Texas Jack Vermilion, and Sherman McMasters. Before setting out again Doc and Wyatt had to have some rest. Moreover, Wyatt suspected that there would be repercussions of what had happened in Tucson which could best be handled on the spot. He ordered a return to Tombstone.

The slaying of Stilwell in Pima County had indeed caused an uproar. The citizens of Tucson had naturally resented having Tombstone's feuds settled in its streets. *The Star* carried an indignant story, and prophesied that Sheriff Bob Paul, then out of town, would make a speedy arrest.

Tombstone, or at least that part of it which was fighting the rustler-county politician team, rejoiced over the demise of Stilwell as strongly as Tucson deplored the incident. ". . . tonight came news," Parsons noted, "of Frank Stilwell's body being found riddled with bullets. . . . A quick vengeance and a bad character sent to Hell where he will be the chief attraction until a few more accompany him."

The Last Chance

Now the Tucson policemen who had found Stilwell had not named any slayer, and, indeed, probably had no specific evidence on which to go. It remained for the indefatigable Ike Clanton to put the finger on Wyatt. Ike waited around until Sheriff Paul returned, and then swore out a warrant, charging Earp with murder. When this had been done, he wired Behan so that he could make the arrest.

It so happened that the telegrapher who received the message in Tombstone was a member of the Law and Order League. Before delivering the message to Behan, therefore, he went to the Cosmopolitan to tell Earp what was afoot. Wyatt asked the operator to hold the message until he had time to make certain preparations.

His position was a ticklish one. An officer of the law who finds it necessary to kill in the line of duty must be prepared to answer for his act when called upon. A refusal would at least jeopardize his office as a deputy U.S. marshal, and he wanted that authority when he hunted out Morgan's other assassins. On the other hand, if he went to Pima County for a protracted trial the men he was after might take occasion to leave Arizona with no forwarding address. He decided to bank on the good will and understanding of Sheriff Paul.

That he made no mistake in so doing was subsequently attested by Parsons. "Paul is here — but he will not take a hand. He is a true — brave man and will not join the murderous posse here. If the truth were known he would be glad to see the Earp party get away with all these murder charges."

To appreciate Paul's attitude it should be borne in mind that he had acted as stage coach guard when Bud Philpot was killed by Crane *et al*. He had also been a member of Wyatt's posse, the one which had captured one of the bandits only to have Behan let him escape. Consequently he knew a great deal about both the outlaw organization in Cochise County and the proclivities of its sheriff.

It was with these facts in mind that Wyatt told his attorney,

The Big Blow Off

Colonel Herring: "You telegraph Bob Paul I'll surrender to him any time." He then went on to make a final disposition of his local affairs. He had decided to leave Tombstone — where it was only a question of on which day he would be shot in the back; although he was by no means through with Cochise County yet.

The five members of his special posse had been summoned. By the time they arrived with word that their horses were saddled, with a rifle at every saddle, Wyatt was ready to release the message demanding his arrest for delivery to Behan. Then he ordered supper to be sent up to his room.

While they were eating Bilicke, the owner of the Cosmopolitan, entered to tell them that Behan and Neagle, the town marshal, were in the lobby. Outside on Allen Street there were eight armed deputies.

"Colonel," Wyatt said to his lawyer, "you'd better wait up here until this is over."

"Not I," Herring was quoted as answering. "I want to see this."

The posse descended the stairs, Wyatt and Herring in front. Holliday, Warren Earp, Vermilion, McMasters, and Johnson trailed them. All were armed with two revolvers apiece, and all were carrying shotguns, with the exception of Holliday, who was not fond of the weapon.

As it turned out, there was not as much to see as Herring had seemingly wished. Neagle approached Wyatt as the latter reached the bottom step, seeking to act as an intermediary for Behan. Wyatt gave him the brush off. Outside, the marshal's posse leisurely strolled toward their horses, ignoring the armed deputies.

Breakenridge, who was one of them, wrote in years to come that the Earp party had hastened out of town while the sheriff's men were scrambling around for their weapons. Why they had not worn such weapons to begin with is explained neither by him nor by the concurring *Nugget*.

Clum had a different account of the departure of the marshal's posse. "As they were about to leave Tombstone," he wrote, "Sheriff Behan appeared and said, 'Wyatt, I want to see you.' Wyatt calmly replied, 'Johnny, you may see me once too often.' No arrests were made."

If this account was also written at the remove of several decades, Parsons' on-the-spot report emphasizes even more strongly the deliberation with which Wyatt and the others left town. "Exciting times again this evening. The Earp party returned this afternoon and Behan tried to arrest him tonight upon a telegram. They refused arrest and retired from town, first though waiting for Sheriff and Neagle to do what they threatened. . . . Sheriff is awake now that one of his friends is killed. Couldn't do anything before. Things are rotten in that office."

If Behan had been anxious to make the arrest at all costs, he wouldn't have had to ride far. Earp and his men bivouacked just two miles out of Tombstone, ready to hit the saddle at daylight. Before they turned in Wyatt received one more report from the coroner's jury which had weighed the case of his brother's death. Follow-up investigation had established the fact that Hank Swilling had been an active agent in the conspiracy to assassinate Morgan. Furthermore the man called Indian Charlie in the initial report had been identified as a half-breed called Florentino Cruz. Wyatt carried this information in the back of his mind when he led his posse for a raid on Pete Spence's ranch.

Spence had taken thought not to be at home, but among several who were present there was a peon who took off for the small timber covering the side of a butte. McMasters, a crack shot with a rifle, halted this flight by nicking the man. Earp still wasn't sure of his identity, but McMasters could speak Spanish almost as well as he could shoot. Under his questioning Cruz admitted his name and his complicity in the plot against Morgan. He also had a great deal to say about the attempts on the lives of Clum and Virgil Earp.

In addition to Stilwell, whom Clum had always suspected, Cruz, alias Indian Charlie, named Ike and Phin Clanton, Johnny Ringo, Curly Bill, Claiborne, and Swilling as the men involved in the assault on the mayor. According to him, Ringo, Stilwell, Ike Clanton, Swilling, and an unknown fifth party had shot Virgil. He also mentioned a case, referred to by Breakenridge, when Stilwell and Ike had tried to ambush Holliday.

Cruz' part in the attack on Morgan had, he first claimed, only been that of a lookout. The business had been plotted by Brocius, Ringo, Stilwell, and Ike Clanton. Curly Bill, Stilwell, and Swilling had been the ones who had gone into the alley as trigger men. The John Doe Freeze cited in the coroner's report had acted as spotter. Ringo, keeping watch on the Fremont Street corner flanking the exit from the alley, had held the horses. Spence and Cruz had stood guard at the Allen Street side.

Earp was inclined to let the half-breed go as a more or less harmless tool of the others. About the time he had reached that decision, however, he asked Indian Charlie one more question. "Neither of my brothers nor I ever harmed you, did we?"

"No," Cruz said.

"Then what," Wyatt wanted to know, "made you help kill my brother?"

Sensing that he was about to go free, Cruz had become more voluble. "Curly Bill, Frank Stilwell, Ike Clanton, John Ringo, they're my friends. They said we'd all make money if you were out of the way, and Curly Bill, he gave me twenty-five dollars."

"For what?"

"For shooting anybody who interfered while he killed the Earps," Indian Charlie replied.

It was this that changed Wyatt's mind about being lenient. "That twenty-five dollar business," he later declared, "just about burned me up."

Maybe an officer shouldn't have acted as Earp then did, but it was an era and locality in which a man's right to direct action hadn't been limited by the unemotional conscience of society. He told McMasters to let Cruz know that he was in for a duel. The terms offered were that the half-breed, who wore two revolvers, could begin drawing right away. Wyatt, on the contrary, would not reach for his gun until he had counted three in Spanish. If Cruz won, he would be allowed to go his way unmolested.

The Last Chance

That looked good to Indian Charlie. His gun was free of its holster before "Tres!" was said; but before he could level the weapon Wyatt drew and drilled him.

That night the marshal and his men again returned to the outskirts of Tombstone for a conference with leaders of the Citizens Safety Committee. Behan had not been idle. What's more he had finally come out into the open as regards his alliance with the outlaws. To start with he had appointed Curly Bill a deputy in charge of a posse which had orders to arrest the Earps or shoot them on sight for the murder of Stilwell. With Brocius rode Pony Deal, Johnny Barnes, Rattlesnake Bill Johnson, Frank Patterson, those fugitives from the Cochise County Jail, the Hicks brothers, and two or three other rustlers. Behan himself had gone forth with another posse, whose nature was sufficiently indicated by Parsons in his entry of March 22. "Excitement again this morning. Sheriff went out with a posse supposedly to arrest the Earp party. . . The cow-boy element is backing him strongly. John Ringo being one of the party."

In taking this course Behan was acting with complete independence, for Paul had not yet pressed charges on behalf of Pima County. Without a request for assistance by Paul, Behan had no authority, as the killing had taken place out of his sphere of jurisdiction. He had, in fact, decreed that men for whom he had no warrant could be shot on sight.

The situation thus created was startling even for the upper San Pedro Valley. On the one hand there was the posse of the Deputy U.S. Marshal for the Tombstone district, legally deputized by the marshal of the territory. These men had been given Federal warrants of arrest for certain known lawbreakers. Yet by the order of a sheriff, backed by no other authority, the members of this posse had been made outlaws in so far as Cochise County was concerned. Deputized to hunt them down were the very men whose names were written on warrants in Wyatt Earp's possession.

So on both sides the seekers were the sought for, as both sides maneuvered for a showdown. Curly Bill, according to the information passed on to Earp, had been given the job of sweeping the west side of the valley. Specifically he was supposed to have headed for the Babocomari sector of the Whetstones. Before the sheriff returned from his first vain pursuit of the marshal, Earp was off across the river in hopes of meeting Brocius. For the guidance of vigilante representatives, who were to follow with messages and certain needed funds, he selected Iron Springs as a rendezvous. This is called Mescal Springs on later maps.

Nearing the oasis in question at the end of a thirty-five mile ride, the marshal's men were tired. The heat made them sleepy, and as they had seen no fresh horse tracks, they allowed themselves to drowse in the saddle. Only Wyatt, stimulated by his fixity of purpose, was fully awake. The approach to the water hole was accomplished without incident, but Earp had the uneasy feeling that trouble was handy. To be in a better position to shoot, if he was right, he dismounted. Then he advanced, thrusting his left arm through the reins in a way that left the hand free to catch at the shotgun he carried in his right.

Still no one challenged him. It was not until he was close enough to look into the hollow cupping of the springs that two men sprang up. Only the fact that they too were taken by surprise saved the life of Wyatt, as well as of McMasters and Vermilion, who were riding close behind him. As things stood, one of them was swift to bring the double-barreled shotgun he held into action. It was Curly Bill.

Coming out of their doze, the other posse members thought they had been ambushed, and they reacted like the experienced men they were. Men on horseback had no business staying in the neighborhood of men with the advantage of shooting from the ground. Warren Earp had been left back at a fork in the trail to await the vigilante messengers, but McMasters, Vermilion, Johnson, and Holliday wheeled and scattered.

Wyatt, however, was not on horseback; he, like the rustler, held a shotgun at the ready, and Brocius was the leader of the men who had killed Morgan. Earp brought his gun to his shoulder, and lived to tell what the moment was like. "I can see Curly Bill's left eye squinted shut," he recalled years later, "and his right eye sighting over that shotgun at me to this day, and I remember thinking, as I felt my coat jerk with his fire, 'He missed me; I can't miss him, but I'll give him both barrels to make sure.' I saw the Wells, Fargo plate on the gun Curly Bill was using and I saw the ivory butts of Jim Hume's pet six-guns in Hume's fancy holsters at Curly Bill's waist as clearly as could be. I recognized Pony Deal, and as seven others broke for the cottonwoods, I named each one as he ran, saying to myself, 'I've got a warrant for him. . . .' "

Taking a little more time than Curly Bill had done, Wyatt did not miss. Both loads from his shotgun, nine balls to the load, hit Brocius in the chest and nearly ripped him apart. That, as the sagas would put it, was his death wound.

Thereafter Earp was alternately engaged in exchanging shots with Curly Bill's men, who had been rallied by Pony Deal, and trying to climb on his panicky horse for a getaway. Groans indicated that he had scored twice more, and he was under the mistaken impression that he had been grazed himself. Yet he finally did mount, only to discover a complication. Vermilion's horse had been killed, and Texas Jack was too stubborn to abandon his weapons and saddle. He was retreating with his impedimenta under cover of Earp's fire when Holliday returned to pick Vermilion up.

Reorganized, the posse members were ready for a counter attack, but Wyatt clamped a veto on that. The position of the rustlers, now dug in amongst the trees surrounding the water hole, was too advantageous. In consequence the Earp party retired without reaching Iron Springs. To that extent they may be said to have lost the battle where they yet scored their most decisive blow. Curly Bill had fallen — a disaster from which outlawry in Cochise County never recovered. Nevertheless, there were still quite a few quills left in that porcupine.

CHAPTER EIGHTEEN

THE PRESIDENT SPEAKS

THROUGHOUT the war between the local titans of law and disorder
the part played by the citizenry of Tombstone should not be overlooked. The town was wracked with intrigue and kept in a per-
petual state of alarm. The vigilantes stood to arms as an all-out
attack on the city by the rustlers was predicted. There was espionage and counter espionage. Within Tombstone nothing was
done by either party which wasn't soon reported to the other. In
the smaller towns and on the range faithful partisans were keeping watch. The telegraph wires were busy, and horseback couriers
dashed all over the place.

Or sometimes they didn't get to go. The two vigilante messengers who were to have met the Earps at Iron Springs were
called Tipton and Smith. Parsons noted with great indignation
that they had been arrested by Behan, who had returned to town
after his first fruitless search for Wyatt and the rest. In the absence
of charges Behan had to let Tipton and Smith go, but he released
them only after their usefulness as couriers had been temporarily
canceled. Meanwhile two other men named Wright and Craker
had set out for the Whetstones.

They did not, of course, meet the Earps at Iron Springs; they
found the rustlers there instead. However, the pair had been
picked because they were unknown to the outlaws, who mistook
them for teamsters engaged in trying to round up some mules they
had lost. Two of the rustlers had been wounded and one of them
was dead. If Craker and Wright were not themselves well known,
they yet easily identified one of the region's men of mark. In the
dead man they recognized Curly Bill Brocius.

The vigilante messengers were not the first to bring the word
about Brocius back to town, because they spent a couple of days
scouring the Whetstones for Wyatt and the others before they

returned. By then the marshal's posse had once more bivouacked near the city for a counsel with vigilante leaders; and Behan had once more charged out in pursuit. But it seems probable, so excellent was the liaison, that a number of men had reported Wyatt's exploit before he could do so.

Tombstone reacted characteristically to the news of Curly Bill's death, which is to say that half of it rejoiced and half chose not to believe it. The newspapers printed divergent accounts — both by avowed eye-witnesses — of what had taken place. *The Epitaph* had positive inside information that the outlaw leader had been killed. *The Nugget* conceded that Wyatt had stood his ground to exchange quite a few shots with Curly Bill's men, but maintained that nobody had been injured.

As to this day partisans of the anti-Earp faction pooh-pooh the statement that Wyatt killed the outlaw leader, a marshaling of the ascertainable facts is pertinent here. They are four in number. Item, by the agreement of everybody a fight did take place at Iron Springs on the date specified, March 23, 1882, between Wyatt Earp's special posse and certain rustlers. Wyatt fired a number of shots at his opponents at close range. Item, Curly Bill had been consistently active in Cochise County up to the very time of the engagement in question. Curly Bill was never seen in those parts again.

Available documents permit assessing the above facts in the light of a quantity of indirect evidence. The fragmentary newspaper files make the earliest date of references to the incident a problematical one. In what is avowedly a follow-up story *The Epitaph* of March 27, 1882, offered the report of a man who claimed he had been approaching Iron Springs from a height overlooking the oasis when the skirmish commenced before his eyes. Pursuant to summarizing a somewhat florid account of the affair, the story continued: "After the road was clear our informant rode on and came upon the dead man who — from the description given — was none other than Curly Bill. . . . Since the above information was obtained it has been learned that during the night the friends of Curly Bill went out with a wagon and took the body back to Charleston, where the whole affair has been kept a profound secret, so far as the general public is concerned." By way of giving both sides a hearing, *The Epitaph* quoted an account which had appeared in *The Nugget*. This report was remarkably like the one which Earp himself subsequently wrote, except for one significant detail. Wyatt's bullets injured no one.

Clum, incomparably the best newspaperman in the Tombstone of the day, retained an unshaken conviction that Brocius was killed by Wyatt. He declared as much in an article written as late as 1929. He did not say how early he received a report on the slaying; but Parsons had word of it within about 48 hours of the event.

"I got strictly private news," he wrote on March 25, "that 'Curly Bill' has been killed at last — by the Earp party and none of the latter hurt. Sheriff Behan has turned all of the cow-boys loose against the Earps and with this lawless element is trying to do his worst. I am heartily glad at this repulse and hope the killing is not stopped with the cut-throat named."

The rustler-politico spokesmen were emphatic about denying the story, although they did not accept *The Epitaph's* challenge to disprove it by the simple method of producing Curly Bill on the hoof. Instead they turned up with the statement that Brocius had been in Mexico for two months past. The men who had fired upon the marshal's posse at Iron Springs were two rustlers with guilty consciences about a robbery in Charleston.

Reasons for urgency in refuting the report of Curly Bill's decease can be easily imagined. His prestige was such that news of his slaying would frighten and dishearten the small change rustlers which supported the outlaw gang proper. On the other hand many small ranchers who had accepted the bullying of Brocius' men would be encouraged to revolt. Thus the loss of Curly Bill could not be conveniently admitted until a new leader — taking over while the old one was supposedly on leave — had established his dominance. Johnny Ringo may or may not have been the brains of the mob, but Brocius was the body. His boister-ous good fellowship combined with his daring, enterprise, and skill with a gun made him a natural chieftain for outlaws of the range. Parsons observed that young outlaws conducted themselves toward Curly Bill like squires given the privilege of attending royalty. A man who can inspire such an attitude is not easily replaced.

But his followers insisted he had gone to Mexico on unnamed business. As he did not rejoin them, the assumption would be that he had abdicated. Why should he have done so at the very time his organization was most successful? For up until the moment of his disappearance the outlaws had the upper hand in the war of attrition with the Earps. Curly Bill's men enjoyed the protection of county officialdom for every act of stock thieving and highway robbery, and their leader was prospering accord-ingly. In view of these facts a motive for his defection is essential to its acceptance, and a likely motive was never produced.

If he was never again seen in Tombstone, Charleston, Galey-ville, and points in between, was he ever seen elsewhere? Nobody ever saw him again with his own eyes, although people who had met somebody who had just seen Curly Bill turned up with the regularity of people who have met somebody who has just seen Judge Crater. And, as in the case of Judge Crater, it was always apt to have been in a different place from the last reported locale. Curly Bill was in New Mexico, Colorado, Wyoming, and Montana. Only once — a good many years later — was he ever in Cochise County again. Breakenridge knew somebody who had just missed seeing Brocius in Benson, when Curly Bill had stepped off a train there for a hurried visit with an old friend.

But could the most notorious outlaw in Arizona go to some other section of the nation without leaving his mark? He could, and for disappointing reasons. One man was told by someone who had seen Curly Bill that he was a changed man when he returned from Mexico. He had foresworn his wicked ways and planned to settle down in Wyoming as a peaceful citizen.

The President Speaks

If all the statements in favor of Curly Bill's survival do not combine to make hogwash, they form something indistinguishable from that commodity. What bird of prey ever left his quarry before the fear of God was administered with a bludgeon? As far as this chronicle is concerned, William Brocius Graham died from shotgun wounds at Iron Springs in the Whetstones.

It is noteworthy that when *The Epitaph* reported the fight, it gave the locality as Burleigh Springs, on the east side of the San Pedro and up the valley from Tombstone. This was done to mislead Behan and to help the Earps to give his large posse the slip.

But the sheriff had a good intelligence service, too. He learned that Wyatt and the rest were in the offing and set out after them a third time. Meanwhile Bob Paul, after having waited as long as he could, finally responded to pressure by arriving in Tombstone with warrants for Wyatt and Doc on the Stilwell killing. When he saw the men whom Behan had enlisted as special deputies, though, he refused to join them. Parsons flatly stated as much, *The Epitaph* concurring. "Sheriff Paul, of Tucson, returned to that city. He refused to go after the Earps, because the posse selected by Behan was notoriously hostile to the Earps, and said that a meeting with them meant blood, with no probability of arrest."

The posse members referred to were what *The Nugget* styled "a brave posse of honest ranchmen." Ike Clanton was one and Johnny Ringo was another. Still others were Phin Clanton, Frank Patterson, Pony Deal, Rattlesnake Bill Johnson, and Hank Swilling. The total was over twenty, and of the lot the only regular deputy was Harry Woods, publisher of *The Nugget*. Breakenridge remarked that he was supposed to go along but refused to do so when Behan turned his horse and equipment over to Ringo. Why Johnny did not have his own was not explained. Probably the truth was the business smelled too bad for a cagey man to want a part of it.

However that may have been, Behan again moved against the

Earps without legal sanction. Sheriff Paul of Pima County, for whom he was supposedly acting, had the warrants for Wyatt and Doc in his pocket when he turned back to Tucson.

When Earp and his associates left the vicinity of Tombstone, they had headed north on a tip from the vigilantes. This was to the effect that Swilling might be nabbed. The latter had again gone to Tucson, this time in the capacity of an additional eye-witness to Stilwell's slaying. The purpose was to prod Paul into ordering the arrest of Earp and Holliday. It seems probable that Paul was already on his way to Tombstone; at any rate the outlaw did not return to Cochise County in his company. Word was sent from Tucson that Swilling had bought a ticket for San Simon, close to the New Mexican boundary, and it was to intercept him that the marshal's posse had taken to the saddle. Wyatt boarded the right train at the medial point of Dragoon Summit, but counter intelligence had been on the job. A rustler partisan had got on at Benson to warn Hank of what was afoot. Swilling promptly got off and rode to join Behan in the hunting of his enemy.

After being disappointed at Dragoon Summit, Wyatt led his men to the Sierra Bonita Ranch of Colonel Henry Hooker, there to await the next messenger from the Citizens' Safety Committee. As president of the Arizona Cattlemen's Association, Hooker was naturally a supporter of Earp's in his struggle against the rustlers. The marshal and his men were warmly welcomed; and they were still enjoying the colonel's hospitality the following evening. At that point one of Hooker's men reported that Behan's posse had been sighted. The colonel offered Earp reinforcements in the shape of his crew of tough cowhands, but Wyatt refused the aid. Instead he withdrew to a nearby hill called Reilley's Butte.

Having camped out no great distance away, the sheriff rode up the next morning to demand the whereabouts of the deputy U.S. marshal. What followed is given in *The Epitaph* of April 10, 1882. Quoting a letter sent from Willcox on April 4th, the paper was in the position of being able to say exactly what it thought of Behan without editorializing. The correspondent had been visiting at the Sierra Bonita when Behan arrived and was a pleased auditor of the conversation between Colonel Hooker and the sheriff. *The Nugget* was to quote Behan to the effect that the colonel had been strangely uncooperative, which was putting it mildly.

The old Sierra Bonita Ranch, of which pictures still exist, was at once a manor and a fortress, and in it Hooker was a baron in his hall. He owned more land than most well-to-do medieval dukes. On it his word was the only word, and blustering sheriffs didn't intimidate him in the least. When Behan asked where the Earps had gone he replied that if he knew he wouldn't tell him.

The other retaliated by warning the colonel that he was putting himself in the position of sheltering murderers and outlaws from officers of the law. That set Hooker off, and he gave Behan both barrels. "I know the Earps and I know you; and I know they have always treated me like gentlemen; damn such laws and damn you and damn your posse; they are a set of horsethieves and outlaws."

"At this," the account went on to say, "one of the 'honest farmers'? of the posse spoke up and said 'damn the son of a b——, he knows where they are, and let us make him tell.' At this Hooker's hostler stepped away for a moment and returned with a Winchester, and drawing a bead on the honest granger said, 'you can't come here into a gentleman's yard and call him a son of a b——! now you skin it back! skin it back! If you are looking for a fight, and come here to talk that way you can get it before you find the Earps; you can get it right here.' . . ."

Behan next had the gall to ask the United States Army to attack Federal officers on the authority of a county sheriff. Specifically he wanted to borrow some Apache scouts and give them the unusual pleasure of going on the warpath against pale faces with the blessings of white officials. *The Nugget* reported that Behan didn't get the scouts because they were on duty elsewhere, but *The Epitaph's* correspondent wrote that Colonel Biddle, in command at Fort Grant, had told the sheriff to go chase himself.

From his camp on Reilley's Butte Wyatt saw the sheriff's posse ride back past Sierra Bonita on the return trip to Tombstone. As Earp observed in a dispatch he sent to *The Epitaph*: "Our stay was long enough to notice the movements of Sheriff Behan and his posse of honest ranchers, with whom — had they possessed the trailing abilities of the average Arizona ranchman — we might have had trouble. . . ."

Wyatt then had six men with him, including Dan Tipton, who had this time succeeded in serving as a messenger from the vigilantes. Behan had twenty deputies; but it may well have been more than the guns and the advantageous position of the marshal's men which made him decide to withdraw. No doubt he, too, had been followed by couriers, and the news they must have brought him gave him much to think about.

To begin with, the sheriff and the Earps had hardly taken their feud north out of gunshot when Tombstone had a new and unrelated series of killings to talk about. These had not been completed when the new governor of the territory paid a visit to Arizona's metropolis.

By virtue of its origins the second event has chronological precedence. Acting-Governor Gosper had, as previously related, used his time in office to launch an attack on territorial outlawry. In particular he had singled out, as he could hardly have failed to do, conditions in Cochise County. It was he who had approved the intervention of the U.S. Marshal in county affairs and the resultant appointment of Earp's special posse. He had also made an effort to arouse public opinion against the criminals. For, and quite rightly, he placed the blame not only on the rustlers and a corrupt officialdom but on citizens willing to play footie with those social elements.

"The people of Tombstone and Cochise County," he put it to them in an official statement, "in their mad career after money have grossly neglected self government until the lazy and lawless element have taken to prey upon the more industrious and honorable classes. . . ." After printing the remark *The Epitaph* enlarged upon it with a combination of further remarks of Gosper and editorial comment. "The acting governor estimates the whole number of cow-boys, which term, he says, includes skilled cattle thieves and highway robbers, in the county of Cochise, where most of the trouble has occurred, from twenty-five to fifty. . . . Besides the cow-boys there is a class much larger in numbers, of the 'good-Lord and good-devil' kind, which keep up a secret partnership with the robbers and profit by their lawlessness."

This attempt of a higher echelon of government to take a hand in its affairs was a new thing for the county of which Tombstone was the seat. That horse had never learned what a saddle was, and paid no heed to the suggestion that such a thing might be imposed upon it. Things went on in the upper San Pedro as before, even after — following representations from Gosper — President Arthur referred rebukingly to the activities of Southwestern citizens described as cowboys in a message to congress.

But Gosper, a stand-in merely, could not pull the weight of a full fledged governor. In due time Arthur appointed F. A. Tritle, a resident of Nevada, to fill that post. The latter took office on March 8, 1882. Tritle had no doubt already been posted on conditions within the territory by Gosper. The governor had hardly had time to warm the gubernatorial chair when Tombstone exploded with the assassination of Morgan Earp. When further dispatches reporting blood and sudden death reached Prescott from Cochise County, Tritle decided to go south and investigate.

Tombstone could not have been an anticlimax to the new governor's expectations.The local papers were lively with accounts of the pursuit of a Federal officer's posse by a sheriff abetted by known outlaws. All the other papers of the territory were broadcasting the scandalous state of affairs. The day after Tritle's arrival, for instance, the Tucson *Star* summed up what was going on in the following words: "The officials of Cochise County, with all the available strength which they can muster, seem to avail nothing in putting down the blood-thirsty class infesting that county. Ex-city and United States officials have taken to the hills as so many Apaches. A lot of loose marauding thieves are scouring the country, killing good, industrious citizens for plunder. . . ."

That very thing had taken place the day before Arizona's chief executive reached the upper San Pedro. Even Tombstone was shocked when M. R. Peel, a young employee of the Tombstone Mining and Milling Co., had been shot down in cold blood at Charleston. The apparent motive had been the robbery of a company safe, although the slayers lost their nerve and fled when their victim fell.

It therefore happened that *The Epitaph* carried a bitter message from the dead youngster's father on the day of the governor's arrival in Tombstone. Addressed to his fellow residents of the community, it took the following form: "Perhaps I am not in a condition to express a clear, deliberate opinion, but I would say to the good citizens of Cochise county there is one of three things you have to do. There is a class of cut-throats among you and you can never convict them in court. You must combine and protect yourselves and wipe them out, or you must give up the country to them, or you will be murdered one at a time, as my son has been. — B. L. Peel."

With the governor in town the sheriff's office had to take action for once, and Breakenridge set out when news was received of the whereabouts of the killers. He wrote in his autobiography that he wanted to go alone, probably anticipating the same cooperation he had generally received from the outlaws. Feeling was running high, though, and a volunteer posse of three men named Allen, Young, and Gillespie respectively, insisted on going with him.

The two suspects were Zwing Hunt, of the traditional fine family, and another young hellion named Billy Grounds. This last was reputed to have been a special protege of Curly Bill. Both had records as trigger men.

Word was sent that the pair had holed up in a ranch house not far from Charleston. The four posse members, according to Breakenridge's account, reached the place before dawn of the next day. Of the house's two doors Gillespie and Young were detailed to cover the one in the rear. The deputy sheriff and Allen advanced toward the front entrance.

Breakenridge had been right. There would have been no trouble, if he correctly reported a statement made to him by one of the murderers. "Hunt told me that they thought it was the Earp party after them, and if he had known who it was, he would not have made a fight." But before the deputy got a chance to introduce the subject of arrest gently, two of his posse undertook to play it tough. One, at least, didn't repeat the mistake.

Gillespie pounded on the back door, demanding surrender, whereupon Hunt stuck a rifle barrel out, killed Gillespie, and put Young hors de combat with a shot in the leg. Grounds also began shooting, knicking Allen in the neck and momentarily knocking him out. In return Breakenridge let drive with a shotgun and scored. At Grounds' yell of agony Hunt came running around the house from the back door. Allen had by then snapped out of it. He and Breakenridge both fired at the rustler. The latter had enough, but his wounds didn't permit a getaway.

Governor Tritle, then, could have seen, and very possibly did see at first hand, the sort of thing that was enabling Tombstone to make the headlines throughout the territory and beyond its boundaries. Six men entered town of whom only Breakenridge was hale enough to straddle a horse. In the wagon he was convoying were one dead and two wounded posse members and two badly shot up bandits.

Tritle had already been in conference with members of the Citizens' Safety Committee before this last development. Under March 27, Parsons jotted in his journal: "Governor Tritle arrived today and Milton and I met him. He took him to his house while I notified the reception committee and looked after the Gov's baggage. . . . This afternoon there was a confab and consultation on law touching matters of great interest to this part of the country. Hope some immediate steps will be taken. . . ."

He was not to be disappointed. What the governor had learned in Tombstone had convinced him of two things. One was the need for prompt and decisive action. The other was that the existing resources of Arizona Territory were inadequate for the emergency. Upon his return to Prescott, in consequence, he drafted an urgent appeal to Chester A. Arthur, President of the United States. What he requested was the authority to create a special force of territorial police, together with the funds necessary to equip and maintain it.

As it turned out, President Arthur shortly heard what was going on in the San Pedro Valley and points east from another prominent official. General William Tecumseh Sherman had been making a tour of the West, and he spent several days in Tombstone. As commanding general of the army, he was chiefly concerned by a local practice which affected international relations. He wrote to notify the nation's chief executive that southeastern Arizona was being used as a base for raids into Mexico.

The president was so stirred by these two communications that he prepared a special message for both houses of Congress. It was delivered April 26, 1882.

"By recent information received from official and other sources, I am advised that an alarming state of disorder continues to exist within the Territory of Arizona, and that lawlessness has already gained such headway there as to require a resort to extraordinary measures to repress it.

"The governor of the territory under the date of the 31st ultimo reports that violence and anarchy prevail, particularly in Cochise County and along the Mexican border; that robbery, murder, and resistance to law have become so common as to cease causing surprise, and that the people are greatly intimidated and losing confidence in the protection of the law. . . ."

Noting that Tritle had advocated raising a state militia to deal with the situation, the president gave it as his opinion that this would not be a strong enough measure. "On the ground of economy as well as effectiveness, however, it appears to me to be more advisable to permit the co-operation with the civil authorities of a part of the army as a posse comitatus."

CHAPTER NINETEEN

THE RING AND THE EPITAPH

THAT message had not been written when Behan returned from his visits to Sierra Bonita and Fort Grant. All that the sheriff knew for certain was that the governor had been in conference with the vigilantes and that reforms had been promised. He and his colleagues were by no means crushed, but they apparently decided to wait and see what would happen. Behan's posse was disbanded, in spite of the fact that the Earps re-entered the county.

If this was not a complete defeat for the politicos, it was a set-back of a critical nature for the outlaws. They had not had an opportunity to reorganize after the death of Curly Bill. They had so far failed in disposing of the Earps that the latter were again taking the offensive. The sheriff had withdrawn his public support. Probably undercover advice was for the rustlers to lay off and make themselves inconspicuous. In any case such prominent ones as John Ringo, Ike Clanton, Hank Swilling, and Pony Deal crossed into Mexico.

This left the lesser outlaws and their semi-pro hangers-on without leadership. The deputy U. S. Marshal's special posse swept the Sulphur Springs Valley without meeting serious opposition. If its members didn't find the key figures for whom they were really looking, they gave religion to many a lesser malefactor, some of whom left the country in anticipation of a visit. By definition gangsters only flourish in gangs. Individually these felt too lonesome to like it when Wyatt read them the riot act. The end result was demoralization such as only a first class leader could have repaired.

This was the more true because some of the top flight outlaws were pulling in their horns. As soon as he heard that Wyatt had returned to the county, Pete Spence fled to Tombstone and Behan. Still feeling insecure, he finally gave himself up to the Federal authorities. According to King he got the protection he was looking for, having been sentenced to two or three years in the penitentiary at Yuma.

Earlier Joe Hill had resigned from outlaw counsels and sought an amnesty with Wyatt by turning informer. Moreover, he got killed, when his horse fell with him, before he could backslide.

The news was not good from any direction. The grape vine brought the word up from Mexico that Hank Swilling had been shot to death in the course of a raid on a Mexican trading post. Then it was reported from Charleston that Johnny Barnes had crossed the San Pedro from where he had taken refuge after the fight at Iron Springs. Improperly cared for, the wound Wyatt had given him had festered. He was dying when he asked the popular saloon keeper, J. B. Ayers, to give him a bed. And he had the strange but common urge of the dying to clear the books before they were closed forever. When he started confessing things to Ayers, the latter sent for his Wells, Fargo superior, Fred Dodge.

The identity of Dodge as a secret express company operative was established not only by Earp but by Clum, who wrote that Dodge was still alive as late as 1929. He thus survived to tell Wyatt's biographer, Stuart Lake, what Barnes had said to him while on his death-bed. Among much that was old stuff there were surprise revelations. He had, for example, been the unknown fifth man of the party which had bushwhacked Virgil Earp. He told of the death of Curly Bill and confirmed the opinion of Craker and Wright that Brocius had been taken to Frank Patterson's ranch for burial.

Subsequently the Wells, Fargo detective pumped Ike Clanton about what had happened at Iron Springs. "Later on Ike Clanton," Dodge wrote to Lake, "who was not in the fight, although his knowledge of it was as good as if he had been, told me all about the whole thing, and his account was the same as Johnny Barnes'...."

The whereabouts of Phin Clanton, Billy Claiborne, and Patterson at this time are nowhere recorded, although it is safe to assume that they took their cue from Ringo, Ike, and Pony Deal. It is improbable that any rustler of note was astir in the county when the Earp party rode to the outskirts of Tombstone for a final conference with representatives of the Citizens' Safety Committee towards the last of April.

The Pima County charges were still hanging over Doc and Wyatt. These, they felt, could be met of themselves; but they feared the state-wide political clique of which the Cochise County group was merely the boldest and most open. In the event that they beat the original rap, a court order might easily be secured by their enemies to have them transferred to the custody of Behan on any charge he might advance. Once in that vindictive sheriff's power they could not, they felt, expect to reach Tombstone alive.

Legal members of the vigilantes came up with a solution of the problem. They advocated going to a neighboring state, thence to send word to Governor Tritle that they would abide extradition proceedings. Thus the validity of the charges against Earp and Holliday would be a matter of territorial, rather than merely county, record. Recognizing the soundness of the counsel, Wyatt elected to go to Colorado. Making a last-minute search for outlaws on the way, he once more led his posse out of Cochise County. Nor did he see Allen Street again.

However, with the Earps afield and the rustlers lying doggo, the contest for the control of Tombstone had already passed to other hands. For more than three weeks the warring elements in town had been narrowed to the vigilantes, supported by *The Epitaph*, and the county government, whose voice was *The Nugget*.

For it takes much more than the disapproval, or even the threats of a governor to drive entrenched office holders from the source of their profits. To remove them on the strength of the record is difficult because they have the means of making documents justify their actions. Moreover, to go from the general to the particular, veterans like Behan, Woods, and Dunbar had learned the lesson that politics are long and public indignation fleeting.

If there would be a cut in their profits through the discontinuance of protection money paid by the rustlers, that, they doubtless reasoned, need not be a permanent condition. The rustlers could be reorganized when the governor forgot about it all, or got tired of being a new broom, and found something else to do. Meanwhile they weren't starving on their salaries, their rake-off from taxes, and the revenue from other perquisites.

So if Behan and the others had been inclined to be more careful when the sheriff returned from his last effort to catch the Earps, they were still in business. Behan put in a bill for his outsize posse of outlaws, based on time, mileage, and supplies for them all. As this bill was submitted to his partner, County Treasurer Dunbar, it was paid in full.

When Pete Spence rode into Tombstone to escape Wyatt, Behan gave him sanctuary in the jail. A few days later, when Pete decided he'd be better off elsewhere, the door was opened for him.

If Wyatt was the main authority for what was done about Spence, what happened in the case of Zwing Hunt was told by Deputy Sheriff Breakenridge, with assists from *The Epitaph* and Parsons. When Hunt and Grounds were brought into town, they were first brought to the undertaker's, but, not dying soon enough, they were removed from these cheerless surroundings and taken to a hospital. Grounds, indeed, never recovered consciousness, and was soon back; but in the instance of young Hunt the visit to the undertaker was entirely unwarranted. He began to recover with astonishing rapidity. Observing this phenomenon, the Citizens' Safety Committee suggested that the outlaw should be taken to jail, but Behan insisted that it would be inhuman to do so.

The Ring and the Epitaph

The man of whom he was so tender was wanted for two murders, as he had been the one who had killed Gillespie after having helped assassinate Peel. Yet no guard was posted in the hospital, even when Hunt's brother came to town. One night, within two weeks of the day Zwing was captured, the Hunt boys drove off in a wagon, headed back for the home stand of Texas.

This was the old days back again. Yet in spite of those signs of confidence regained, there was one factor — probably not reckoned with — which was against the politicos. The outlaws had served them in more ways than one. By stealing the headlines, for instance, they had diverted public attention from the subtler thievery of crooked politics. There had long been some grumbling about what was going on, but now there was no gunfire at once to drown out the protests and to make them seem relatively unimportant.

As early as the spring of 1881 Parsons had begun to mutter about the activities of Behan and his deputies. "King the stage robber escaped tonight early from H. Woods who had been previously notified of an attempt at release to be made. Some of our officials should be hanged. They are a bad lot."

Similar remarks were scribbled in his journal from time to time during the ensuing months, but the wording indicated he was inveighing against the sheriff's office. It wasn't until considerably later that he intimated any knowledge of an organization of crooked political officers and their backers. Then he began using such phrases as "feeling is growing against the ring."

Now this was a favorite term of *The Epitaph*, which usually enlarged it to "ten per cent ring." Under Clum's aegis the paper had been fighting the coalition of rustlers, county officers, and, of course, *The Nugget* more unremittingly than any other force in Tombstone. It was, in all probability, not Clum the mayor but Clum the editor whom the rustlers had tried so earnestly to rub out. For if the public is often willing to let bygones be bygones while prosperous times keep it soothed, nothing will appease the wrath of a crusading journalist with his teeth in a cause.

And Clum was good. Also, as was to be expected of a man with his record for guts in dealing with the Apaches, he had not been frightened into silence by gunmen who had tried to finish him. After returning from his almost fatal trip to Washington, he had carried on with his campaign. What fragments of it survive still make good reading.

For he knew his readers. In spite of the fact that Westerners have been a favorite subject of romance writers, the temperament of the natives — born and self adapted — leans toward an ironic realism. Likewise Clum knew a truth about human nature in general which many reformers never learn. He was aware that indignation can become a bore and defeat its purpose, where ridicule, by entertaining, can keep the interest of the reader alive.

At first he specialized in attacking the county administration indirectly through their allies, the rustlers. *The Nugget* had adopted the practice, earlier referred to, of calling the outlaws "cowboys." The inference was that the meanest thing they ever did from one Fourth of July to the next was to brand a calf. When they fired guns it was in self-defense, or out of exuberance. Those, like the Earps, who opposed the "cow-boys" were persecuting honest working men. When any harm befell a "cow-boy" *The Nugget* bore the burden of public grief.

The Epitaph had jumped on this whitewashing term with joy. On some days it greeted it with a raucous crow-laugh; at others it gravely accepted the designation while it reported how certain "cow-boys" had acted. Eventually its columns made the term "cow-boy" synonymous with criminal, not only in Cochise County but elsewhere in the West. Furthermore Clum succeeded, through dispatches and paper-swapping, in making *The Nugget* a journalistic laughing stock. This was so not only among papers in the territory but of those in adjacent territories and states.

Perhaps his greatest triumph in this respect was an item printed in *The San Francisco Exchange* under the date of November 2, 1881. "A cow-boy met the natural fate of all cow-boys in Camp Rice yesterday, being riddled with bullets. The Tombstone *Nug-*

get should send down a special reporter to weep over the remains. That journal is now recognized in Arizona Territory as the great obituary organ of all slaughtered cow-boys."

It was probably Clum who coined the phrase, "the ten per cent ring." The significance of it was that when the sheriff collected the taxes which supported himself and his associates, he mulcted an additional tithe to reward himself for the time and effort involved in tax collection.

How this worked out in practice can be grasped by *The Epitaph's* comment relative to Behan's "posse of honest ranchmen," which never got too near the Earps. "Mileage still counting up for our rascally sheriff," Parsons had complained. "He organizes posses, goes to within a mile of his prey and then returns. He's a good one." Clum's remark, made after the bill had been submitted, was more explicit. "We understand that the tax-payers of Cochise County will be called upon to pay about $3000 for the employment of cow-boy deputy sheriffs in a fruitless endeavor to capture the Earps. Add to this the ten per cent for collection ($300) and a diamond pin, and you'll see how dearly we pay for the whistle."

This persistent heckling got under the normally impenetrable hides of case-hardened politicians for a particular reason. During 1881 they hadn't paid too much attention; but as 1882 began to unroll it was borne in upon them that their appointive positions would not belong to them indefinitely. In November of that year the voters would elect officers of Cochise County for the first time.

Then after the series of episodes which began with the assassination of Morgan Earp and ended with a personal investigation by the new governor the accusations of *The Epitaph* took on an added significance. Governor Tritle had taken no overt steps, as far as they knew, but the politicos certainly didn't want him stirred up by adverse publicity. In addition there were signs of trouble for them within the Democratic party. Some of its leaders in the territory were becoming leery of six-shooter politics. The scandal in Cochise County was a party scandal which they no longer felt comfortable about countenancing. Unless the dirt ceased to fly, there was a chance the territorial party would use its influence to oppose the incumbents. And still *The Epitaph* kept at it.

The solution was to buy the paper out, and this was finally done. That the move was a blow to Clum is evident from his editorial comments, but he had two partners, Messrs. Sorin and Reppy. Probably they held the moneybags, or if not, they could outvote him, and in any case the deal was put through. In late April of '82 *The Epitaph* announced that it would change both hands and political affiliations.

The man brought in by the ring as publisher was Sam Purdy, a politician and newspaperman from Yuma. From his post on the Colorado River, he had often commented on Tombstone affairs, backing *The Nugget* and sniping at *The Epitaph*. In particular Purdy had expressed indignation over the constant attacks made upon Behan's conduct in office. "If," he wrote, "*The Epitaph* continues in its bitter persecution of Sheriff Behan, it will make him the most popular man in Arizona."

"If this is a fact, Mr. Purdy," *The Epitaph* commented by way of pinning a price tag on a purchased man, "you should continue the persecution for upon Behan's popularity depends your success in the future." Clum also wished the politics of the new publisher in Purdytion, and fixed his policy for him. "Mr. Purdy will doubtless advocate a continuation of the economical administration of county affairs. . . . We are confident that he will oppose a higher rate for collection of taxes than ten per cent. . . ."

But the ring could afford to read that passage with a certain amount of complacence, for it embodied the war cry of a dying enemy. On May 1, 1882, Clum wrote "30" for the paper of his guidance in two different strains. The one about the Republican party losing its strong right arm in Cochise county need not be given in full. "On this bright spring evening," the other one ran, "while the birds are singing in the grease-wood bush and the Apaches are howling through the mountains, *The Epitaph* wraps itself in an American flag and dies like a son of a gun. Ta-ta! We will meet again, Clemantha."

The Ring and the Epitaph

At this point, however, the ring was no longer in the mood to rejoice at the overthrow it had financed. On April 26th the president had delivered the message to Congress quoted at the end of the last chapter. The politicos were still gasping from that blow when Arthur struck again. In his message he had suggested that martial law should be invoked with special reference to Cochise County. On May 3rd he made a proclamation which showed that he had gained Congressional support for the move.

". . . whereas," that proclamation stipulated, "it has been made to appear satisfactorily to me, by information received from the Governor of the Territory of Arizona and from the general of the army of the United States . . . that in consequence of unlawful combinations of evil disposed persons who are banded together to oppose and obstruct the execution of the laws it has become impracticable to enforce by the ordinary judicial proceedings the laws of the United States within that territory . . . and

"Whereas the laws of the United States require that whenever it may be necessary in the judgment of the President to use the military forces for the purpose of enforcing the faithful execution of the laws of the United States, he shall, by proclamation, command such insurgents to disperse. . . ."

So far this declaration of intent, like the message to Congress, had been directed at the outlaws, but now it went on to point a finger directly and unmistakably at their political protectors. ". . . therefore, I, Chester A. Arthur, President of the United States, do hereby admonish all good citizens . . . against aiding, countenancing, abetting, or taking part in any such unlawful proceedings; and I do hereby warn all persons engaged in or connected with said obstruction of the laws to disperse . . . on or before noon of the 15th day of May."

This was notification from the highest authority that Cochise County had been annexed to the United States; but the members of the ring were by no means the only residents of Tombstone who were unhappy about it. Even many of those who had hoped that Governor Tritle would take action were aghast to learn that their community had been made the object of Congressional action. They were commercial and professional men, and the town where they made their living had been held up for the obloquy of the nation. It was not only a disgrace, it was bad for business.

There were indignation meetings. Protests were drafted, and counter propaganda was distributed. Significantly *The Epitaph* and *The Nugget* now sang in chorus of a land where a competent officialdom permitted no law-breaking.

Tucson, always jealous of Tombstone, the city which had so quickly supplanted it as the metropolis of the territory, would not let this pass. *The Arizona Weekly Citizen* retorted on May 7th in an article which dragged out all the old scandals, "Statements sent by the Tombstone associated press agent and the papers of that city to the effect that no lawlessness exists in Cochise County are simply presuming upon the ignorance of a public who have been treated to an almost daily dose of horrors from the same source. Officers in Tombstone will not or cannot arrest and there is a reign of terror there. Jails will not hold their inmates and jurors dare not convict. It is a well established fact that stage lines, express companies, ranchmen, and miners find themselves forced to purchase immunity from robbery. . . ."

Yet if the citizens wailed their indignation and the ring fumed, Uncle Sam had nevertheless put his big foot down. Conditions would improve by May 15th or the troops would be ordered to take over. The rustlers had reappeared after the departure of the Earps, but — perhaps under instructions from the ring — had made themselves inconspicuous. Even Tucson papers conceded a change for the better. "The outlaws remain but are quiet," the *Citizen* declared on May 21st, "and crime which has run riot in Cochise County for two years has made way for peace and quiet."

Only a few days earlier, however, the ring had demonstrated that it was neither beaten down nor without power. Wyatt and Doc had reached Colorado and from there had wired Paul of their whereabouts and intentions. Learning of this, Behan moved

The Ring and the Epitaph

to obtain custody of the prisoners, but, as a Tucson news dispatch said: "Governor Tritle has placed requisitions in the hands of Sheriff Paul who leaves for Denver tomorrow. The Tombstone 'cowboys' are very indignant that the Governor has commissioned Sheriff Paul for this business. They wanted Sheriff Behan of Tombstone to have the requisitions and bring the Earps to Cochise County in order that they might have an opportunity to murder them. . . ."

But due to the political alliances of the ring neither Governor Tritle nor Sheriff Paul felt that they could keep Earp and Holliday from being turned over to Behan, once the prisoners were in Arizona, and they so advised Governor Pitkin of Colorado. Pitkin consequently refused to honor the extradition request, ruling that the charges in the Stilwell killing had been pressed solely for the purpose of nabbing Earp and Holliday after they had been disarmed by the law.

But *The Epitaph* did not rejoice at the release of Doc and Wyatt, whose cause had once been its own. The sheet was now in the ranks of those who sought to vindicate the ring by maligning its enemies, and Wyatt was still ring enemy number one. The line taken can be judged from the journal of L. Vernon Briggs, an Easterner who spent three or four days in Tombstone in 1882. While there he was shocked to learn that a group of peace officers named Arp had murdered harmless citizens in the city streets. Worse, they had been supported in this felonious conduct by a judge, (Spicer) a postmaster, (Clum) and a newspaper, (*The Epitaph* of other days).

CHAPTER TWENTY

OF SUNDRY ENDINGS

THE epitaph for Russian Bill, meanwhile, had not been written in the Cyrillic alphabet. Probably late in 1881 or early in 1882 Bill had saddled up with one Sandy King, planning to make a raid into New Mexico. In or near Shakespeare, in that territory, the two had stolen some horses. The Shakespearians, who held strong views on property rights, had caught them.

It has been affirmed and denied that Bill and Sandy were hanged from the rafters of a Shakespeare eating joint and were left dangling while their executioners finished their meal. The more likely version is that they were strung up on a tree outside the boarding house by men who left them there when they answered the summons of the dinner gong.

For Tombstone the significance of Russian Bill's passing was that one less outlaw of stature was present to help reestablish the shattered rustler organization when Johnny Ringo, Ike Clanton, and Pony Deal returned from Mexico. Phin Clanton and Billy Claiborne were still around, but remaining names on the roster couldn't compare with those of the illustrious missing. Among the ones who had answered roll call less than a year before, and who now failed to, were Curly Bill, Old Man Clanton, Frank McLowry, Tom McLowry, Billy Clanton, Johnny Barnes, Pete Spence, Indian Charlie, Joe Hill, Hank Swilling, Jim Crane, Harry Head, Bill Leonard, Luther King, who may or may not be identical with the Sandy King who was hanged with Russian Bill, and Frank Stilwell.

Even so the rustlers might have planned to reorganize and commence operations on a county-wide scale again when the storm had blown over, and the Federal government had turned its eyes elsewhere. But before enough time had elapsed to make it feasible, the one man who might have succeeded in refashioning the structure of outlawry in Cochise County died. On July 14, 1882, the body of John Ringgold was found near what is now known as Turkey Creek in the foothills of the Chirichuas.

Sam Purdy's *Epitaph*, in addition to printing a "noble Roman" type of elegy for the deceased, expressed the opinion that Johnny Ringo had committed suicide by shooting himself. That story has been current ever since, and has gained support from the deposition of one Robert M. Boller, who was a member of the self appointed coroner's jury which assembled to gaze upon Ringo before the latter was buried where he died. Mr. Boller said that all the jurymen had agreed on a verdict of suicide.

That may have been true, but it is distinctly *not* what the coroner himself decided after weighing the facts in the case. His official decision, still to be found in the records of Cochise County, was "Cause of death unknown but supposed gunshot wound."

The reasons for the coroner's hesitation about coming to a conclusion can be picked from the report made to him by the volunteer jurors. He himself never saw the body. "There was found by the undersigned John Yoast the body of a man in a clump of oak trees about 20 yards north from the road leading to Morse's mill and about a quarter mile west of the house of B. F. Smith. The undersigned viewed the body and found it in a sitting posture facing west the head inclined to the right. There was a bullet hole in the right temple, the bullet coming out on the top of the head on the left side. There is apparently a part of the scalp gone including a small portion of the forehead and part of the hair, this looks as if cut out by a knife.

"These are the only marks of violence visible on the body. Several of the undersigned identify the body as that of John Ringo, well known in Tombstone. He was dressed in a light hat, blue shirt, vest, pants and drawers, on his feet were a pair of hose and undershirt torn up so as to protect his feet. He had evidently traveled but a short distance in this foot gear. His revolver he grasped in his right hand, his rifle rested against the tree close to him. He had on two cartridge belts, the belt for the revolver cartridges being buckled on upside down. The under-noted property were found with him and on his person:

"1 Colt's revolver Cal. .45 No. 222, containing 5 cartridges.

"1 Winchester rifle, octagon barrel Cal. .45, model 1876 No. 21896, containing a cartridge in the breech and 10 in the magazine.

"1 cartridge belt containing 9 rifle cartridges.

"1 cartridge belt containing 2 revolver cartridges.

"6 pistol cartridges in pocket. . . ." Certain minor personal belongings and a letter of unrevealed contents were also itemized.

People who had seen Johnny just the day before his body was found — Breakenridge was one of them — testified that the outlaw had been on a protracted bender. Proponents of the suicide theory hold that Ringo's horse had strayed off while Johnny was sleeping it off. In support they cite the tradition that the animal was found the next day with the rustler's boots still dangling from the pommel of the saddle. The picture then drawn is that of a man with a morning after thirst in Arizona in July shooting himself in despair at not being able to locate water. Others, however, have found two fallacies in this theory. When discovered, Ringo was within a short distance of water in a country with which he was thoroughly acquainted. Moreover, it is specifically stated that the rags with which he sought to protect his feet in the absence of his boots showed that he had not walked far in them, let alone wandered desperately for miles until all hope was gone.

Yet even if the motive could be allowed, logic would still be baffled. The question that must have stumped the coroner, although it has not elsewhere been raised, is: "what could Ringo have shot himself with?" Aside from the fact that it was evidently leaning against a tree, as if placed there, the rifle had a cartridge, not an empty shell, in the breech, and a lever action gun does not have automatic ejection and loading. True, Ringo had his revolver in his right hand, but the cylinder of the weapon was declared to have contained five cartridges. A man who knew anything about revolvers — and nobody in the world knew much more about

Of Sundry Endings

handling them than Johnny Ringo — never loaded more than five chambers, there's no such thing as piecemeal ejection in a revolver, and all the bullets were accounted for. The term used for what was found in the weapon was "5 cartridges." Men as familiar with weapons as the residents of Cochise County then were do not say "cartridge" when they mean the empty casing.

Some people, for no particular reason except for the facts that he was a skilled gunman and had been seen in the vicinity decided that Buckskin Frank Leslie had killed Ringo; but there was no solution which made sense until Stuart Lake got in touch with Fred Dodge. The reports which the latter had turned into the president of Wells, Fargo & Co. were destroyed in the San Francisco fire of 1906, but Dodge remembered what he had found out about Ringo's death.

By his account Johnny-behind-the-deuce had drifted back into Cochise County, where there was no warrant for him; it was only in Pima County, of which that region was no longer a part, that he was sought for murder. This was the man whom Curly Bill and Ringo had thought it would be fun to have lynched by usually law abiding citizens for the shooting of Schneider, the engineer. Ringo and Brocius had led the chase from Charleston to Tombstone and had prompted the mob which surged down Allen Street toward where O'Rourke shivered in Vogan's bowling alley.

Johnny-behind-the-deuce wasn't in the high brackets either as a gambler or a gunman. He couldn't shoot it out with the fellow who had inspired others to fire upon him while he was unarmed, and to call for his blood, but he could play a sure thing. Passing along the road, he had seen the outlaw leader sleeping off his drunk under a tree some twenty yards away. Recognizing his enemy, John O'Rourke had let John Ringo have it. Dodge had apparently nothing to say about the hide removed from the rustler's head; but there would be nothing far fetched in the assumption that Johnny-behind-the-deuce, like many of the old time Westerners, had lived with Indians enough to have prized a scalp lock as a trophy of vengeance.

The Last Chance

As far as Tombstone was concerned, however, it made no difference with which foot Ringo kicked the bucket. He was dead, and the stones piled on his grave might as well have been piled on that of crime, in any large scale, thereabouts. Petty rustlers remained and gunmen with bad dispositions remained, but neither ever again affected the economics of the city in any important respect or constituted a major threat to the lives of its citizens. The days when the civic-minded men of the town had to garrison it against armed invasion were over.

So quickly do public attitudes respond to change that within a few months the old "cow-boy" attitude toward the law could be treated as a grotesque novelty. An example is the account of a gun battle which took place in Charleston toward the end of 1882. Messrs. O'Brien and Lee, both identified as citizens of Calabasas, west along the Mexican border, became excited to combat and so wounded each other that they ended up side by side in bed, their coffins waiting. The beginning of the action is thus presented by a reporter seemingly well versed in Mark Twain's *Life on the Mississippi.*

"When they got their guns and mounted their horses O'Brien gave a hurroo. He announced himself to be a son of a blank from Bitter Creek and resided pretty high; that he lived whole seasons on rattlesnakes and scorpions; that the first shirt he ever wore was made of rawhide, and that he was born on the top of a freight car when the train was speeding along at the rate of fifty miles an hour. He said that he could out-drink and out-shoot any sucker he ever met, and that he was a darned son of a sea cook if he did not kill somebody right away and run the darned town. At the expiration of the last sentence he turned his pistol loose. . . ."

Several things are notable about the report. One is that *The Epitaph*, although now a ring paper, could report the activities of "cow-boys" with detachment. They were no longer important enough to be protected. The incident was unusual where such things had once been commonplace, and so the paper could afford the space to give it a colorful presentation. The characters involved had nothing to do with any criminal organization. Most remarkable of all, they did not come from the law-abiding Tombstone district at all. They were from out of the county, hailing from that never-never land of screwball disreputability, Calabasas, Arizona.

With the disappearance of the stock thieving and stage robbing mob, the ring was doomed. As Acting Governor Gosper had pointed out, it had been tolerated and supported by many residents of Tombstone because they shared the gravy. Others strung along and paid dues because they feared the guns of the outlaws. Now, lacking the weapons of intimidation and profit sharing to hold their followers in line, the politicos were in a bad way.

Behan did not run for sheriff in November of '82; and as far as can be discerned from the imperfect records none of the appointive officers of the county was elected. Those who did get in office were no doubt affiliated with the old politicos, for a predominantly Democratic electorate voted for a complete Democratic slate; but the tax payers were in revolt against the practices of the "ten per cent ring."

In the latter part of 1882 Parsons several times referred to some action being taken against the county organization. Its nature was unspecified but as Behan was hauled into court a couple of times, it was probably a grand jury investigation. Finally on January 26, 1883, he indicated that the revolt was about to succeed. "Tombstone quite aroused now — a good sentiment is growing. Put them through they say meaning 'the ring.' Their fun is over. The day of reckoning is at hand."

Probably there was no heavy reckoning, for it usually takes a bigger storm than any county can stir up to make a veteran political crook lose his footing. Yet there can be no doubt that the old machine was routed, for some of its stalwarts left to find softer pickings elsewhere in the territory.

By then it could be said with finality that Tombstone was not the individual place it had been. The prospectors were turning to other fields. Gambling for high stakes had gone the way of gangster politics. The city, allowing for general Western and particular mining variations, had been absorbed into the normal pattern for American provincial towns.

Everything pointed to steady growth. The mines were holding up. No longer hampered by big-scale rustling, the cattle raising industry was thriving. By every sign Tombstone should have gone on being the metropolis of the territory — when the bottom fell out. The town which had thriven on the conditions imposed by outlawry and a rogue regime faded when the factors had seemingly become entirely favorable.

Tranquil good times lasted only during 1883. Allison's rider to the Bland act of 1878 had permitted the government to purchase only a limited amount of silver annually for coinage. As silver production in the West increased, the amount the treasury could use was overmatched by the supply, driving the price of the metal gradually downward. By 1884 the price was so low that the absentee owners of the Tombstone mines no longer felt able to pay the top wages of $4.00 per day.

Tombstone was a union town, and union workers, then as now, were not concerned with economic factors. They wanted their dough, and never mind where it came from. The offer of $3.50 was greeted by a strike and violence. Not only the hoisting works of the mines but the good health of managerial employees, as innocent about lowering the salaries as the miners themselves, were threatened.

The strike caused the closing of most of the mines on May 1, 1884. The Contention, the biggest of the lot, had not lowered its wages, but by then the strikers were in the spirit of the thing. They tried to burn the hoisting works of that mine, too, forcing it to shut up shop.

The miners also decided that it would be a good idea to lynch the superintendent of the Grand Central Mine. The man thus menaced was the former vigilante leader, E. B. Gage. His home on the outskirts of the town was so situated that any attempt on his part to escape could have been easily spotted; and the time to go get him had been set by the strikers. These last didn't know that their plans had leaked out; but some hours before the deadline Nellie Cashman left her boarding house in a wagon. At a leisurely pace she drove to Gage's abode, and drove as slowly off after he had mounted up beside her. Everybody who wasn't in on the secret assumed that the mine superintendent had left on a brief pleasure jaunt; but when Nellie returned, Gage did not.

Curiously enough it was at this time that President Arthur's threat to clamp the lid of martial law on Tombstone was belatedly made good. The humdrum business town got the troops which had been withheld from the city besieged by outlaws. Under the supervision of the soldiers from Fort Huachuca the strikers quieted. Just the same it was months before the mines reopened; and when they did so it was on a smaller scale of operation. Meanwhile another pillar supporting the town's prosperity had been cut out from under it. On May 10, 1884, the Safford and Hudson Bank permanently closed its doors.

Aside from the strike the quiet of the year 1884 was broken by one other example of mass violence. During the preceding December a gang of toughs had robbed a Bisbee store filled with people engaged in Christmas shopping. A group of trigger-happy amateurs, they had become nervous and fired at random into a crowd which included quite a few women and children before they made their getaway. The men were later identified as Owen Semple, James Howard, Daniel Dowd, and William Delaney.

The man who seemed to be most enraged over what was called "the Bisbee massacre" was a fellow named John Heith. He insisted upon joining the sheriff's posse and proved himself a veritable bloodhound on the scent. The only trouble was that it was the wrong scent, and in time the rest of the posse became certain that he was deliberately trying to lead them astray. Arrested, Heith turned out to be an associate of Semple, Howard, et al. Indeed, he was held to be the leader of the killers, who were also soon captured.

The Last Chance

However, as Heith had not actually shot anyone, he was tried as an accessory only in the Cochise County Courthouse, which had been rebuilt on Tough Nut Street after the old one on Fremont had been destroyed by the fire of May, 1882. The others were sentenced to swing, but Heith was merely given a prison sentence. Holding this a miscarriage of justice, a mob from Bisbee set out to rectify it. They snatched Heith out of the county jail and strung him up not far away.

The citizens of Tombstone were sympathetic to the endeavor and approved of the result, yet a corpse had been left in their town which had to be accounted for. Those who sat on the coroner's jury knew what had been done and by whom, but they did not wish to make any statement which might cause a charge or indictment to be brought against any of the Bisbeeites. To crack this impasse while preserving the legal proprieties Dr. Goodfellow penned the following verdict: "We the undersigned find that J. Heith came to his death from emphysema of the lungs — a disease common to high altitudes — which might have been caused by strangulation, self inflicted or otherwise."

As the rope awaited the remaining four members of the gang in any case, they were not mishandled by the mob. Being a matter of routine, this execution probably wouldn't have been remembered if so many people had not wanted to witness it. The seating arrangements provided by the county fell far short of accommodating the expected crowd — a fact which impressed a local opportunist. He built a grand stand on a spot overlooking the scaffold; and he would have cashed in, too, if it hadn't been for Nellie Cashman.

According to the passes issued by the sheriff, one or two of which are still extant, the execution was set for one o'clock on March 28, 1884. In the meantime Nellie had succeeded in persuading a lot of men that the project to commercialize such a spectacle was in the nature of a civic disgrace. On March 27 she led a band of them to the offending structure and asked them to go to it. The grand stand was smashed to pieces and for good measure its promoter was issued an accepted invitation to leave Tombstone. Thereafter Dowd, Delaney, Semple, and Howard were hanged with decorum.

Tombstone was dying peaceably, too, although it wasn't yet ready to accept the fact. The town still held together, in spite of a loss of population, for two more years, living on the hope that the campaign for free silver coinage would bring back good times again. Then in 1886 the gun nobody knew was loaded went off. In arid Arizona of all places — in Arizona where rivers traffic in small moisture or none — water rose mightily in the mines from some vast subterranean source.

They manned the pumps, but it was no use. The mines remained awash, and a town dependent upon them was bankrupt. Two thirds of the remaining population cleared out, to leave the rest amidst the forlorn remnant of what had once been the largest and most promising city between San Antonio and the Pacific Ocean.

There were two lesser booms to break the monotony of the sleepy succeeding years. In 1890, in answer to a renewed demand for silver, the companies spent a fortune on pumping devices, but the expense of keeping the water low consumed the profits. Again in 1902 there was an attempt backed by so much optimism that its own spur of railroad, breaking off from the line which ran down the San Pedro Valley at Fairbank, at last reached Tombstone. But this try for the great wealth still in the veins of the Lucky Cuss, the Contention, the Grand Central, and the Tough Nut was also a failure.

The flooding of the mines was even rougher on Charleston and Contention City than it was on the parent town. As long as a steady supply of water was handy, there was no use in having the stamping mills so far from the source of the ore. Contention and Charleston became such ghost towns that a visitor could not tell where the streets had once been; and Galeyville likewise became not much more than a memory.

There is talk now, which is to say in 1949, of a renewed effort to exploit the mines, which hold copper, lead, and zinc as well as silver and a reasonable amount of gold. If the effort is made, modern mining methods may bring prosperity back to Tombstone; but they will not retrieve the individualistic days of its unique story.

That story is almost told in so far as the available records permit. The tale of Sheriff John Slaughter, the lone hunter of lone rustlers, is a great tale of Cochise County, but it is not, in the sense that the town was gravely affected, or that its citizens felt that their destiny was at stake, a tale of Tombstone. A few threads of the main story remain to be followed, however.

CHAPTER TWENTY-ONE

A NECROLOGY AND BOOT HILL

JOHNNY-BEHIND-THE-DEUCE did not have long to gloat over his vengeance on Ringo. We have Fred Dodge's word for it that Pony Deal, who had attached himself to Ringo after the death of Curly Bill, suspected the gambler and accordingly shot him.

After Ringo's demise only five of the Tombstone area's notorious killers remained alive, at large, and in the vicinity. Four — Deal, Ike and Phin Clanton, and Claiborne — were survivors of the rustler mob. The fifth was Buckskin Frank Leslie, who, although not classified as an outlaw, was without law whenever he felt so inclined.

Of the five Pony Deal was apparently the first to go, but no date for his passing can be located. In any case he was killed in a gunfight in Greenlee County, north of Cochise and forninst the boundary of New Mexico. Then there were four, but not for long. On November 14, 1882, Claiborne and Leslie staged the last of Tombstone's famous gun duels.

If the quarrel had any origins aside from Claiborne's bad humor at the time they are lost to history. What is known is that Billy entered the Oriental, where Frank was tending bar, at an early hour of the day in question. Drunk and in a mean mood, he horned in on what Frank considered a private conversation. Whereupon Leslie gave Claiborne the bum's rush into an adjoining room.

Billy then, according to witnesses, left the saloon with the meaningful remark: "See you later."

"While I'm in Tombstone," Frank was quoted as retorting, "you can see me any time."

Claiborne didn't keep him waiting very long. He soon reappeared at the corner of Fifth and Allen Streets with a rifle. Making no secret of what he intended to do, he took his stance in front of the main or Allen Street entrance of the saloon. Upon being informed of this, Leslie emerged from a side entrance with a revolver and called Billy's name. Claiborne whirled and fired two shots to Leslie's one. That one, however, was all that was needed.

"He shot and killed the notorious Kid — Claiborne this A.M. circa 7:30," Parsons jotted in his journal, "making as pretty a center shot on the Kid as one can wish to see. The Kid threatened and laid for him near the Oriental with a Winchester but Frank got the drop on him. . . ." Parsons went on to remark on the victor's composure. "Frank didn't lose the light of his cigarette during the encounter."

Five years later destiny caught up with the remaining two Clantons. Like Pony Deal they had shifted their bases of operations to Greenlee County, where they were jointly leaders of a small gang of rustlers. Their luck held out until 1887, but in that year they were trapped by a posse led either by the famous sheriff, Commodore Perry Owens, or by one of two different deputies of that officer. At all events Ike disobeyed the order to surrender and was shot while trying to flee. Phin was captured and put in ten years at the Yuma penitentiary before he took up stock raising in a legal fashion.

Phin had only been at Yuma three years when he was joined by Buckskin Frank Leslie, who had taken to heavy drinking that soured him. He was reputed to have killed twelve men without incurring any penalty, and he probably would have got away with slaying Six-shooter Jim, which he did while in a fit of jealousy compounded with drunkeness; but he also shot Molly Bradshaw. Molly, who sang at the Bird Cage — for the year was 1890, and Tombstone was having a brief revival — was a leading figure in the redlight district; but she was a woman, and in the Old West it was bad luck to shoot one of her sex. Frank went to Yuma where he stayed until 1897. Later he went to California, where Wyatt Earp recognized him in a broken down old saloon swamper.

Dr. Goodfellow also went to California, where he became a

prominent San Francisco surgeon. At the other end of the state his old friend and patient, George Parsons finally found in Los Angeles the prosperity which had been denied him in Tombstone. Clum, like Goodfellow, went to San Francisco for a while, and there became one of the original editors of the *Examiner*. But he was in the Yukon when that gold rush got under way, and, as already mentioned, when the fever sent men stampeding into Alaska, he was commissioned by the United States government to organize postal service for the territory. Both in the Yukon and Alaska he met Nellie Cashman, still in the business of making homes for the homeless.

While Frank Leslie and Phin Clanton were in Yuma they were, as it happened, the responsibility of John Behan. When Tombstone's tax payers ceased to support him, the territorial political organization of which he had long been a wheel horse took care of him. The post of assistant to the warden of the territorial prison was secured for him; and in due time he was promoted to warden. He spent quite a few years at Yuma, where Sam Purdy, late of *The Epitaph*, had become district attorney; but later he made his home in Tucson, where he died in 1912.

William Breakenridge remained a deputy under Behan's successor before leaving for a better position in Tombstone and a succession of other jobs which eventually qualified him to be considered the dean of Arizona's old timers. Finally he, like Behan, went to Tucson, to which place Clum also came to spend his last years. In patriarchal retirement both wrote of their Tombstone days, taking, of course, opposite sides of the old controversies, in particular the one about the rights and wrongs of the Battle of the O. K. Corral.

Of the remaining Earps the youngest died first. Warren, who had become a detective for the Arizona Cattlemen's Association was killed by a rustler in Lordsburg, New Mexico, in the course of a poker game. The year was 1900. Virgil lasted six years longer before dying a natural death in the Nevada mining town of Goldfield. Wyatt died in Los Angeles in 1929. Among his honorary pall bearers were two men, soon to pass on themselves, who had backed his play as vigilantes in the old days in Tombstone. These were John P. Clum and George Whitwell Parsons.

In the intervening years Wyatt had continued to seek out boom towns, going to the Yukon and again to Alaska to find the sort of life he liked; but after the frontiers ran out on him, in coincidence with the approach of years which made hectic living undesirable, he became a man of affairs. As competent in real estate and financial dealings as he had been in other things, he became a very prosperous, even a wealthy, man when he died, a brief time before his 81st birthday.

His friend, John Holliday, did not fare so well, although he lived longer than he expected. Doc had always bet that the time would come when he wouldn't draw his gun quick enough, yet he died of tuberculosis in a Colorado sanatorium, during or about 1895. His last words and actions were passed on by Wyatt to his biographer. Up to the day of his passing Doc had drunk hard liquor in quantities to make strong men shiver. On D-day he asked for and drank a tumbler of neat whiskey. "This is funny," he said, referring to the fact that he wasn't wearing his boots; and therewith he closed his eyes for good.

William Barclay Masterson finally became, of all improbable things, a sports writer in New York City. Bat died there in 1921, eight years before Wyatt but long after their mutual friend, the quiet and dangerous Luke Short. The latter, contrary to all expectations except possibly his own, died peacefully — in Kansas City, Missouri.

Curiously enough the year of Wyatt Earp's death was that of Tombstone's ultimate disaster and renewed hope. Bisbee's copper mines had continued to produce long after the silver mines north down the San Pedro Valley had become steeped in water. Bisbee, therefore, took Tombstone's place as the largest town in the county, and eventually, in 1929, used its electoral power to vote itself into being the county seat.

With the emptying of the court house on Tough Nut Street,

everything which Tombstone had once possessed had been stripped from it except the memory of its heroic age. The town which had always boasted that it was too tough to die pulled up its slacks and went to work at the business of making its traditions a source of profit.

When they took stock of their assets, most of the old buildings had collapsed or been torn down. The court house, the town hall, the Bird Cage Theatre, and Schieffelin Hall were about all that remained to let people know that the village on Goose Flats had ever been a city. Of all the saloons which had once made Allen Street a haven for the thirsty only the Crystal Palace remained to indicate how lively a place Tombstone had been.

There were land marks, of course, such as the site of the old O. K. Corral and the yawning hole of the Million Dollar Stope, and then there was Boot Hill. Or rather there was a heap of rubbish under which Boot Hill had long lain hidden. Nobody quite knew what was under the refuse or remembered just who had been buried there.

Ed Schieffelin had not, for one. When the old prospector died on the West Coast, it was found that his will contained instructions for his body to be returned to Tombstone, and this was done. Fittingly, though, he was planted at Watervale on a rise above the old camp site near his first great discovery, the Lucky Cuss. A rugged little stone and mortar monument marks where he lies.

Not too much of anything marked the graves of Boot Hill when that cemetery was finally cleared. The boards had fallen down, or rotted away. In some cases they had been stolen by souvenir collectors.

Had the investigation been delayed another ten years, it would have been too late to do anything. A good few of the old residents were still alive then, however, and for one of them, an E. C. Nunnelley the rehabilitation of Boot Hill became a labor of love. He collected the old headboards, pored over old records, and talked with or wrote to anybody who might remember where a marker belonged or how an epitaph had been worded.

His honest work has since been stultified by tourist-hungry opportunists. With no respect for the rights of either history or ghosts they have assigned graves there to Curly Bill and Johnny-behind-the-deuce, for instance. But Boot Hill as reconstructed by Nunnelley was impressive and interesting. When he could find out nothing, he didn't try to supply the deficit, and about half the markers he placed on the graves read: "Unknown." Yet the ones on which other things were written constituted a sort of tabloid history of old Tombstone: "Conly Shot by Doc Holliday," "Ben Smith and A. L. Bennet Ambushed by Apaches," "Mrs. Clum," "Old Man Clanton," "Dick Jobey Killed by Sheriff Behan," "China Mary — Mrs. Ah Lum," "Marshal White Shot by Curly Bill," "W. M. Grounds died of Wounds," "Margarita Stabbed by Gold Dollar," "Charlie Storms Killed by Luke Short," "George Johnson Hanged by Mistake," and so on.

Some of the slayings referred to in the Boot Hill markers were incorporated in the Helldorado celebration, the pageant by which Tombstone annually seeks to improve its present by commemorating its past. This show, which yearly attracts larger crowds from all over the nation, is held on the nearest week end to October 26th, the date when the Earps and the Clantons met at the O. K. Corral.

The pageant, complete with the staged gun fights, and the unstaged riding, drinking, and gambling, is considered a successful piece of evocation; but there are mysteries which can't be called back from Boot Hill either for pay or pleasure. Who was the protagonist of that drama written in thirteen words on three grave markers not thirty feet apart: "Red River Tom Shot by Ormsby," "Bronco Charlie Shot by Ormsby," "Ormsby Shot"?

And what of a country and a time when all men knew about a fellow at his burial was that he called himself Tom and that he had once sojourned in a distant river valley? What can be said of "Stingin' Lizard Shot by Cherokee Hall"? These men were adrift in a region almost as vast and almost as empty as an ocean without even a real name for a sea anchor. "Black Jack 1881," "Kansas Kid,"

"Shoot 'em up Jack"; and it went for women, too, "Dutch Annie 1883." The era of that epic loneliness and self-dependence can be momentarily glimpsed during the reading of such inscriptions.

Editorializing was very rare among the epitaphs in Boot Hill, although the headboard of Billy Clanton, for instance, stated that he had been murdered. A similar comment was made in a dozen other cases; but usually just the facts were given: the name or nom de guerre, the manner of death, the executioner if known, and the burial year.

Among the few which said anything else, one headboard bore the ultimate in tributes: "Jack Williams — he done his damndest." That could stand for a final judgment on about every man Joe and woman Josephine in the old mining town in its early years. For the great thing about Tombstone was not that there was silver in the veins of the adjacent hills, but that life flowed hotly and strongly in the veins of its people.

BIBLIOGRAPHY

Adams, Ward R. and Sloan, Richard E. — HISTORY OF ARIZONA, 4 vols.— Phoenix, 1930.

Alliott, Hector — BIBLIOGRAPHY OF ARIZONA — Los Angeles, 1914.

Anonymous — HISTORY OF ARIZONA TERRITORY — San Francisco, 1884.

———— JOURNALS OF THE ELEVENTH LEGISLATIVE ASSEMBLY OF THE TERRITORY OF ARIZONA — Prescott, Ariz., 1881.

Bakarich, Sarah Grace — GUN SMOKE — Tombstone, Ariz., 1947.

Bancroft, Hubert H. — HISTORY OF THE PACIFIC STATES OF NORTH AMERICA, Vol. 12: ARIZONA AND NEW MEXICO — San Francisco, 1888.

Barnes, Will C. — ARIZONA PLACE NAMES — Tucson, Ariz., 1935.

Barnes, Will C. and Raine, William McLeod — CATTLE — Garden City, N. Y. 1930.

Bechdolt, Frederick R. — WHEN THE WEST WAS YOUNG — New York, 1922.

Benton, Jesse James — COW BY THE TAIL — Boston, 1943.

Bishop, William H. — CALIFORNIA, ARIZONA, AND NEW MEXICO — New York, 1883.

Blake, W. P. — TOMBSTONE AND ITS MINES — New York, 1902.

Breakenridge, William M. — HELLDORADO — Boston, 1929.

Briggs, L. Vernon — ARIZONA AND NEW MEXICO 1882, CALIFORNIA 1886, NEW MEXICO 1891 — Boston, 1932.

Burnham, Frederick R. — SCOUTING ON TWO CONTINENTS — Garden City, N. Y., 1928.

Burns, Walter Noble — TOMBSTONE: *An Iliad of the Southwest* — Garden City, N. Y., 1927.

Clum, John P. — IT ALL HAPPENED IN TOMBSTONE — "Arizona Historical Quarterly," October, 1929.

———— NELLIE CASHMAN — Ditto, January, 1931.

Clum, Woodworth — APACHE AGENT: *The Story of John Clum,* Boston, 1936.

Coolidge, Dane C. — ARIZONA COWBOYS — New York, 1938.

———— FIGHTING MEN OF THE WEST — New York, 1932.

Bibliography

Cunningham, Eugene — TRIGGERNOMETRY — Caldwell, Idaho, 1934.

Dobie, J. Frank — GUIDE TO LIFE AND LITERATURE OF THE SOUTHWEST — Austin, Tex., 1943.

Farish, Thomas E. — HISTORY OF ARIZONA, 8 vols.— Phoenix, Ariz., 1915.

Gardner, Raymond Hatfield — ADVENTURES OF ARIZONA BILL — San Antonio, 1944.

Haley, J. Evetts — JEFF MILTON: *A Good Man with a Gun* — Norman, Oklahoma, 1948.

Hamilton, Patrick — RESOURCES OF ARIZONA — San Francisco, 1884.

Holbrook, Stewart H. — LITTLE ANNIE OAKLEY AND OTHER RUGGED PEOPLE — New York, 1948.

Horn, Tom — LIFE OF TOM HORN: *Government Scout and Interpreter;* written by himself — Denver, 1904.

Hughes, Dan de Lara — SOUTH FROM TOMBSTONE — London, 1938.

Hume, James B. and Thacker, John N. — REPORT OF JAMES B. HUME AND JOHN N. THACKER: *Special Officers, Wells, Fargo & Co.'s Express* — San Francisco, 1885.

King, Frank P. — WRANGLIN' THE PAST — Pasadena, Calif., 1935.

Lake, Stuart N. — WYATT EARP: *Frontier Marshal* — Boston, 1931.

Lesley, Lewis Burt — UNCLE SAM'S CAMELS — Cambridge, Mass., 1929.

Lockwood, Frank C. — THE APACHE INDIANS — New York, 1938.

—————— ARIZONA CHARACTERS — Los Angeles, 1928.

—————— PIONEER DAYS IN ARIZONA — New York, 1932.

Lloyd IV, Elwood — ARIZONOLOGY — Flagstaff, Ariz., 1933.

Love, Alice E. — HISTORY OF TOMBSTONE TO 1887 — Unpublished thesis in library of University of Arizona, Tucson.

McClintock, James H. — ARIZONA, THE YOUNGEST STATE, 3 vols. — Chicago, 1916.

Monaghan, Jay — THE LAST OF THE BAD MEN — Indianapolis, 1946.

Mowry, Sylvester — ARIZONA AND SONORA: *The Geography, History and Resources of the Silver Region of North America* — New York, 1866.

Parsons, George W. — THE PRIVATE JOURNAL OF GEORGE WHITWELL PARSONS — Phoenix, Ariz., 1939.

Paulison, C. M. K. — ARIZONA, THE WONDERFUL COUNTRY — Tucson, Ariz., 1881.

Bibliography

Raine, William McLeod — GUNS OF THE FRONTIER — Boston, 1940.

Raine, William McLeod and Barnes, Will C. — CATTLE — Garden City, N. Y., 1930.

Rockfellow, John A. — LOG OF AN ARIZONA TRAIL BLAZER — Tucson Ariz., 1933.

Santee, Ross — APACHE LAND — New York, 1948.

Schieffelin, Edward L. — HISTORY OF THE DISCOVERY OF TOMBSTONE, ARIZONA — Tucson, Ariz., 1926.

Sloan, Richard E. and Adams, Ward R. — HISTORY OF ARIZONA, 4 vols., Phoenix, 1930.

Sonnichsen, Charles L. — BILLY KING'S TOMBSTONE — Caldwell, Idaho, 1942.

Thacker, John N. and Hume, James B. — REPORT OF JAMES B. HUME AND JOHN N. THACKER: *Special Officers, Wells, Fargo & Co.'s Express* — San Francisco, 1885.

Walters, L. D. — TOMBSTONE'S YESTERDAYS — Tucson, Ariz., 1928.

Willson, Clair E. — MIMES AND MINERS: *A Historical Study of the Theater in Tombstone* — Tucson, Ariz., 1935.

Willson, Neill V. — TREASURE EXPRESS: *Epic Days of the Wells-Fargo* — New York, 1936.

ADDITIONAL MATERIAL

THE early files of two Tombstone newspapers are available in the Library of the Arizona Pioneers Historical Association in Tucson: the 1881 volume of the daily *Nugget,* (fairly complete) and the 1882 weekly *Epitaph.* The latter contains many columns reprinted from the daily of the same name. The files of the Tucson *Arizona Star,* also available, are reasonably complete for the years 1880-1886. In addition the library has a wealth of material in the form of depositions, dossiers, newspaper clippings, and legal documents.

The Criminal records and coroner's records for Cochise County may be examined at the county court house in Bisbee.

INDEX

Index

Behan, John H., *continued*
    warrants obtained by, for the
    Earps and Holliday, 189-190
Benson, rail point, 48; Mayor Clum
    went to, 177
Berry, George, killed, 191-192
Berry, J. B. (Prairie Jack), 82
Biddle, Col., at Fort Grant, 209
Big Minnie, 75
Bignon, Joe, 75
Billicke, Albert, 93; owner of Cos-
    mopolitan Hotel, 197
Billy King's Tombstone, 116
Bird Cage Theatre, 53, 70-71, 75, 241
Bisbee, copper mines, 15, 240; files
    of Cochise County records at, 246;
    seat of Cochise County, 55, 182,
    234, 240
Bishop, William, 56, 86
Blackfeet Indians, 19
Bland Act of 1878, 232; Allison's
    rider to, 232
Blasts for excavation, 41-42
Boller, Robert M., stated all jurymen
    considered John Ringgold a suicide,
    227
Boot Hill, 54, 241
Bourland, Addie, 171, 174
Bowie knives, 67
Brand changing on cattle, 83, 102
Breakenridge, William M., 25, 103,
    129, 136-139, 166; deputy sheriff
    of Maricopa County, 118, 188, 197,
    218; tax collector, 142; sought Pell
    killers, 212-214; went to Tucson,
    239
Briggs, L. Vernon, comment on
    Tombstone affairs, 225
Bronco, Frederic,
    see under Brunckow
Brown, Neal, presented with a
    "Buntline Special" revolver, 129
Brunckow, Frederic, 17
Brunckow Mine, 18
Buffalo Bill Cody, 63

Buildings in Tombstone, 241; adobe,
    brick, frame, 50
Bullion, theft of, 89
Buntline, Ned, 128
"Buntline Special," revolver made by
    Colt for Ned Buntline, 128
Burleigh Springs, 207
Burnham, Maj., Frederick R., mem-
    oirs, 87-88; *Scouting on Two Con-
    tinents*, 244
Burns, Walter Noble, *Tombstone:
    An Illiad of the Southwest*, 23
Burros, The, 15

Calabasas, on Mexican border of
    Arizona, 230-231
Camp Rice, 220
Camp Rucker, 147
Campbell and Hatch's Pool Hall, 191
Can-Can Chop House, 50, 53
Carr, John, succeeded John P. Clum
    as Mayor of Tombstone, 186
Cashman, Nellie, 233; in Alaska and
    the Yukon, 239; prevented com-
    mercializing scene at hanging of
    Bisbee mob, 234-235; *see also* Bib-
    liography, 244
Cattle, introduced into Arizona by
    Father Kino, 80; markets a prob-
    lem, 81; ranges, 81; steady growth
    in industry, 232; stolen, 102
Cattlemen, 80-86, 188; forays of, in
    Mexico, 119; in Cochise County,
    tax problems, 142
Census of 1880 and 1890, 49
Charleston (Town), 38, 86; gun bat-
    tle of O'Brien and Lee, 230; suf-
    fered from mine floods, 235
China Mary (Mrs. Ah Chum), 76-77
Chinese, in Tombstone, 58
Chirichuas (Indians), 21-22
Chirichuas Mountains, 21-22, 227
Church services in Tombstone, 38
Churches, 51

Index

Churchill, Winston, 87
Cibola, 16
Citizen, The, 47
Citizens of Tombstone, safety of, 90
Citizens' Safety Committee, 59, 117, 153, 164, 181, 187, 208, 211; conference with Gov. Tritle, 213; consultation with Wyatt Earp, 200; swore out warrants for Clanton, Stilwell and Swilling, 186
Civic improvement, efforts for, 78-79
Claiborne, William, 86, 94, 153-154, 159-160, 165-170, 226; in Tombstone again, 237; involved in assault on Mayor Clum, 198; killed in gun duel, 236-237
Claim brokers, 42-43
Claim prices, 30-33, 41
Clanton, Joseph Isaac (Ike), 84, 137, 146, 149-154, 159-163; arrival in Charleston, 152; in Tucson, 193; involved in assault on Mayor Clum, 198; in Wells, Fargo and Co. holdup, 183; Iron Springs events, 216; killed by posse in Greenlee County, 238; return from Mexico, 226, 237; testimony at Earp's trial, 168-169, 171-174
Clanton, N.H. ("Old Man Clanton"), 84, 146, 151, 159-160; built ranch house near Lewis Springs, 85; killed by Mexicans, 151; outlaws chief, 118-120
Clanton, Phineas, 84, 128, 146, 226; involved in assault on Mayor Clum, 198; returned to Tombstone, 237; sent to Yuma penitentiary for ten years, later took up stock raising, 238
Clanton, William, 84, 127-128, 146, 156, 161-163, 166, 173, 175; took part in theft of mules, 147-148; went to Charleston, 152-154
Clapp, Milton, cashier of a local bank, 40-41, 164

Clark, Dick, purchased the Alhambra, 61
Clark, Gray and Co. real estate firm, 107-110
Clements, Mannen, famous "killer," 112
Climate of Tombstone, 15
Clum, John P., agent of San Carlos Apache Reservation (1874-1877), 123; comment on death of Curly Bill, 206; crusade against bad politics and outlaws, 219-220; in Alaska and the Yukon, 239; last days in Tucson, 239; mayor of Tombstone (1881), 25, 77-78, 91, 102, 123-124; one of original editors of San Francisco *Examiner*, 239; pall bearer for Wyatt Earp, 240; postmaster, publisher, 49, 61, 176; quoted, 110, 175-176, 197-198
Cochise (Apache), 19-21, 31, 81; death, 22
Cochise County, 46, 84, 89-90, 236; cattlemen, 188; formed, 130; records of, 94; seat now Bisbee, 55
Cochise County Courthouse, John Heith tried at, 234
Cochise culture, 16
Cochise's Stronghold, 22
Coleman, R. J., 155
Colorado River mining towns, 17
Colton, Calif., home of Earp family, 192
Comanche tribe, 17
Communications, primitive, 89
Contention City (mill town), 39, 178, 189; suffered from mine floods, 235
Contention Consolidated Mining Co., 34
Contention mine, 32, 49, 232-233, 235
Copper in Tombstone mines, 235
Copper Queen Mine in Bisbee, 151
Corbin brothers of Connecticut, 59

249

Index

Index

Earp, Virgil, 64, 115, 130-131, 133, 139-140, 147, 167, 192; Chief of Police, 145, 153; died in Goldfield, Nev. (1906), 239; elbow injury, 185-186; men who killed him, 198, 216; moved to Cosmopolitan Hotel, 187; official power reduced, 186-187; Town Marshal, 110-111, 137; went to Colton, Calif., 193

Earp, Warren, 64, 188; detective for Arizona Cattlemen's Ass'n., 239; killed by rustler in Lordsburg, N. M., (1900), 239; member of U. S. Marshal's posse, 193, 195, 197

Earp, Wyatt, 24-25, 39, 93, 103, 126-128, 141, 153; attempt on his life, 190-191; biographical notes, 63-64, 85, 112-117; Clanton-Earp feud, 146, 152-160; Deputy Sheriff of Tombstone, 105; Deputy U. S. Marshal for Tombstone district 105, 111, 145; died in Los Angeles (1929), 239-240; duel with Florentino Cruz, 199; entered real estate field; became prosperous, 240; hired by Wells, Fargo and Co. to guard bullion stages, 104; in Colorado, 224-225; McLowry mule theft, 147-148; moved to Cosmopolitan Hotel, 187; offered Ike Clanton bribe, 150; official power reduced, 186-187; presented with a "Buntline Special" revolver, 129; public opinion at trial after shooting episode, 165-168; shot Frank Stilwell, 194-195; special posse of, begins to function, 190; Town Marshal, gave orders to rustlers, 160; trial of, 166-167; Wells, Fargo and Co. thief arrested, 182; went to Colorado, 218

Eating, cost of, 55

Eccleston, 109, 124

Engineers at Tombstone, 41

Episcopal Church, 51

Epitaph, The (newspaper of Tombstone), 47, 49, 102, 122, 144, 177, 179, 181, 183, 207; accusations of become significant, 221-222, 224; Acting-Gov. Gosper's message, 210-211; comment on feud between Clantons and Earps, 165, 167, 175; rustlers vote, 129; did not rejoice at release of Holliday and Wyatt, 225; early files, 246; founded by John P. Clum, 61; John Carr opposed by, 186; message to, from B. L. Peel, 212; new attitude towards cowboys, 230-231; quoted Col. Biddle's remark to Sheriff Behan, 209; quoted letter from Willcox, 208; reaction to President Arthur's proclamation, 224; report on Curly Bill's death, 204-205; ridiculed whitewashing of outlaws, (cowboys), 220-221; sale of; Sam Purdy new publisher, 221-223; stage holdup story, 183; supported the vigilantes, 217; "ten per cent ring" comment, 219, 222-223; Wyatt Earp dispatch to, 210

Evans, Joseph, Deputy U. S. Marshal at Tucson, 193

Excavation by blasts, 41

Fairbank (mill town), 14, 39

Faro (gambling game of the West), 65-66

Fay, E. A., original publisher of *The Nugget*, 122

Federal Government, indifference of, 90

Federal Grand Jury in Tucson, 190

Ferguson, Lark, known as Pete Spence, *see* under that name

Feud, between business men and miners, 40; county and town governments, 126, 145; Earp-Clanton affair, 146, 165, 171-172

Index

Fifth Ave. Comedy Co., 52
Fire, in 1881, 55-56; in 1882, 49, 56
Fisher, Big Nose Kate, 116, 141
Fly, F. C., photographic studio, 157, 170
Flynn, constable in Tombstone, 187
Food in Tombstone excellent, 50
Fort Buchanan, 19
Fort Grant, 215
Fort Huachuca, 27, 233
Foy, Eddie, 53-54
Free Silver coinage campaign, 235
Freeze, John Doe, accused in killing of Morgan Earp, 192
Fremont, Gen. John C., Gov. of Arizona, 101, 104-105
Fremont street (Tombstone), 37
Fuller, Wesley, 154, 156, 168-170

Gadsden Purchase (1853), 14, 17
Gage, E. B., prominent mining man, 176; threat to lynch him, 232-233
Galeyville, 39, 86, 151, 235
Gambling, forms of, 65, 77
Gas installed for lighting, 50
Gates, Deputy Sheriff, 148
Geronimo, captured by John P. Clum, 61
Gila River, 14
Gillespie, 212-213
Gilette, Dan, 33
Gird, Richard, 30-34, 38, 88, 135
Gold in Tombstone mines, 235
Goodfellow, Dr. George, 60, 172, report on death of John Heith, 233; went to California; because prominent San Francisco surgeon, 239
Goose Flats, 35, 38, 241
Gosper, Acting Governor John J., 188, attack on outlaws, 210
Graham County, 82
Graham, William Brocius ("Curly Bill"), 95-96, 110, 112, 119, 127-128, 132, 153, 200-202; assisted in tax collecting, 142; at Huachita,

Graham, William Brocius, *continued*
151; involved in assault on Mayor Clum, 198; in Wells, Fargo and Co. holdup, 183; killed by Wyatt Earp, 202; most famous outlaw in Arizona, 85, 216; raid into Sonora, 151; suspected in Morgan Earp murder, 192; took part in theft of stock, 147
Gramma grass, 81
Grand Central mine, 32, 49, 232, 235
Grand Central Mining Co., 34, 178
Grand Hotel, The, 55
Graveyard claim, 30
Graveyard inscriptions at Boot Hill, 242
Gray, Mike, justice of the peace, 107
Greene, Bill, built copper mining empire in Mexico, 82
Greene, William C., owned the Cananea copper mines in Sonora, 61-62
Greenlee County, rustlers in, 238
Griffith, William, 29
Groton (Mass.), school for boys, 60
Grounds, Billy, 119, 218; reputed protege of Curly Bill, 212-213
Gunmen, Texas Jack Vermilion, Turkey Creek Jack Johnson and Sherman McMasters, 187
Guns, Methods of using, 96-100

Hafford's saloon, 155, 181
Haley, installed water supply for Tombstone, 50
Hamilton, Patrick, 15, 48-49
Hammond, John Hays, 87
Hancock, Louis, 94
Hardin, John Wesley (swift killer), 85, 99
Hardware stores, 47
Harper, Tom, 93
Haslett brothers of Huachita, 151
Hatch, Bob, 191
Head, Harry, 119, 137, 139, 149-150-151

Index

"Healey Bros.," 54

Hearst, Senator George, of California, 59

Heith, John, killed by mob, 234; leader in "Bisbee Massacre," 233

Helldorado, *pseud.*, *see* William M. Breakenridge

Helldorado celebration (pageant), 242

Herefords in Arizona, 82

Herring, Col. William, attorney, 164, 189-190, 197

Hickey, James, 153

Hickok, Wild Bill, 62

Hicks, John, 93, 200

Hicks, Milt, 144, 200

Hicks, Will, 144

Highwaymen, 89

Hill, Joe, 150-151; killed by fall from horse, 216

Holdups in Cochise County, 180

Holliday, Dr. John H. (dentist), 64, 152-154, 157-163, 167, 187-188; biographical notes, 115-117, 139-141, 149, 193-198, 201; died of tuberculosis in Colorado sanitorium about 1895, 240

Homes, one-story, 55-56

Hooker, Col. Henry C., 82, 85, 208-209

Hop Town, Chinese settlement, 48

Horn, Tom, 67, 86

Horse thieves, 85

Howard, James, in Bisbee robbery, 233-234

Howard, Gen. O. O., 21

Hoyt, George, slain by Wyatt Earp, 113

Huachita, store robbery at, 151

Huachuca Mountains, 14, timber source, 33

Huachuca Water Co., 185

Hualapai Indians, 26-27

Hughes, Dan de Lara, autobiography of, 76

Hume, James B., detective for Wells, Fargo and Co., 138, 181-182-184

Hunt, Zwing, 119, 212-214, 218-219

Hurst, Capt. (of the U.S. Army), 147

Indian Charlie, *see* Florentino Cruz

Indian policy of U. S. Government, 123

Indians, conversions by Jesuits, 16; hated Mexicans, 18

Indignation can defeat its purpose in journalism, 220

Investment values, 43-44

Iron Springs (later, mescal springs), 201

Jackson, Frank, with Sam Bass at Round Rock fight, 87

Jails in Tombstone, 224

James boys, 86

Jesuits, Missions, 16

Joe Hill, 86

Johnson, Rattlesnake Bill, 200

Johnson, Turkey Creek Jack, gunman, 65, 117, 187-188, 195, 197, 201

Jones, Al, County Recorder, 143

Jones, Councilman, 108

Jones, Harry, 138

Jurors of Tombstone dared not convict, 224

Killeen, Mike, wife of, 95

"Killers" famous in Kansas, 85, 112

King, Billy, 25, 68, 74, 93, 116

King, Luther, 137-139, 149, 151, 182, 219, 226

King, Roger, 93

King, Sandy, 226

Kino, Father Eusepio, Jesuit founder of two Spanish Missions, 80

Knights of Pythias, 51

Index

Index

Miners, purchased immunity from robbery, 224; strikes, 232-233
Mines, production, 48; slump in, 232-233
Mining, 80, affected by price changes, 232; reduced operations, 233
Mining claims, 17
Mission Indians, 80
Mohave county, 118
Mohaves, 68
Mowrey, Lt. Sylvester, 47
Mule Pass, 14, 36
Mules, 14-15

Names in Boot Hill graveyard inscriptions, 242
Neagle, David, action in Wyatt Earp case, 197-198; elected Town Marshal of Tombstone, 186
Nellie Boyd Dramatic Co., 52
New Mexico, 17
Newspapers, 47; clippings on record, 246; fire loss of early files, 91
Nobles, Milton, 52
Noon, A. H., 69-70
Nosey Kate, 116
Nugget, The, 122, 139-141, 179, 181, 197, 207-209; attitude towards outlaws, 121, 219; called outlaws "cowboys"; supported them, 220; comment on feud between Clantons and Earps, 165, 174-175; on reported death of Curly Bill, 203-205; early files of, 246; made a laughing stock by Clum, 220; organ of county politics, 122-123; reaction to President Arthur''s proclamation, 224; started in 1879, 47; supported Mark Shaffer, candidate for mayor of Tombstone, 124-125; the county government, 217
Nunnelley, E. C., rehabilitation of Boot Hill, 241

O'Brien and Lee, gun battle, 230
O'Day, Pat, 95
O. K. Corral, 155-163, 169, 189; site of, 241
Oliver, John, 32
O'Neil, Capt. William (Bucky), of Roosevelt's Rough Riders, 61
Opium houses of the Chinese settlement, 77
Ordinances in Dodge City, 130-131
Oriental, the, saloon and entertainment center, 47
O'Rourke, John, 131-135, assumed murderer of John Ringgold, was shot by Pony Deal, 229-230, 237
O'Shea, Con, 74
Outlaws, 85-86, 118-120, 149-150, 183-184, 216, 219; acting Gov. Gosper launched attack on, 210; kept an eye on the Earps, 187; losses, 226; opposed authorities sent to control them, 189; setback for, 215
Owens, Commodore Perry, Sheriff, 238

Packard, B. A., 82
Parsons and Redfern, title searching and mining agency, 44
Parsons, George Whitewell, comment on Stilwell's death, 196; criticism of Behan and deputies, 219-221; journal of, 24, 37-41, 56, 58, 70, 195; met Gov. Tritle upon his arrival, 213; nose injury, 184-185; pall bearer for Wyatt Earp, 240; quoted, 108-109, 124-125, 187, 190, 231; trip to Ft. Huachuca with the Rev. Endicott Peabody, 60; went to Los Angeles, 239
Patterson, Frank, 147, 200
Paul, Robert (Bob), guard for bullion stages, 136-137, 139; informed of Frank Stilwell's death, 196-197; issued warrants on Stilwell killing,

Index

Index

Sierra Bonita Ranch of Col. C. Hooker, 208

Sierra Bonita Springs, Col. Henry C. Hooker ranch at, 82, 215

Signal, 29-30

Silver, lure of, 13, 18; price slump, 232; supply of at Tombstone, 49

Silver King Mine at Globe (Arizona), 29

Simmons, Pink, 99

Sioux Indians, 19

Sippy, Ben, 130, 135, 145

Skeleton Canyon, 119, 151

Slaughter, John, Cochise County's greatest sheriff, 82, 85, 336

Sledge hammer risks, 42

Smith, vigilante messenger, 203

Smith, B. F., 227

Smith, Marcus Aurelius, lawyer, 59-60

Smuggling, 88

Sobaipuris (subdivision of the Pimas), 16-17

Soldier Holes, in Sulphur Springs Valley, 147

Sonora, Curly Bill raid, 151

Source material, 23-25

Southern Pacific Railway, 46, 81, 188

Spangenberg's gun shop, 154

Spanish Missions, at Tubac and Tucson, 80

Spanish settlers, 16

Spence, Pete (real name said to be Lark Ferguson), 86, 119, 182, 190, 218; accused in killing of Morgan Earp, 192; in Wells, Fargo Co. holdup, 183; raid on his ranch, 198; sentenced to several years in Yuma penitentiary, 216

Spicer, Judge Wells, 166-174

Stabbing frowned upon, 96

Stages, regular service begun, 89; protection at a price, 224; robberies, 147, 180-182; six horse, 46

Star, The, of Tucson, 195, 211

Statehood for Arizona, 50

Stilwell, Frank, 86, 119, 144, 180, 190; shot by Wyatt Earp, 194-195; stage robber, 148, 182, 193-194

Stilwell, Jack, Texas scout, 180

Stillwell, Judge William H., 143

Stinkem (town), 38

Stope mining, 49

Storms, Charlie, 65, 94-95, 99

Sulphur Springs Valley, 36, 82

Sutton, Fred, 97

Swilling, Hank, 185, 208; involved in assault on Mayor Clum, 198; shot to death in Mexico, 216; suspected in murder of Morgan Earp, 192-194

Sycamore Springs, 49

Tax collection in Cochise County, 142; irregularities practiced, 221

Telegraph service, in 1880, 50

"Ten per cent ring," 219, 222-223, 231

Territorial Legislature at Prescott, 122

Texas Rangers, 87

Thacker, John, an officer of Wells, Fargo and Co., 181-182

Theatres, 51

Thompson, Ben (swift killer), 85, 112

Tilghman, Bill, 129

Timber source, 38

Tipton, Dan, Vigilante messenger, 203, 210

Tolliday, John, 93

Tombstone, 13-14; armed camp atmosphere, 187; became a metropolis, 48; citizens' attitude towards crime, 90-92; citizens of, 45, 58; city of, 46; celebrated approach of Southern Pacific Railroad, 46; David Neagle elected town marshal, 186; establishment of town, 31-32, 36-37; in Pima County, 91;

Index

Index

Williams, W. S., deputy district attorney for Cochise County, 171
Willson, Claire E., 52
Wilson, Johnnie, 93
Windlassing, 42
Wood, Capt. Leonard, 60
Woods, Harry M., 138, 207, 219; publisher of *The Nugget* in 1881 and 1882, 122; Undersheriff at Tombstone, 139
Wright, Vigilante messenger, 203; perhaps same as John B. Wright, 52
Wright, John B., lawyer, 52

Xaralampo, Georges (Greek George), 67-68

Yavapai County, John H. Behan in, 117
Yoast, John, report on death of John Ringgold, 227-228
Young, —, 212-213
Younger brothers, 86
Youth, early maturity of, 50-51
Yuma territorial prison, 96

Zinc in Tombstone Mines, 235